HOPELESS SAVAGES

WRITTEN BY
JEN VAN METER

ILLUSTRATED BY
CHRISTINE NORRIE

LETTERED
BY ANDY LIS

FLASHBACKS AND
"STICKS AND STONES"
ILLUSTRATED BY
CHYNNA CLUGSTON-MAJOR

COVER, LOGO,
CHAPTER BREAKS,
AND "ROMANCE #1"
COLORING BY
ANDI WATSON

EDITED BY JAMIE S. RICH

BOOK DESIGN BY K. SEDA

Lettering font provided by
Larry Young

"Sticks and Stones"
colored by Guy Major
lettered by Amie Grenier

"Open House" and "Good Fences"
colored by Christine Norrie

Published by Oni Press, Inc.
Joe Nozemack, publisher
Jamie S. Rich, editor in chief
James Lucas Jones, associate editor

www.onipress.com
www.spookoo.com

First Oni Press edition: June 2002
ISBN 1-929998-24-4

1 3 5 7 9 10 8 6 4 2
PRINTED IN CANADA.

This book collects all four issues of the Oni Press comic book series *Hopeless Savages*, as well as short stories from various sources.

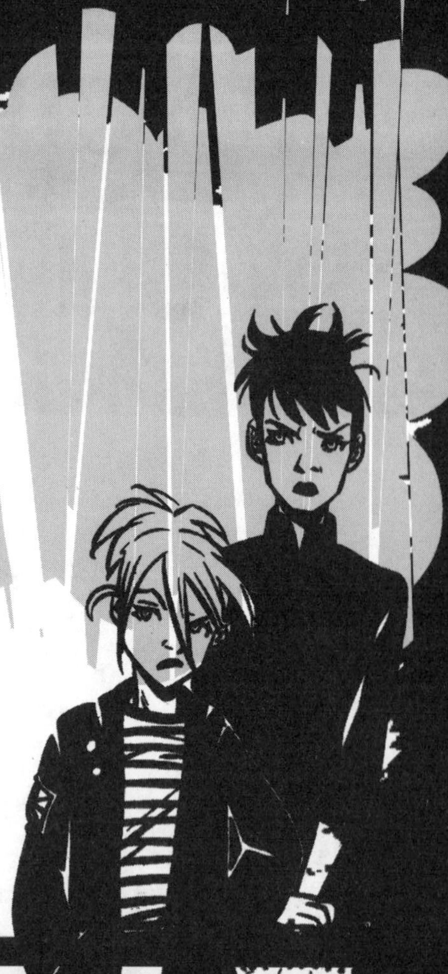

ONI PRESS, INC.
6336 SE Milwaukie Avenue, PMB30
Portland, OR 97202
USA

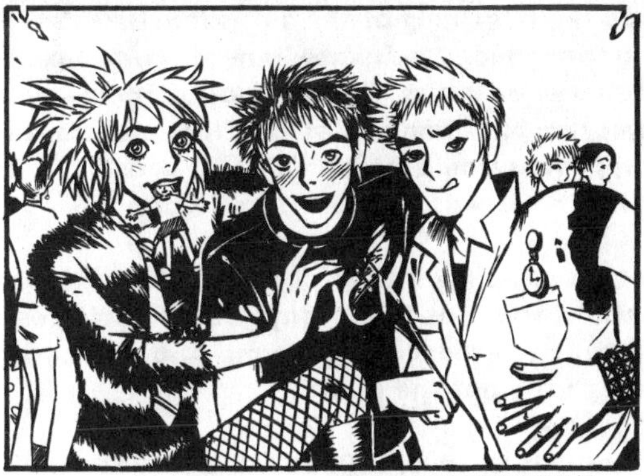

PHOTO BY CHYNNA CLUGSTON-MAJOR '77

THERE WAS RIOTING IN THE STREETS...OR SO WE LIKE TO THINK.

1977 was a long time ago, and we all like to remember ourselves as a lot bigger than when we were. I know most of my stories have taken on legendary proportions. Not only did I burgle the Louvre one Friday night, but my accomplices were Joe Strummer and that guy who played Jimmy in *Quadrophenia* (you know, the "Parklife," loves-a-bit-of-it guy). Winston Churchill drove the getaway car wearing a Mohican wig so no one would recognize him. It was mental.

It's the sort of thing where, yeah, if you really remember it, you weren't there. If you have a pretty good idea of how dank and nasty a lot of it was—how much urine there was in the street, the proliferation of gobs on the wall, the warmness of the beer—you probably have seen it in picture books or watched one of the countless documentaries meant to cash in on the occasional punk rock fever. You know, like when Green Day turned into Sum 41 and suddenly kids were putting chains on their wallets again. Which, come to think of it, is the perfect fashion accessory to separate the real deal from the mallrat poseur. If you look like several feet of bad medicine with leather and studs and hair that airport security would be worried to let you board with, do you really need to be concerned about some stupid pickpocket nicking your wallet? Didn't think so.

So, yeah, most of you weren't there.

But some of you were. I mean, somebody had to be there otherwise it would never have happened, if you catch my drift. And like I said, it was mental. It may not be as crazy as they tell you, but it's as crazy as we pretend to recall.

And I remember seeing Dirk Hopeless for the first time. It was around that period where labels were snatching up anything that came on black plastic and was wrapped in a little paper sleeve. A lot of cack was getting signed, pressed, and played on BBC to scare the grandmothers while they chomped their biscuits—but it hadn't gotten so bad that you couldn't yet tell the true from the false. Dirk Hopeless was no fake. Like those aliens in those movies that burn holes in metal when they bleed, Dirk's sweat was like acid to the opportunists who wanted to put the boot into good, old fashioned, we-hate-you rock-and-roll. Dirk on stage was like Neil Armstrong on the moon. A boy of seventeen couldn't help but let his jaw drop and think, "This...this is better than anything anyone has ever done *ever*."

Keep in mind, this was the beginning of the set, even. Nikki Savage hadn't yet made one of her amazing appearances. You know how she was—like Bowie wanted to be, had he really needed to wear a bra. Their sexuality, their smolder, their passion—this wasn't some come-on, Mick Ronson letting Ziggy make sweet kisses to his frets so the California surf jocks could be all, "Ewww, gross." It was all that sweaty, fumbling backseat stuff *rawk* was supposed to be about.

I was lost forever. I pierced my ear that night with a book of matches and a ballpoint pen. Thankfully, this was in the days before DNA testing, coz I left trails of earlobe blood all over the museum while me and Joe and Jimmy went running through its halls...but that's not the point.

The point is, in big capital letters, DIRK HOPELESS AND NIKKI SAVAGE WERE THE SPONSORS OF MY TEENAGE REBELLION, AND NOW THEY HAVE FOUR FREAKIN' KIDS, A HOUSE IN THE SUBURBS, AND THEY DON'T EVEN DO DRUGS! WHAT IN GOD'S NAME HAPPENED?

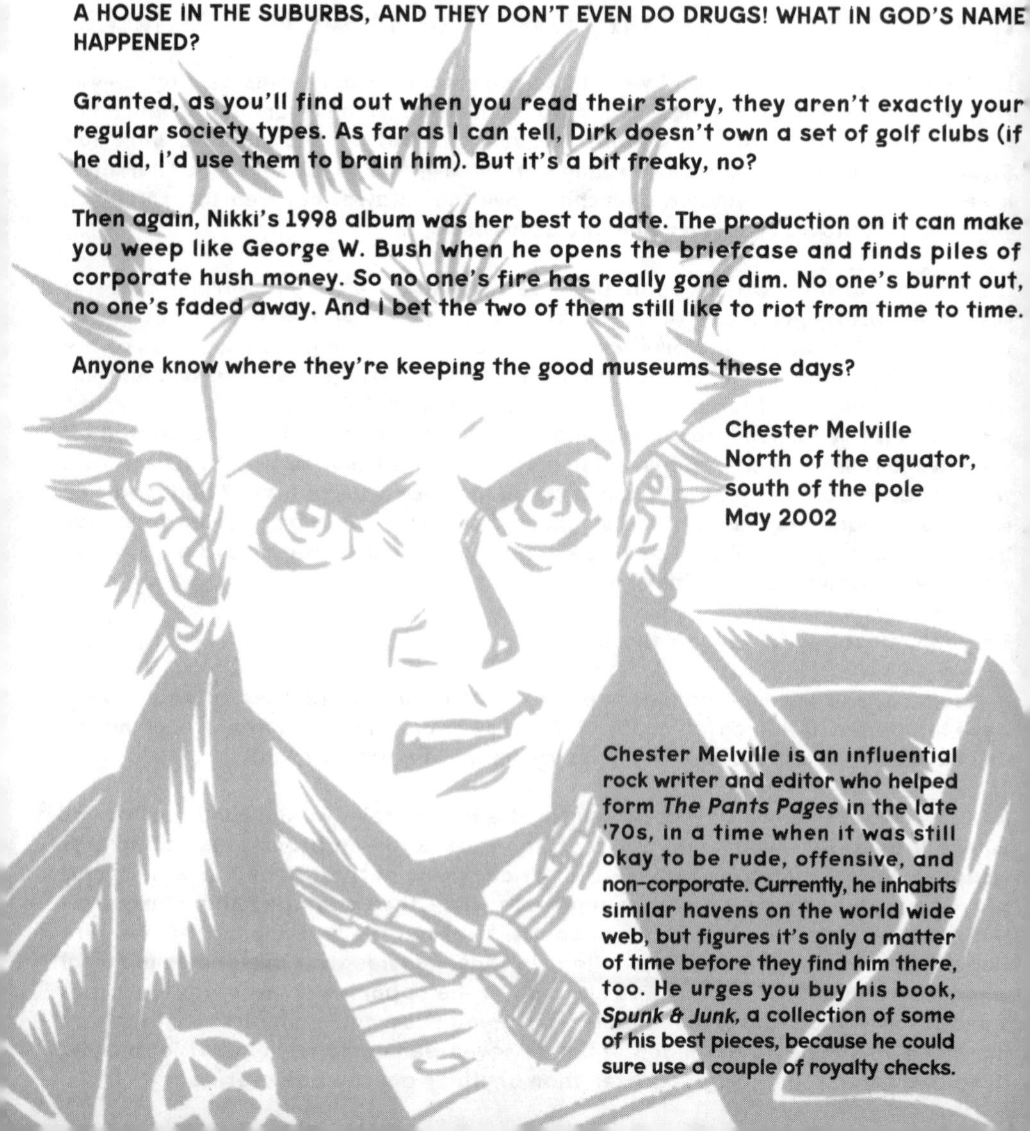

Granted, as you'll find out when you read their story, they aren't exactly your regular society types. As far as I can tell, Dirk doesn't own a set of golf clubs (if he did, I'd use them to brain him). But it's a bit freaky, no?

Then again, Nikki's 1998 album was her best to date. The production on it can make you weep like George W. Bush when he opens the briefcase and finds piles of corporate hush money. So no one's fire has really gone dim. No one's burnt out, no one's faded away. And I bet the two of them still like to riot from time to time.

Anyone know where they're keeping the good museums these days?

Chester Melville
North of the equator,
south of the pole
May 2002

Chester Melville is an influential rock writer and editor who helped form *The Pants Pages* in the late '70s, in a time when it was still okay to be rude, offensive, and non-corporate. Currently, he inhabits similar havens on the world wide web, but figures it's only a matter of time before they find him there, too. He urges you buy his book, *Spunk & Junk*, a collection of some of his best pieces, because he could sure use a couple of royalty checks.

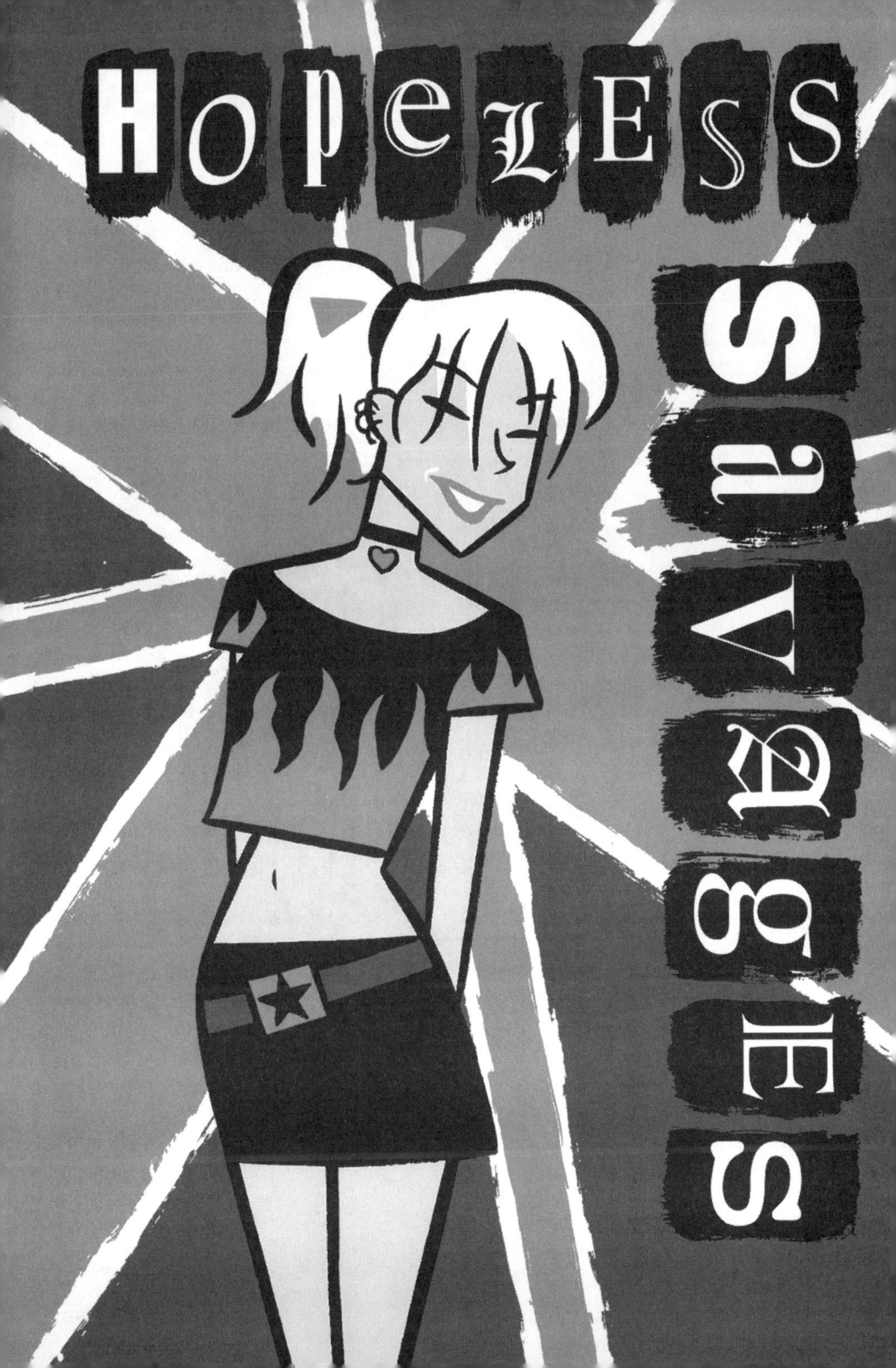
HOPELESS
SAVAGES

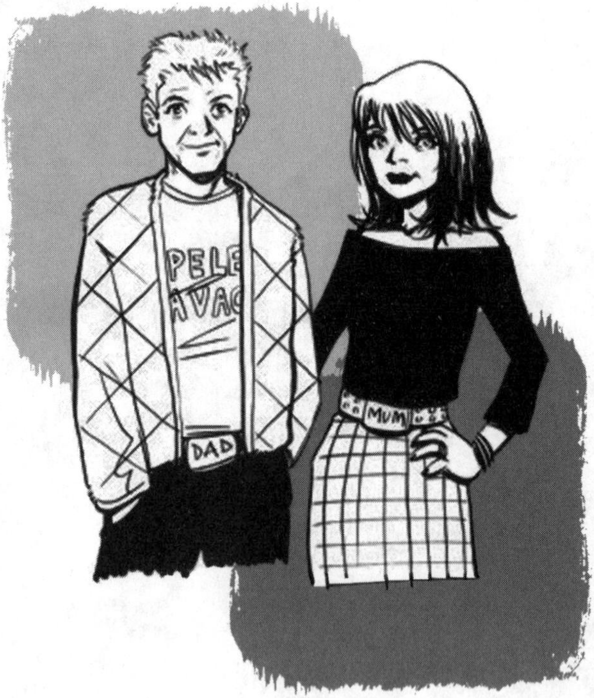
PELE
DAD
MUM

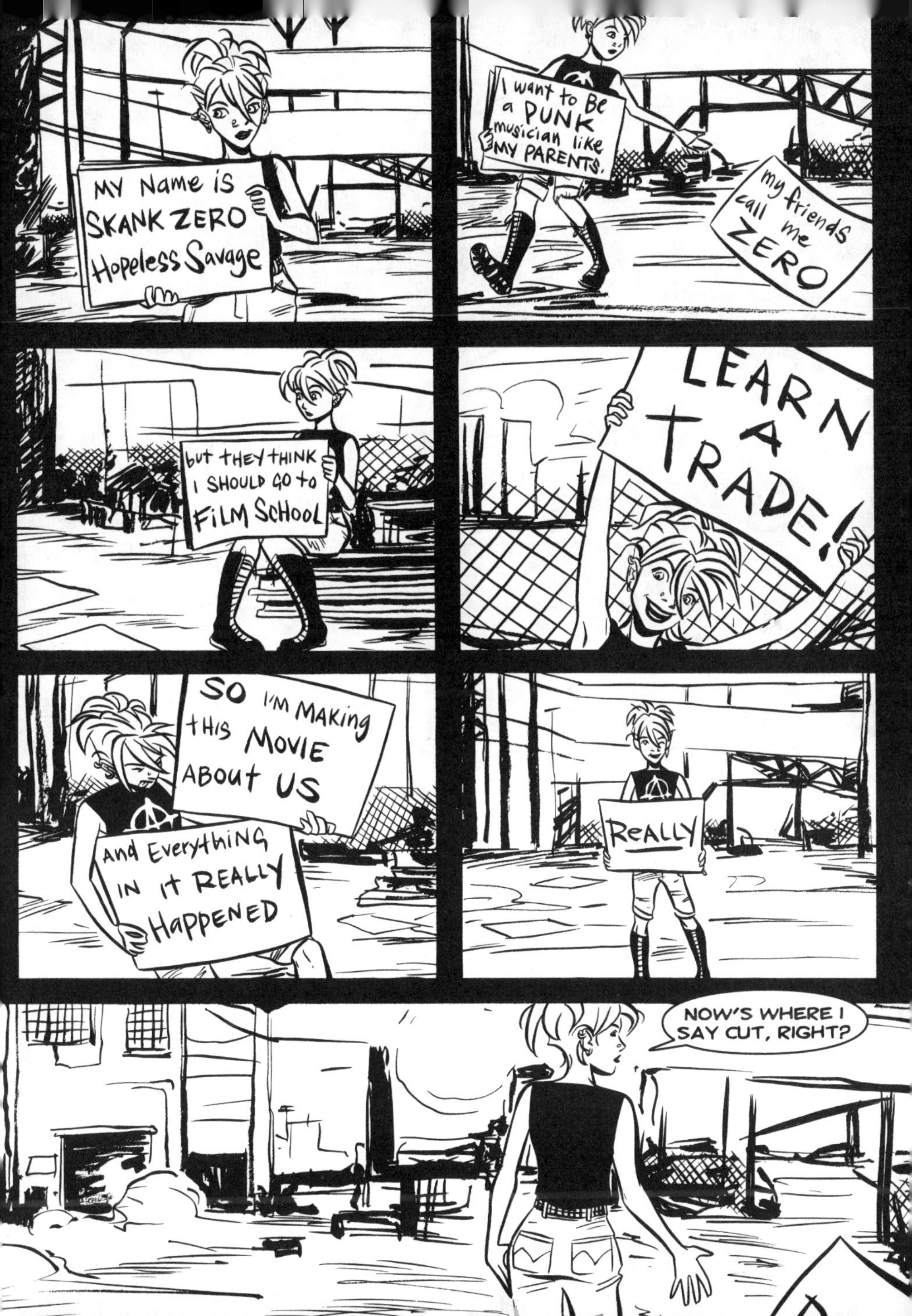
MY Name iS
SKANK ZERO
Hopeless Savage
I want to Be a PUNK musician like MY PARENTS.
my friends call me ZERO
but THEY THINK I SHOULD GO to FILM SCHOOL
LEARN A TRADE!
SO I'M MAKING THIS MOVIE ABOUT US
And Everything IN IT REALLY HAPPENED
REALLY
NOW'S WHERE I SAY CUT, RIGHT?

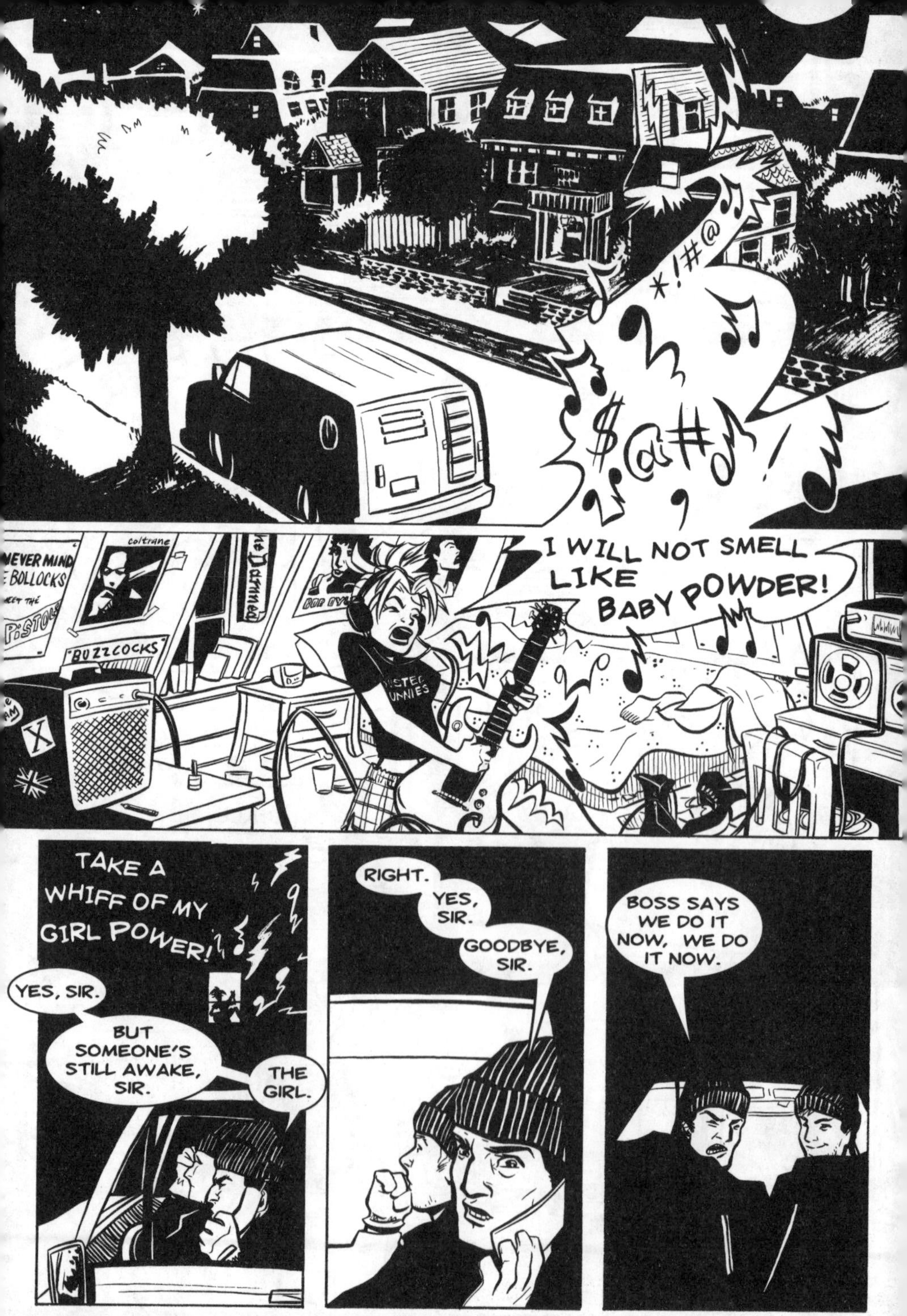
*!#@
$@#
I WILL NOT SMELL LIKE BABY POWDER!
NEVER MIND THE BOLLOCKS
PISTOLS
coltrane
BUZZCOCKS
The Damned
X
TAKE A WHIFF OF MY GIRL POWER!
YES, SIR.
BUT SOMEONE'S STILL AWAKE, SIR.
THE GIRL.
RIGHT.
YES, SIR.
GOODBYE, SIR.
BOSS SAYS WE DO IT NOW, WE DO IT NOW.

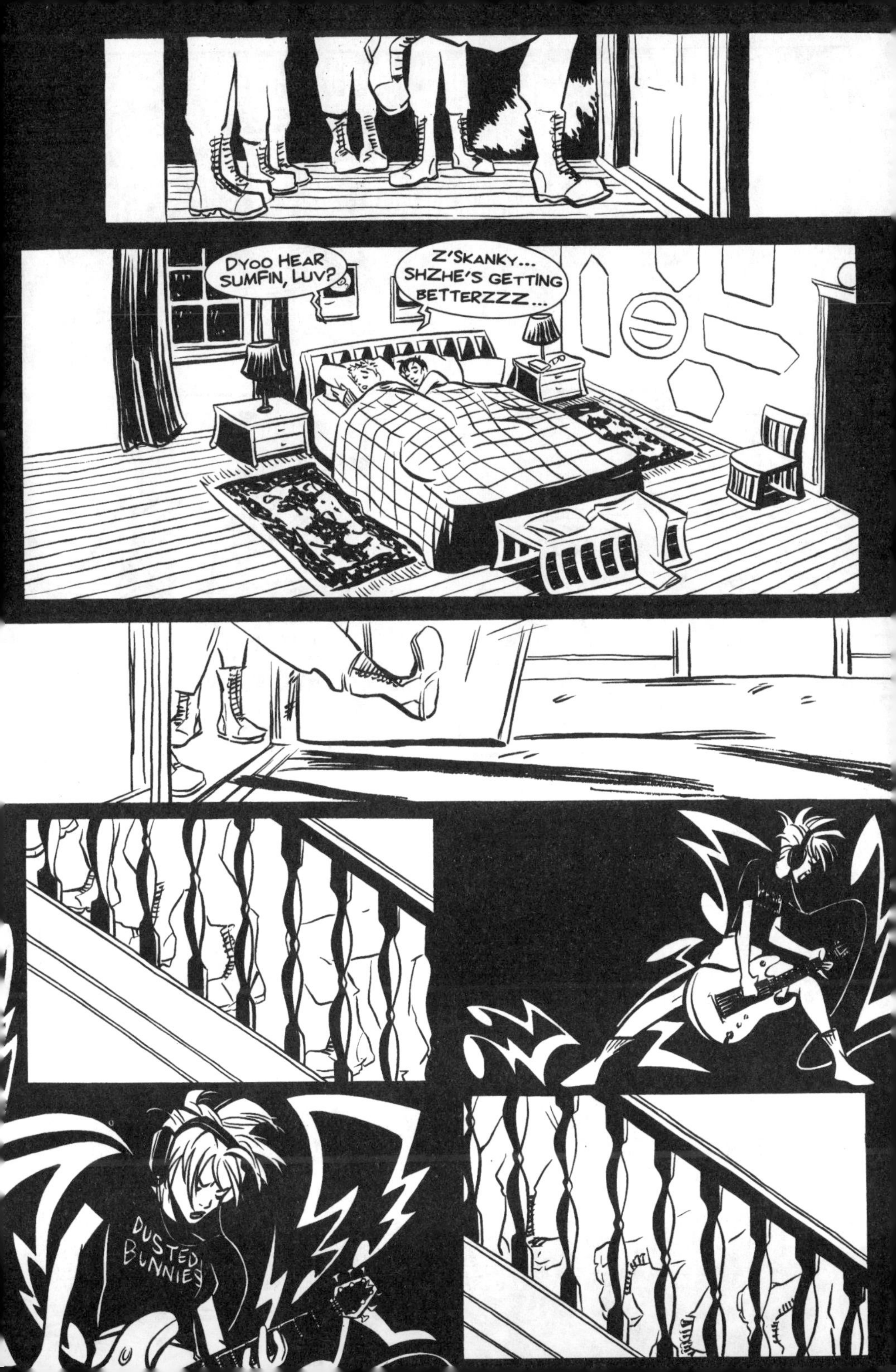
DYOO HEAR SUMFIN, LUV?
Z'SKANKY... SHZHE'S GETTING BETTERZZZ...
DUSTED BUNNIES

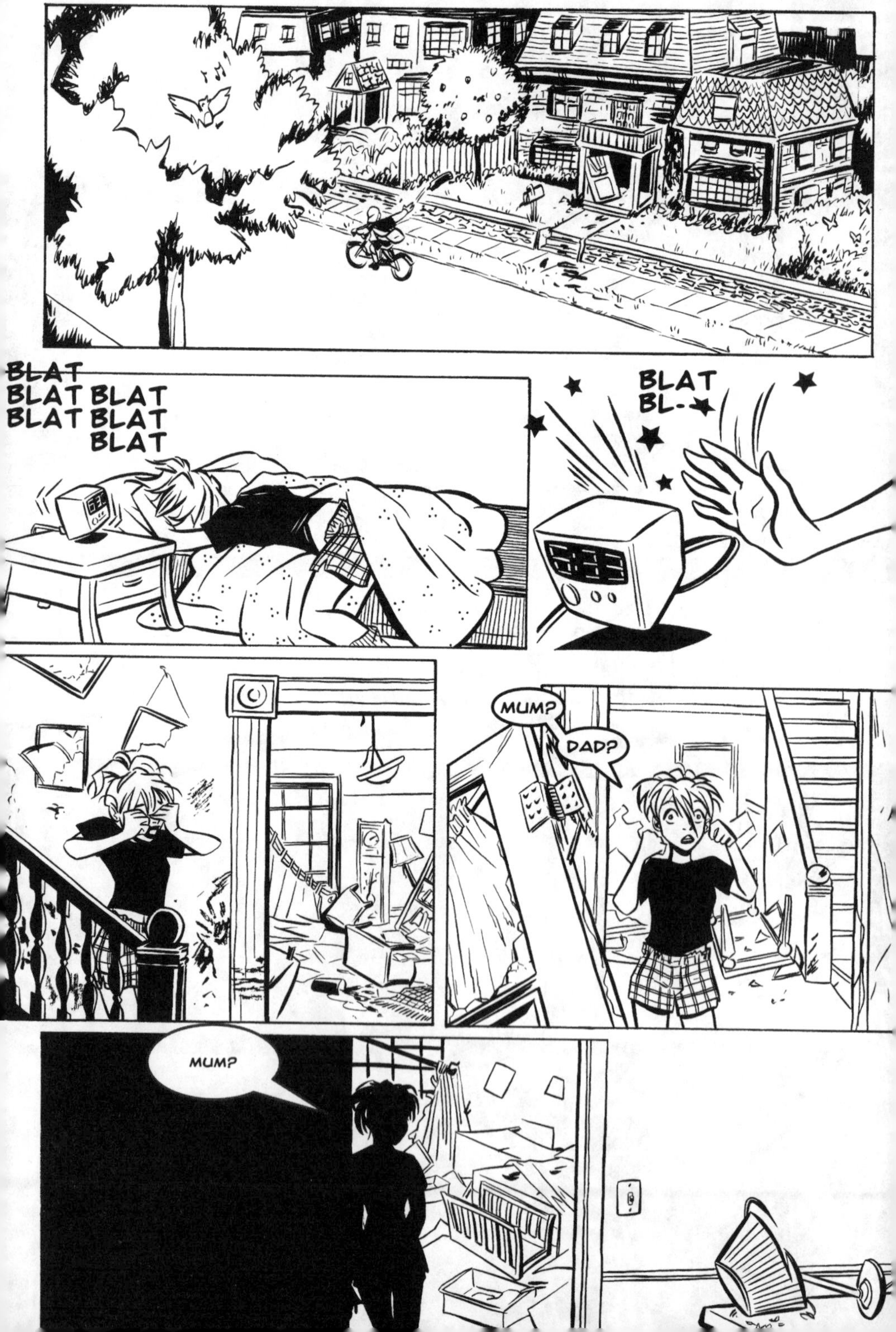
BLAT
BLAT BLAT
BLAT BLAT
BLAT
BLAT
BL-
MUM?
DAD?
MUM?

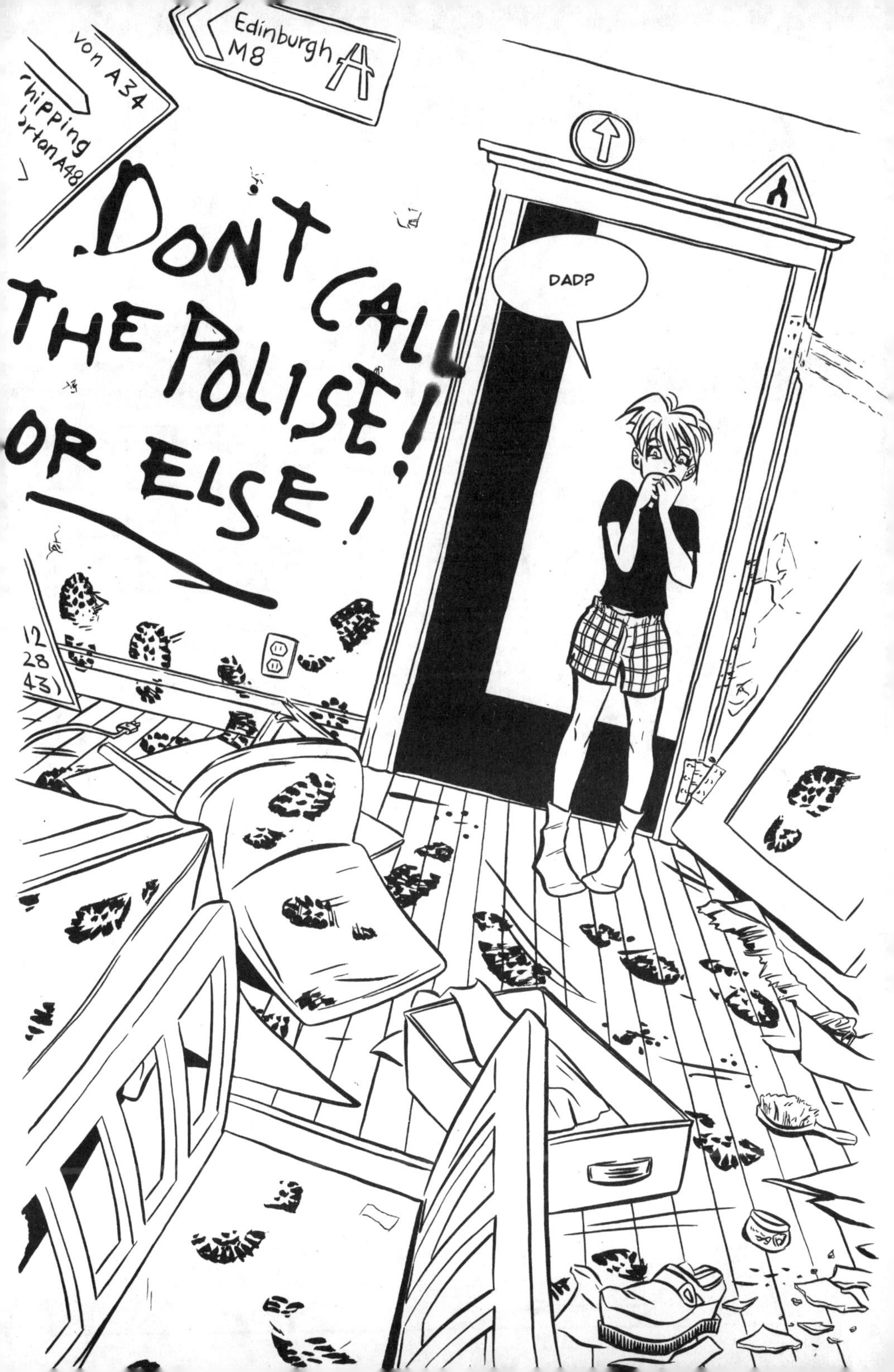
Edinburgh
M8
von A34
hipping
orton A48
DONT CALL THE POLISE! OR ELSE!
DAD?
12
28
43)

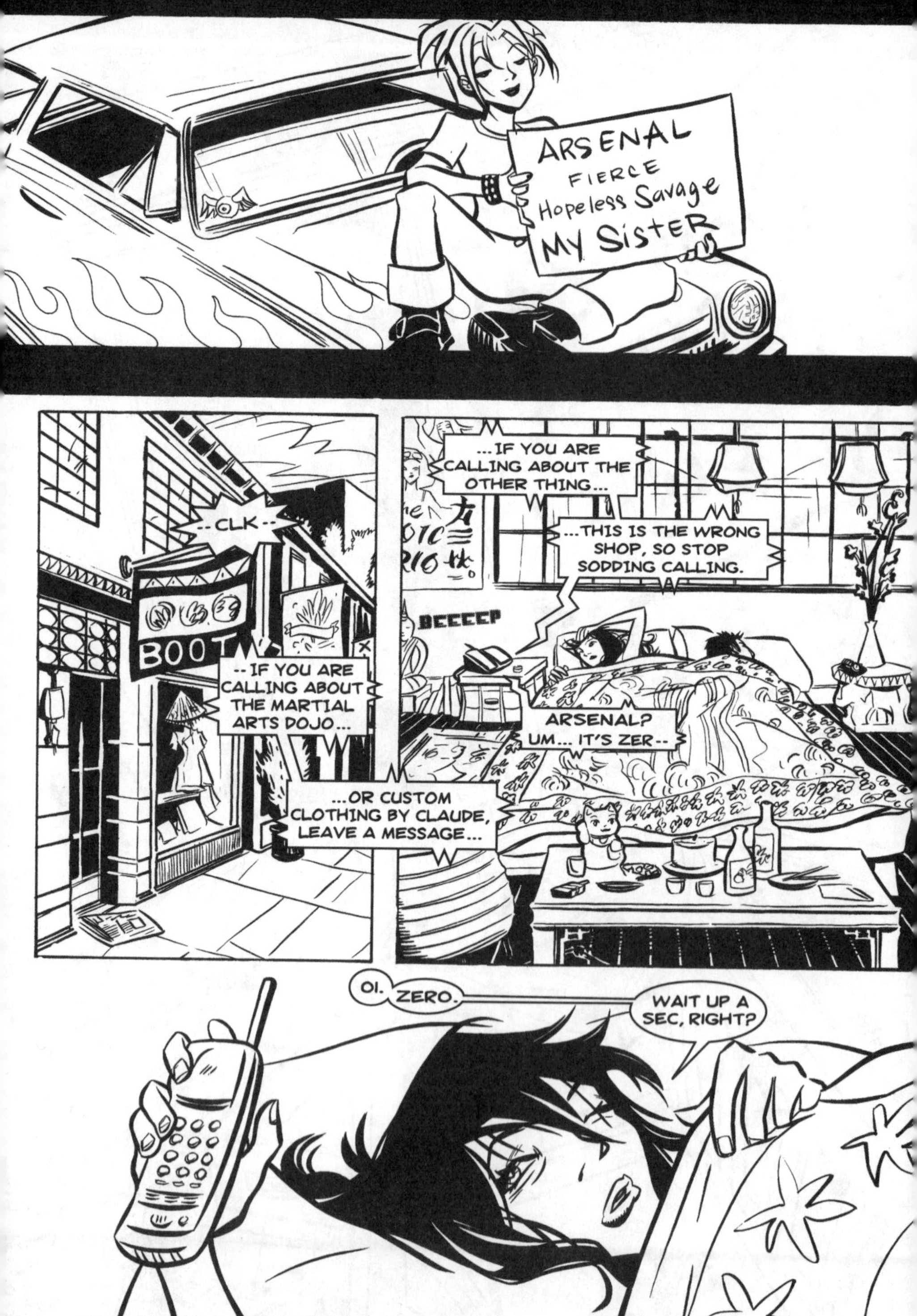
ARSENAL
FIERCE
Hopeless Savage
MY SISTER
--CLK--
BOOT
--IF YOU ARE CALLING ABOUT THE MARTIAL ARTS DOJO...
...OR CUSTOM CLOTHING BY CLAUDE, LEAVE A MESSAGE...
...IF YOU ARE CALLING ABOUT THE OTHER THING...
...THIS IS THE WRONG SHOP, SO STOP SODDING CALLING.
BEEEEP
ARSENAL? UM... IT'S ZER--
OI.
ZERO.
WAIT UP A SEC, RIGHT?

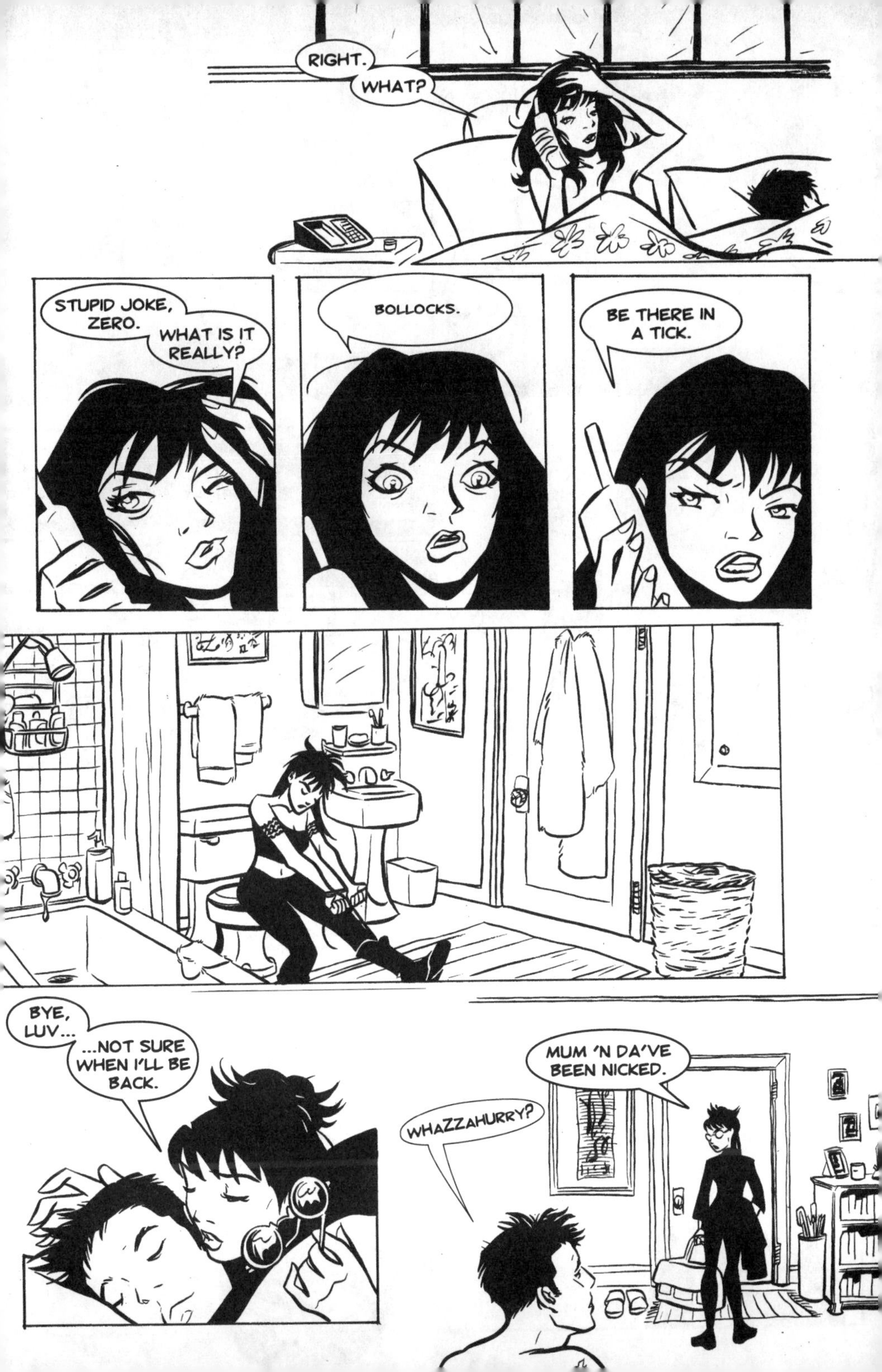
RIGHT.
WHAT?
STUPID JOKE, ZERO.
WHAT IS IT REALLY?
BOLLOCKS.
BE THERE IN A TICK.
BYE, LUV...
...NOT SURE WHEN I'LL BE BACK.
WHAZZAHURRY?
MUM 'N DA'VE BEEN NICKED.

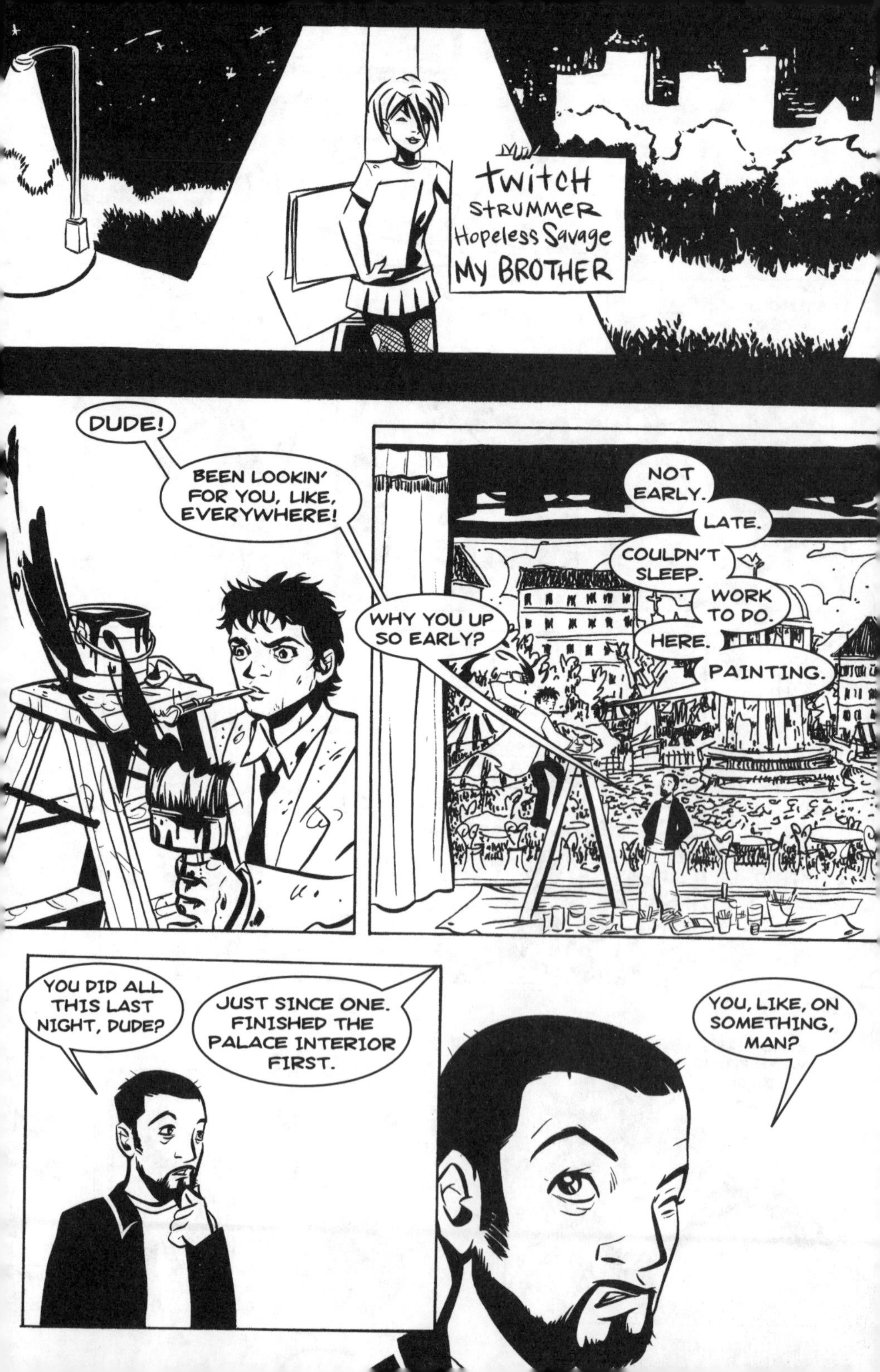

twitch
strummer
Hopeless Savage
My BROTHER
DUDE!
BEEN LOOKIN' FOR YOU, LIKE, EVERYWHERE!
WHY YOU UP SO EARLY?
NOT EARLY.
LATE.
COULDN'T SLEEP.
WORK TO DO.
HERE.
PAINTING.
YOU DID ALL THIS LAST NIGHT, DUDE?
JUST SINCE ONE. FINISHED THE PALACE INTERIOR FIRST.
YOU, LIKE, ON SOMETHING, MAN?

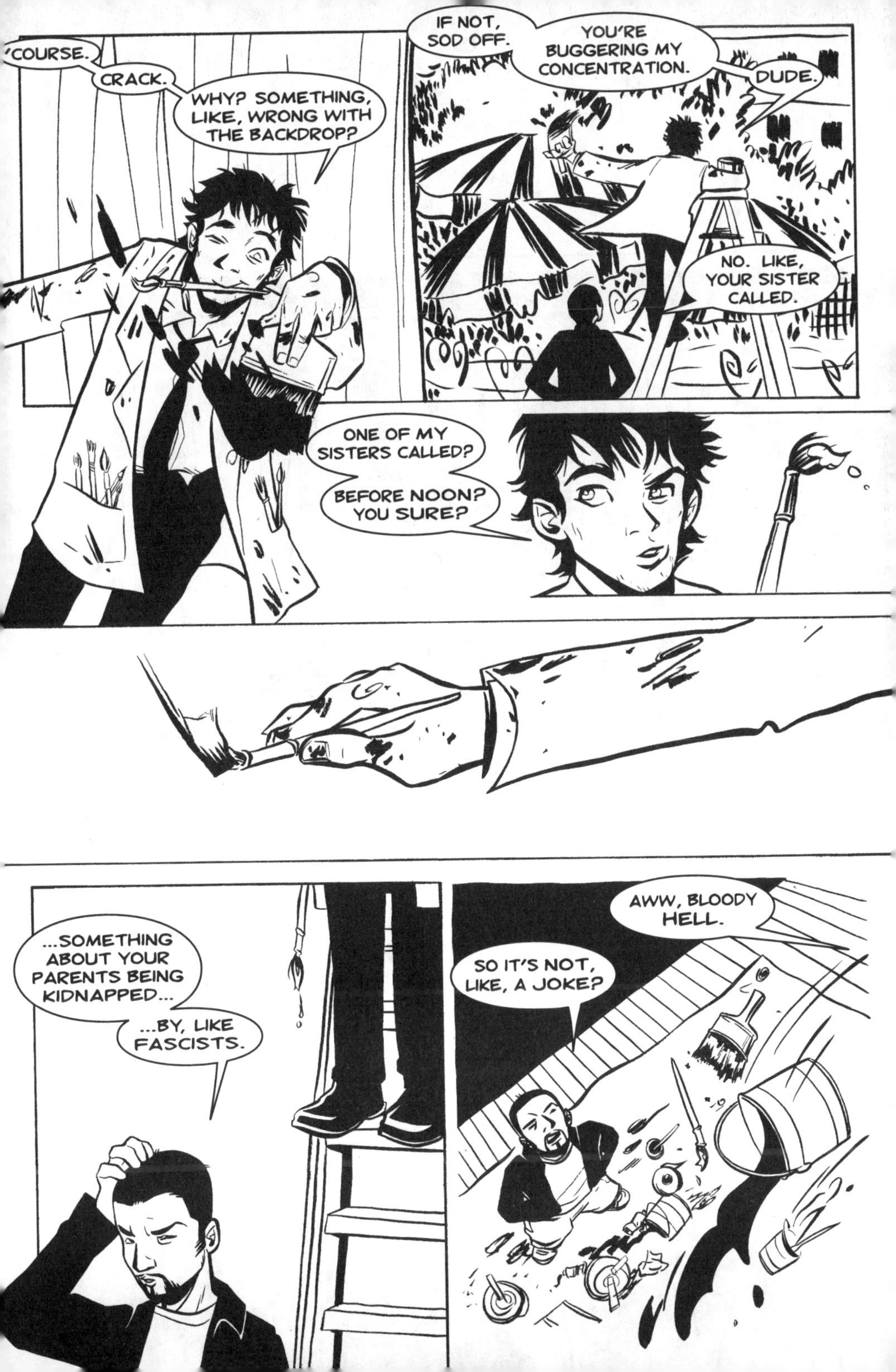
'COURSE.
CRACK.
WHY? SOMETHING, LIKE, WRONG WITH THE BACKDROP?
IF NOT, SOD OFF.
YOU'RE BUGGERING MY CONCENTRATION.
DUDE.
NO. LIKE, YOUR SISTER CALLED.
ONE OF MY SISTERS CALLED?
BEFORE NOON? YOU SURE?
...SOMETHING ABOUT YOUR PARENTS BEING KIDNAPPED...
...BY, LIKE FASCISTS.
SO IT'S NOT, LIKE, A JOKE?
AWW, BLOODY HELL.

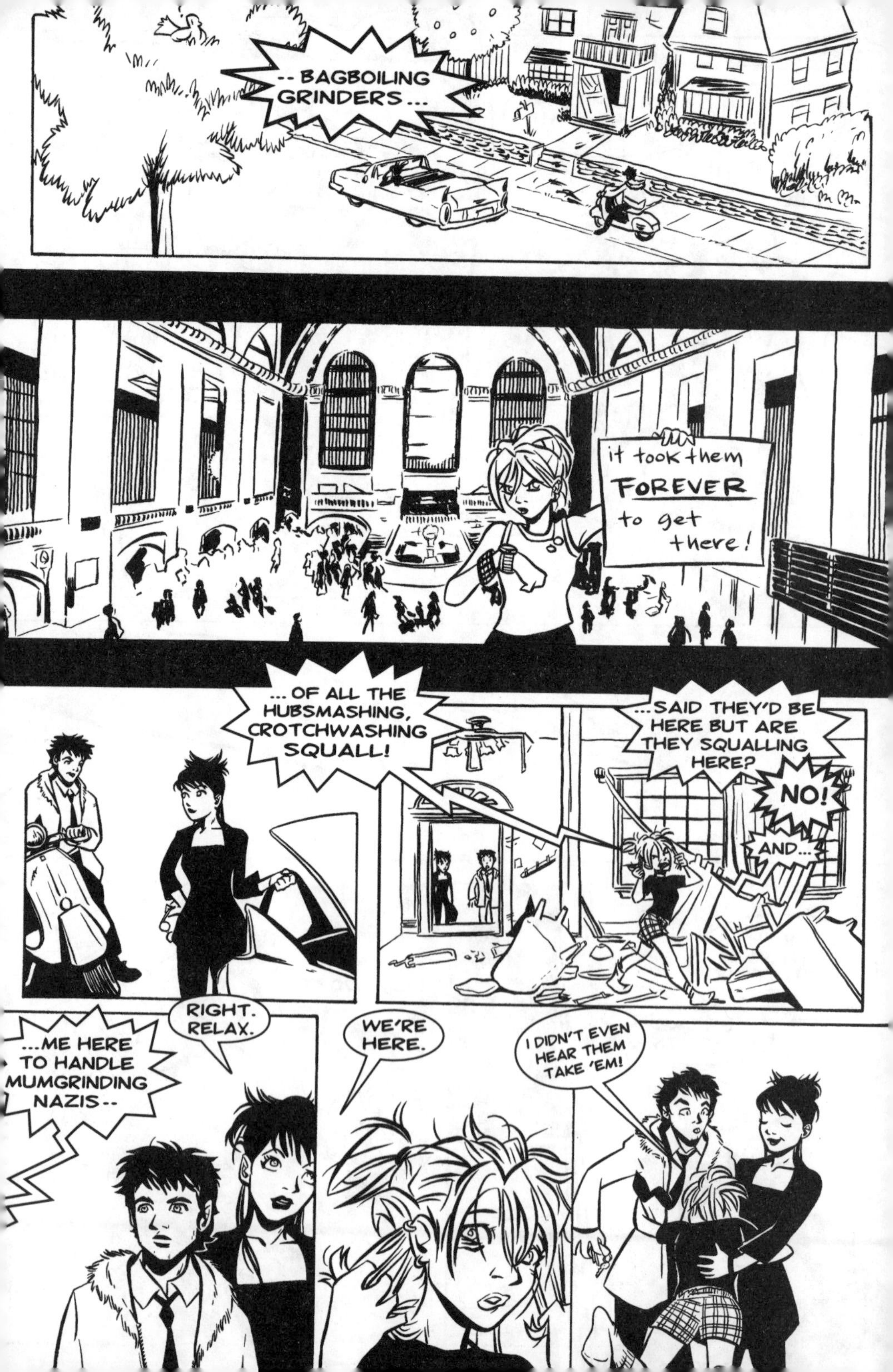
-- BAGBOILING GRINDERS ...
it took them FOREVER to get there!
... OF ALL THE HUBSMASHING, CROTCHWASHING SQUALL!
... SAID THEY'D BE HERE BUT ARE THEY SQUALLING HERE?
NO!
AND...
... ME HERE TO HANDLE MUMGRINDING NAZIS --
RIGHT. RELAX.
WE'RE HERE.
I DIDN'T EVEN HEAR THEM TAKE 'EM!

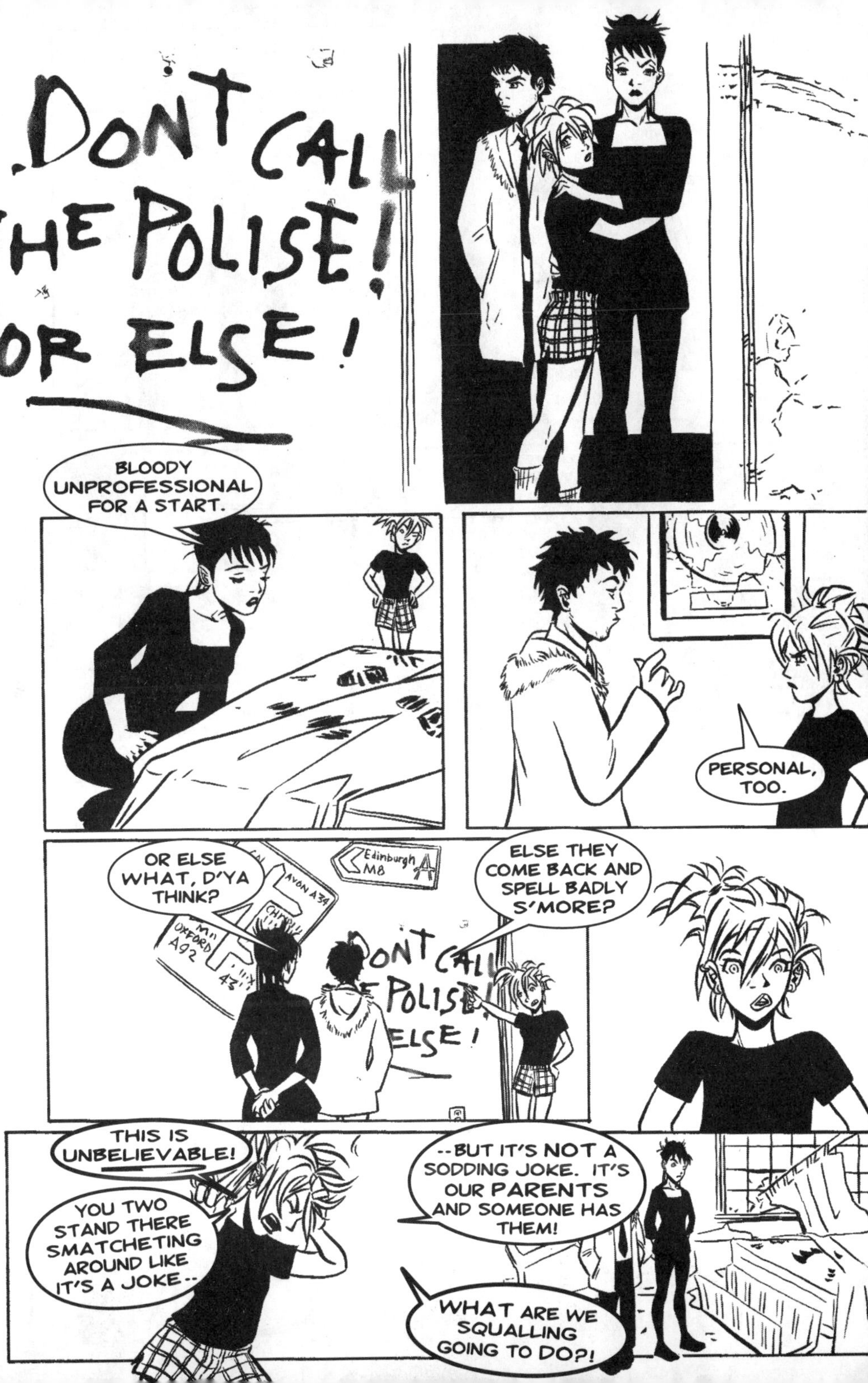

DON'T CALL THE POLISE! OR ELSE!
BLOODY UNPROFESSIONAL FOR A START.
PERSONAL, TOO.
OR ELSE WHAT, D'YA THINK?
Edinburgh M8
AVON A34
OXFORD A92
ELSE THEY COME BACK AND SPELL BADLY S'MORE?
THIS IS UNBELIEVABLE!
YOU TWO STAND THERE SMATCHETING AROUND LIKE IT'S A JOKE--
--BUT IT'S NOT A SODDING JOKE. IT'S OUR PARENTS AND SOMEONE HAS THEM!
WHAT ARE WE SQUALLING GOING TO DO?!

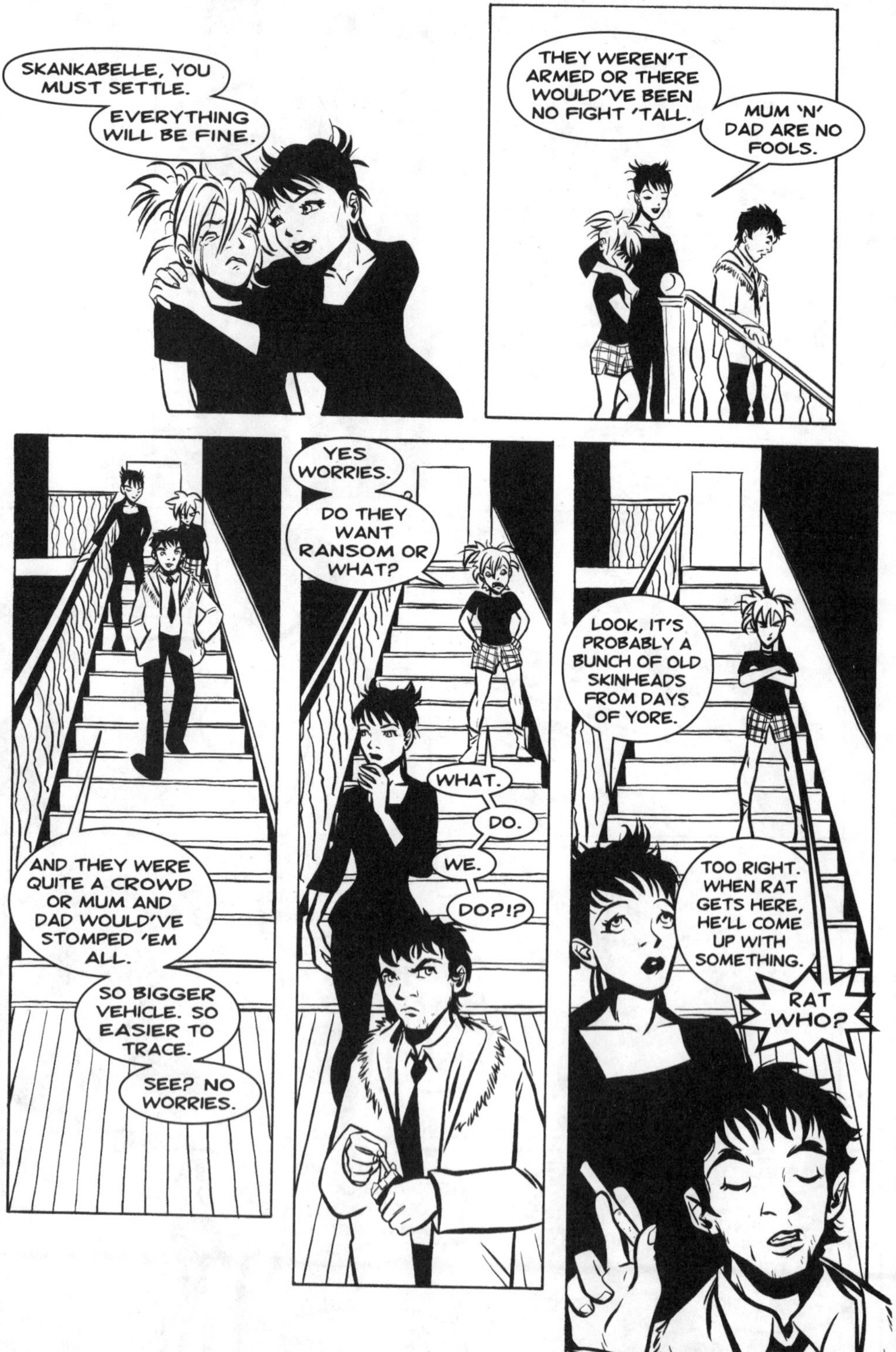
SKANKABELLE, YOU MUST SETTLE.
EVERYTHING WILL BE FINE.
THEY WEREN'T ARMED OR THERE WOULD'VE BEEN NO FIGHT 'TALL.
MUM 'N' DAD ARE NO FOOLS.
AND THEY WERE QUITE A CROWD OR MUM AND DAD WOULD'VE STOMPED 'EM ALL.
SO BIGGER VEHICLE. SO EASIER TO TRACE.
SEE? NO WORRIES.
YES WORRIES.
DO THEY WANT RANSOM OR WHAT?
WHAT.
DO.
WE.
DO?!?
LOOK, IT'S PROBABLY A BUNCH OF OLD SKINHEADS FROM DAYS OF YORE.
TOO RIGHT. WHEN RAT GETS HERE, HE'LL COME UP WITH SOMETHING.
RAT WHO?

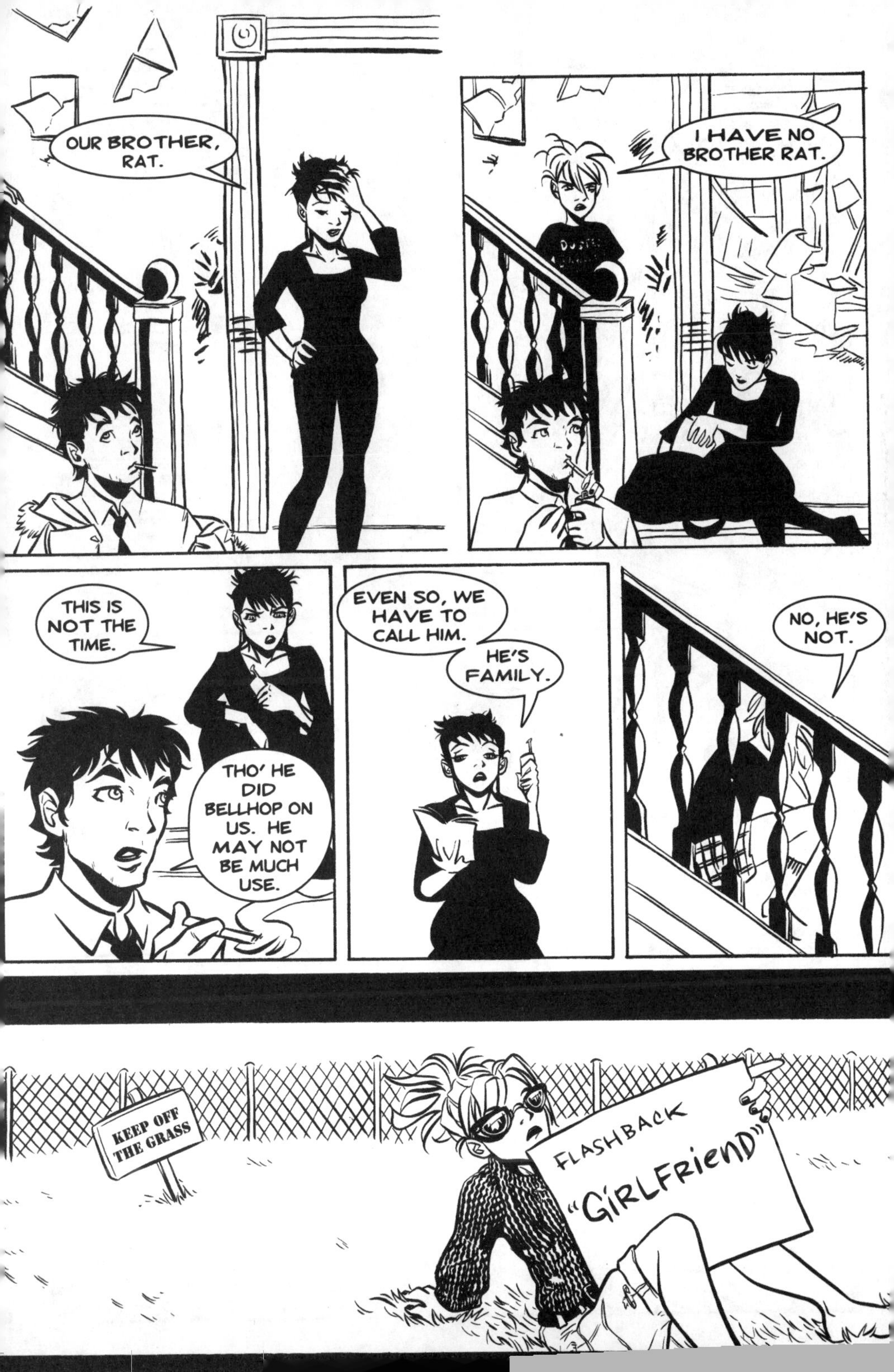
OUR BROTHER, RAT.
I HAVE NO BROTHER RAT.
THIS IS NOT THE TIME.
THO' HE DID BELLHOP ON US. HE MAY NOT BE MUCH USE.
EVEN SO, WE HAVE TO CALL HIM.
HE'S FAMILY.
NO, HE'S NOT.
KEEP OFF THE GRASS
FLASHBACK
“GIRLFRIEND”

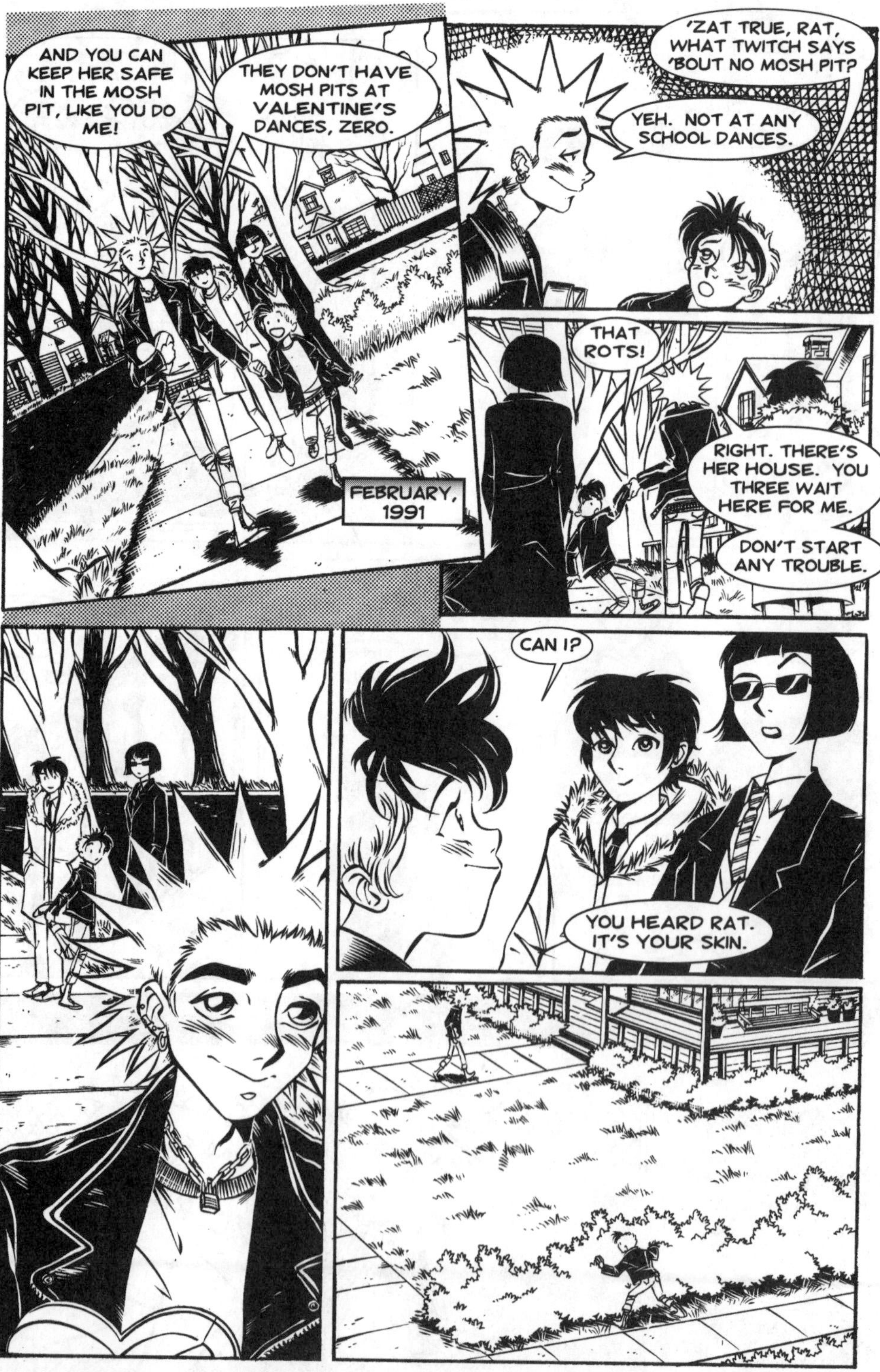
AND YOU CAN KEEP HER SAFE IN THE MOSH PIT, LIKE YOU DO ME!
THEY DON'T HAVE MOSH PITS AT VALENTINE'S DANCES, ZERO.
FEBRUARY, 1991
'ZAT TRUE, RAT, WHAT TWITCH SAYS 'BOUT NO MOSH PIT?
YEH. NOT AT ANY SCHOOL DANCES.
THAT ROTS!
RIGHT. THERE'S HER HOUSE. YOU THREE WAIT HERE FOR ME.
DON'T START ANY TROUBLE.
CAN I?
YOU HEARD RAT. IT'S YOUR SKIN.

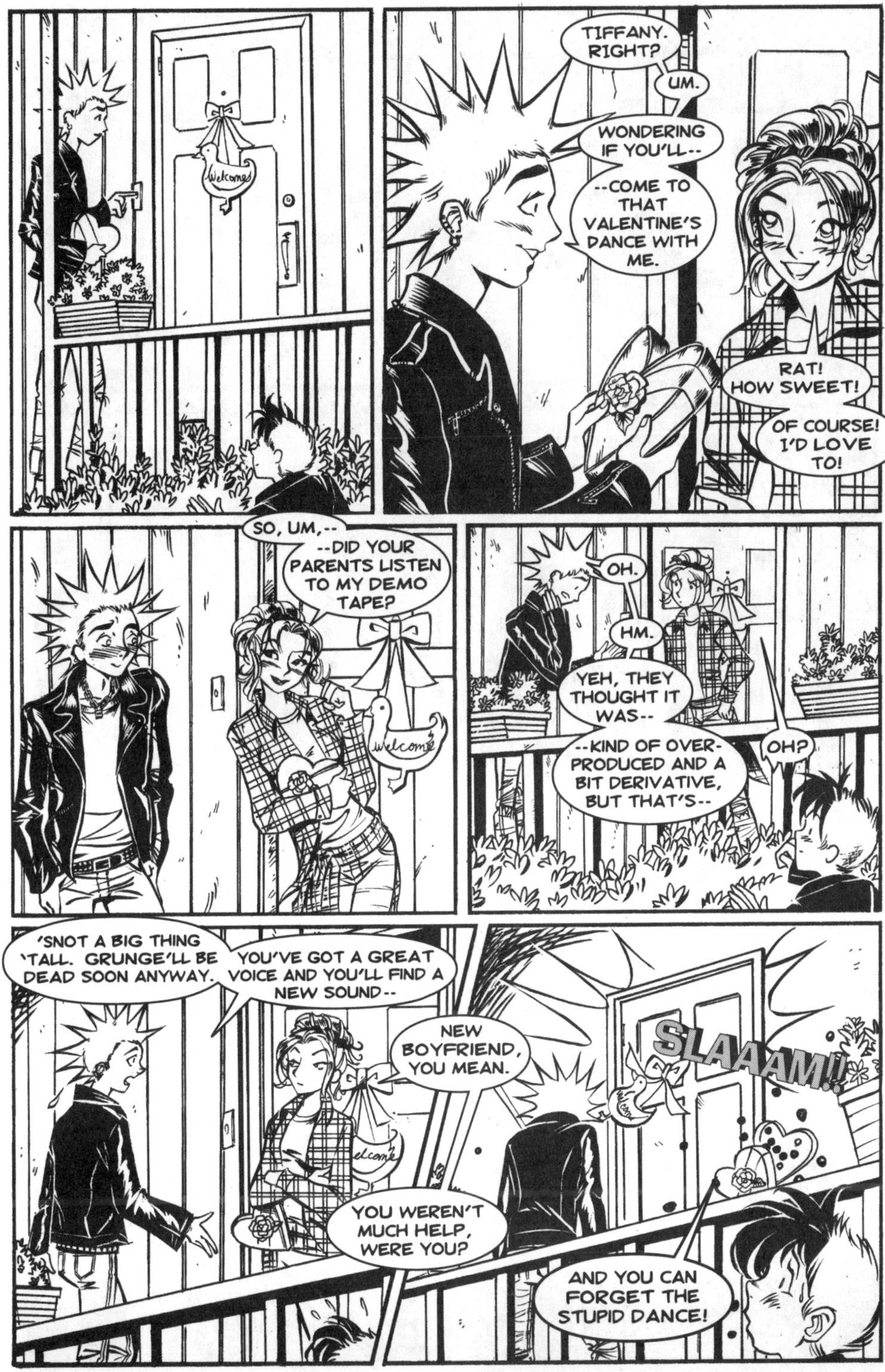

TIFFANY. RIGHT?
UM.
WONDERING IF YOU'LL--
--COME TO THAT VALENTINE'S DANCE WITH ME.
RAT! HOW SWEET!
OF COURSE! I'D LOVE TO!
SO, UM,--
--DID YOUR PARENTS LISTEN TO MY DEMO TAPE?
OH.
HM.
YEH, THEY THOUGHT IT WAS--
--KIND OF OVER-PRODUCED AND A BIT DERIVATIVE, BUT THAT'S--
OH?
'SNOT A BIG THING 'TALL. GRUNGE'LL BE DEAD SOON ANYWAY.
YOU'VE GOT A GREAT VOICE AND YOU'LL FIND A NEW SOUND--
NEW BOYFRIEND, YOU MEAN.
SLAAAM!!
YOU WEREN'T MUCH HELP, WERE YOU?
AND YOU CAN FORGET THE STUPID DANCE!

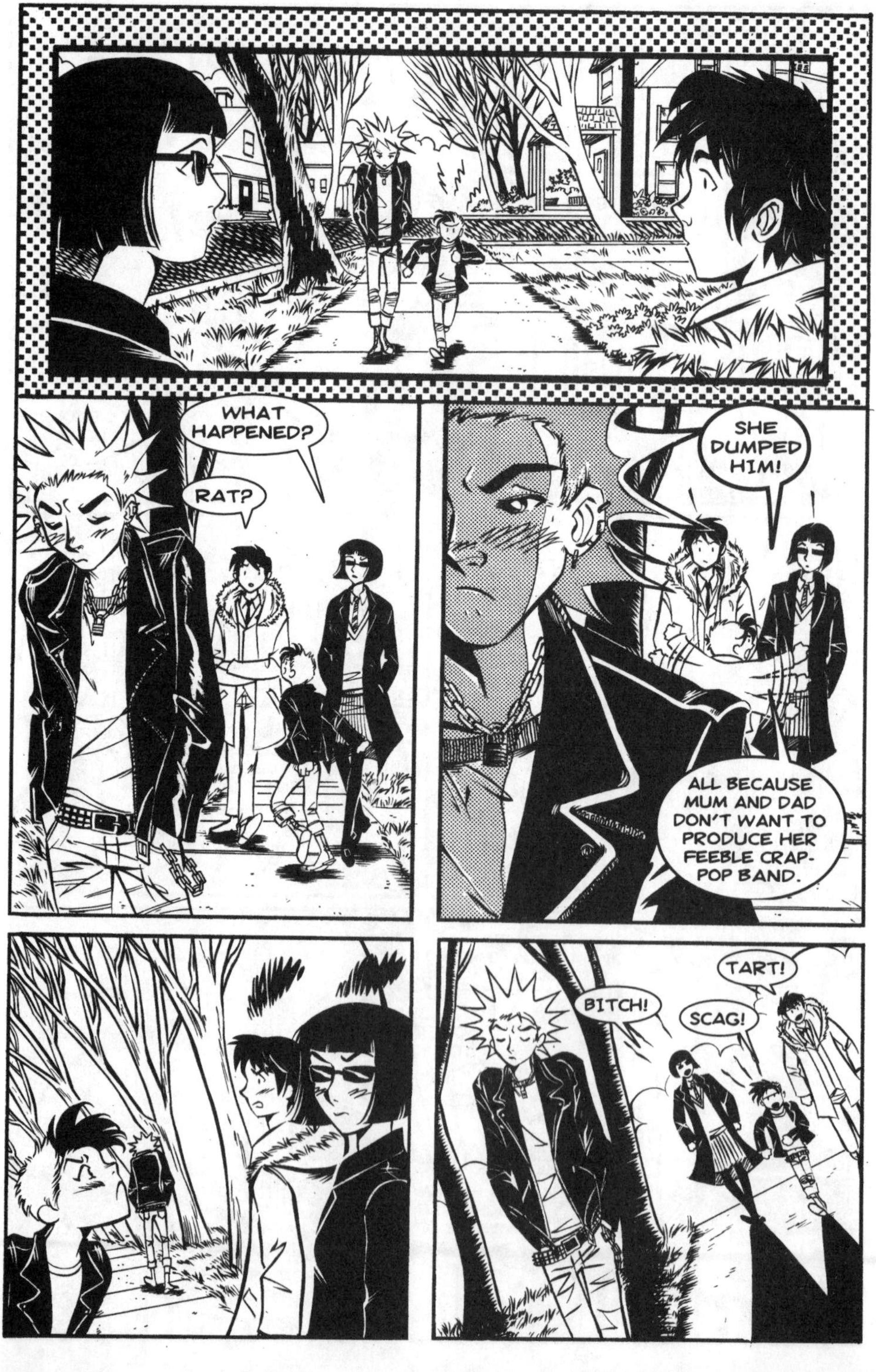
WHAT HAPPENED?
RAT?
SHE DUMPED HIM!
ALL BECAUSE MUM AND DAD DON'T WANT TO PRODUCE HER FEEBLE CRAP-POP BAND.
BITCH!
SCAG!
TART!

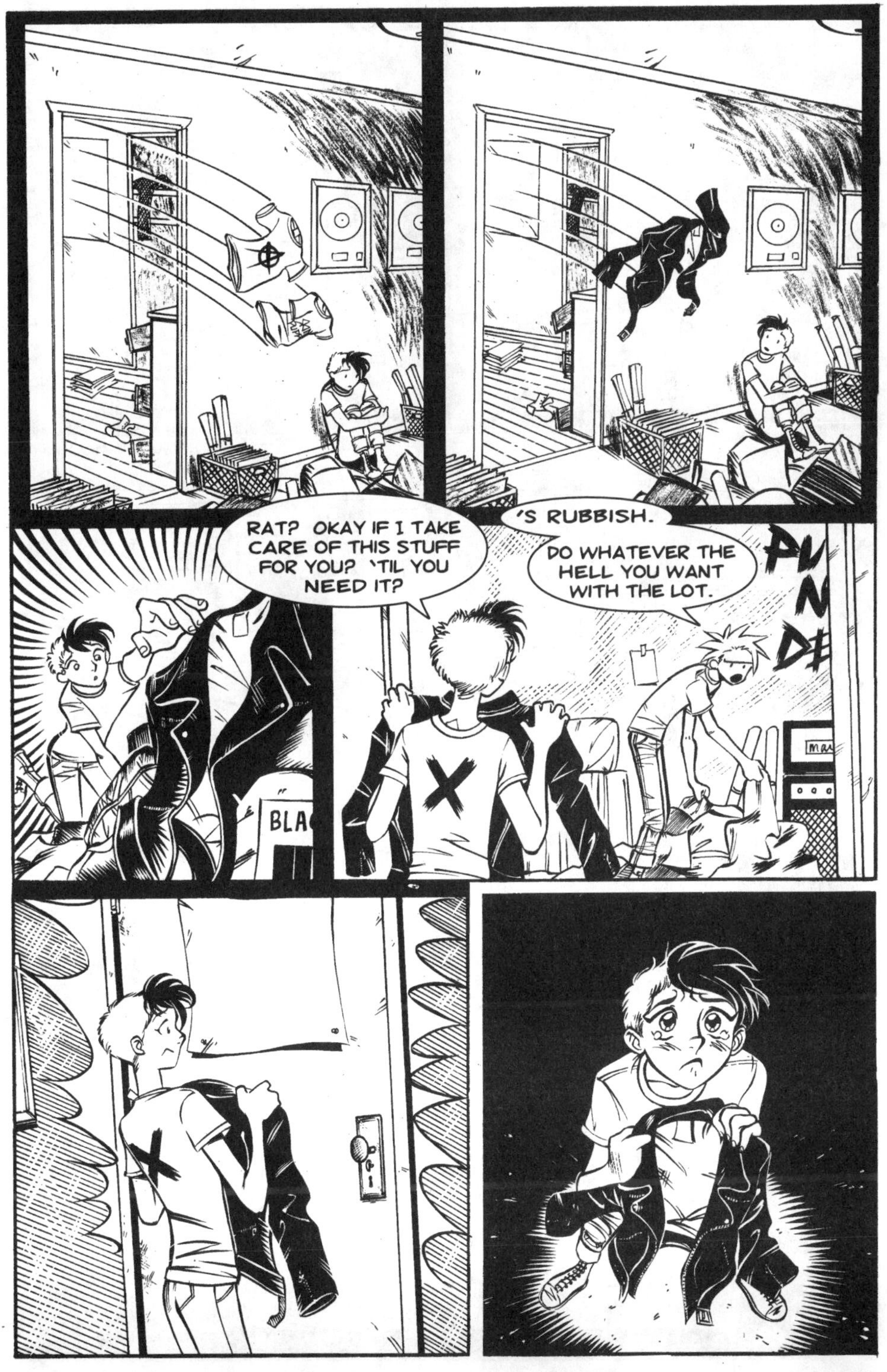
RAT? OKAY IF I TAKE CARE OF THIS STUFF FOR YOU? 'TIL YOU NEED IT?
'S RUBBISH.
DO WHATEVER THE HELL YOU WANT WITH THE LOT.

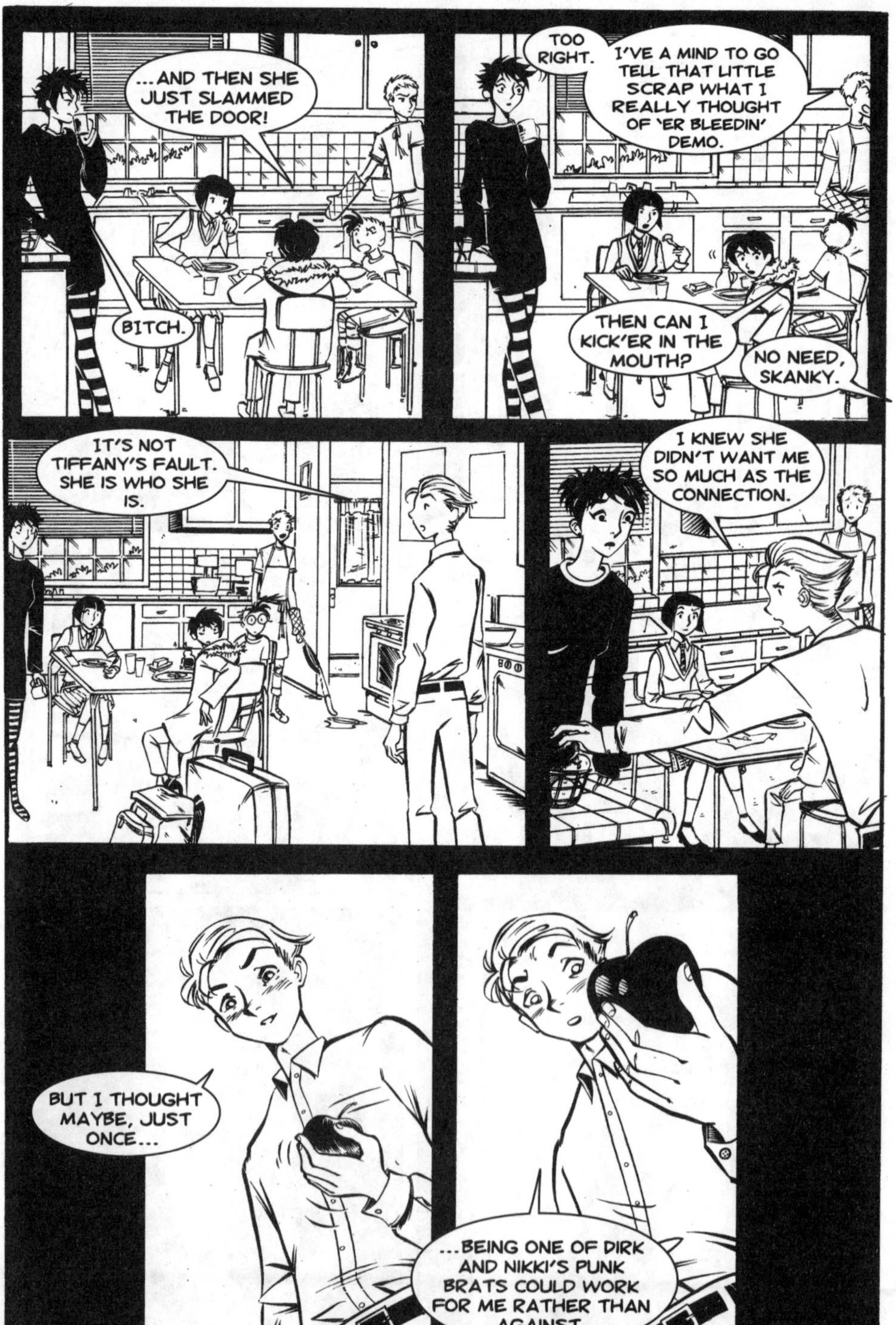
...AND THEN SHE JUST SLAMMED THE DOOR!
BITCH.
TOO RIGHT.
I'VE A MIND TO GO TELL THAT LITTLE SCRAP WHAT I REALLY THOUGHT OF 'ER BLEEDIN' DEMO.
THEN CAN I KICK'ER IN THE MOUTH?
NO NEED, SKANKY.
IT'S NOT TIFFANY'S FAULT. SHE IS WHO SHE IS.
I KNEW SHE DIDN'T WANT ME SO MUCH AS THE CONNECTION.
BUT I THOUGHT MAYBE, JUST ONCE...
...BEING ONE OF DIRK AND NIKKI'S PUNK BRATS COULD WORK FOR ME RATHER THAN AGAINST.

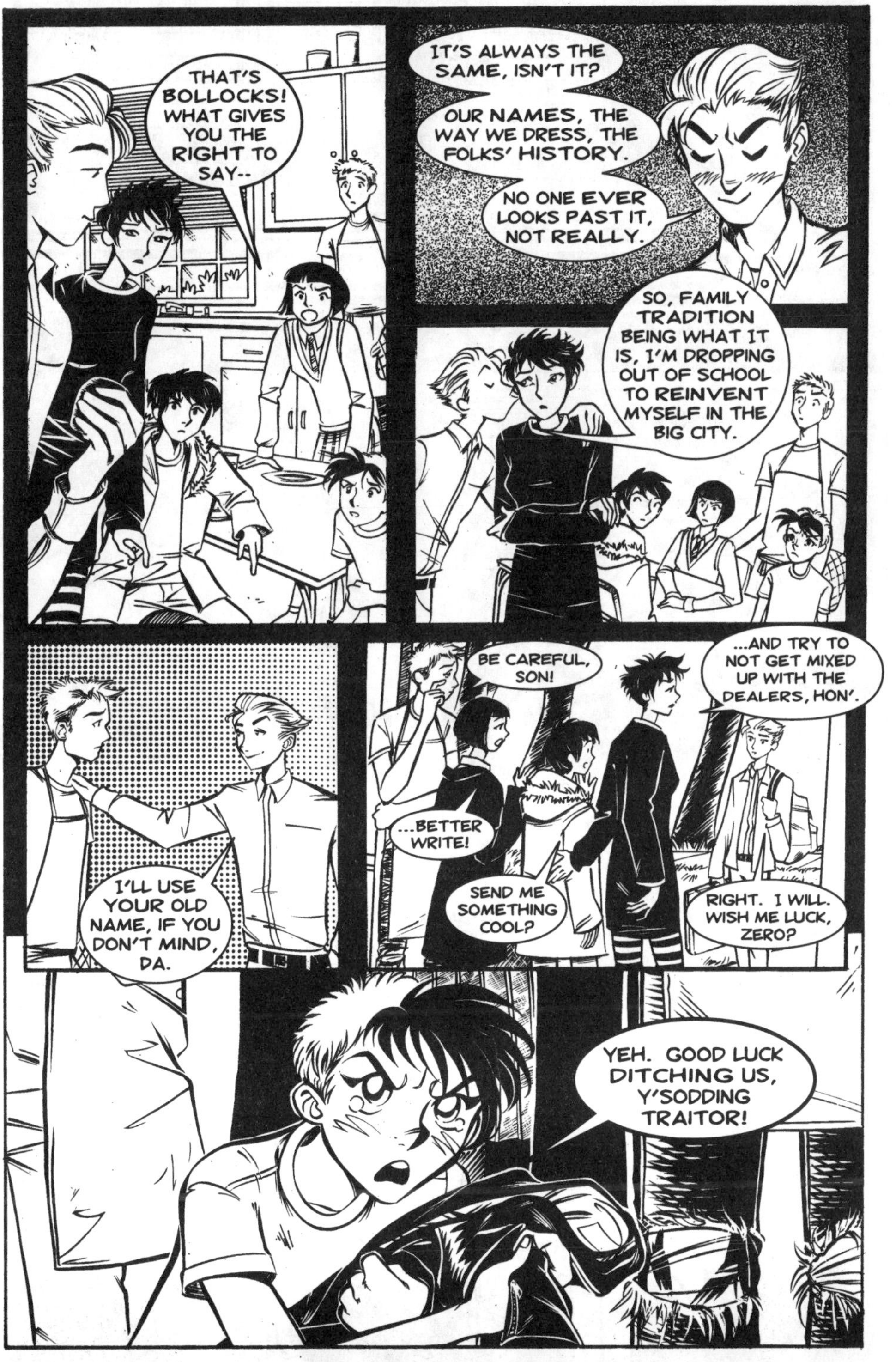
THAT'S BOLLOCKS! WHAT GIVES YOU THE RIGHT TO SAY--
IT'S ALWAYS THE SAME, ISN'T IT?
OUR NAMES, THE WAY WE DRESS, THE FOLKS' HISTORY.
NO ONE EVER LOOKS PAST IT, NOT REALLY.
SO, FAMILY TRADITION BEING WHAT IT IS, I'M DROPPING OUT OF SCHOOL TO REINVENT MYSELF IN THE BIG CITY.
I'LL USE YOUR OLD NAME, IF YOU DON'T MIND, DA.
BE CAREFUL, SON!
...AND TRY TO NOT GET MIXED UP WITH THE DEALERS, HON'.
...BETTER WRITE!
SEND ME SOMETHING COOL?
RIGHT. I WILL. WISH ME LUCK, ZERO?
YEH. GOOD LUCK DITCHING US, Y'SODDING TRAITOR!

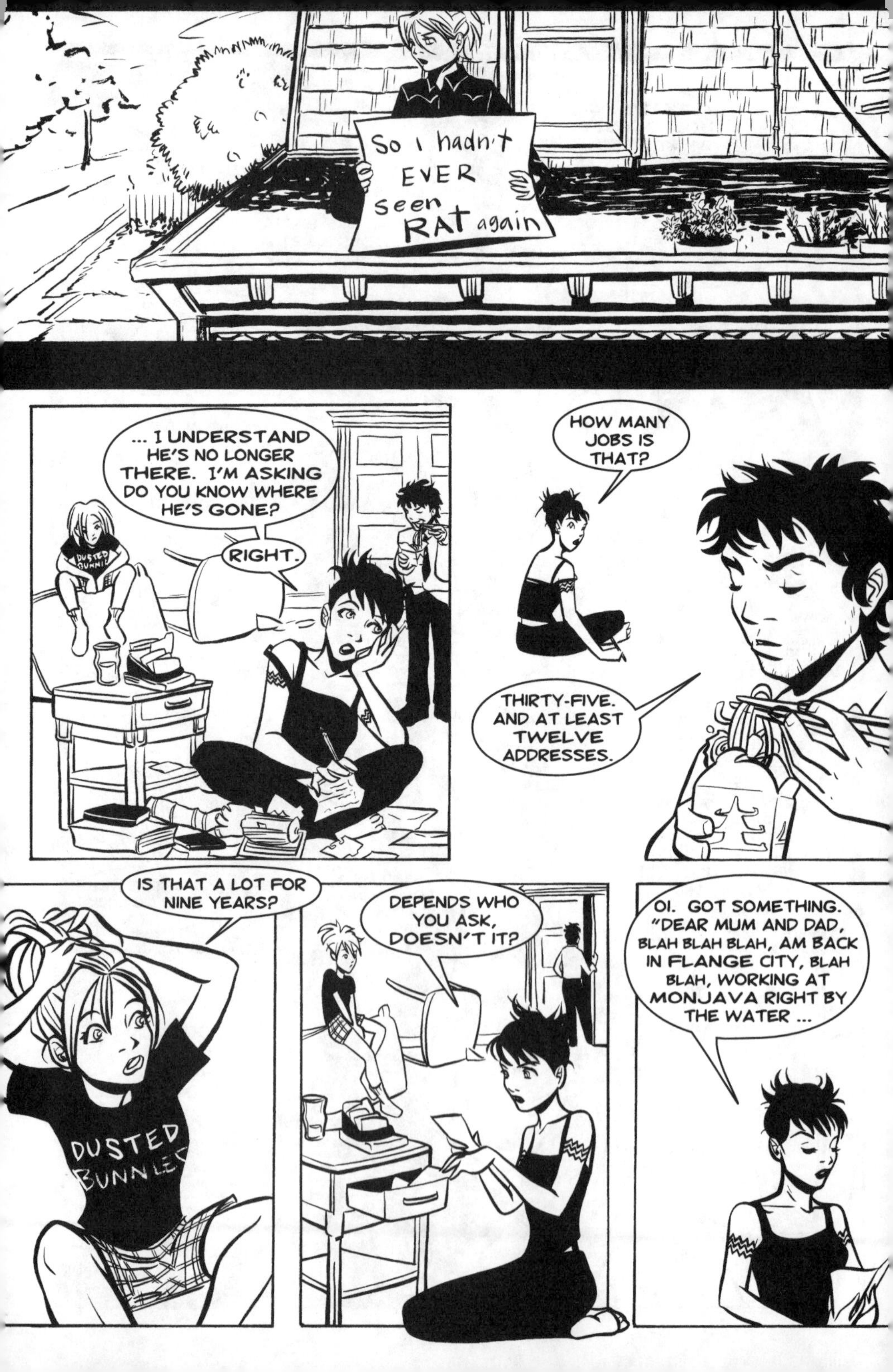
So I hadn't EVER seen RAT again
... I UNDERSTAND HE'S NO LONGER THERE. I'M ASKING DO YOU KNOW WHERE HE'S GONE?
RIGHT.
HOW MANY JOBS IS THAT?
THIRTY-FIVE. AND AT LEAST TWELVE ADDRESSES.
IS THAT A LOT FOR NINE YEARS?
DEPENDS WHO YOU ASK, DOESN'T IT?
OI. GOT SOMETHING. "DEAR MUM AND DAD, BLAH BLAH BLAH, AM BACK IN FLANGE CITY, BLAH BLAH, WORKING AT MONJAVA RIGHT BY THE WATER ...
DUSTED BUNNIES

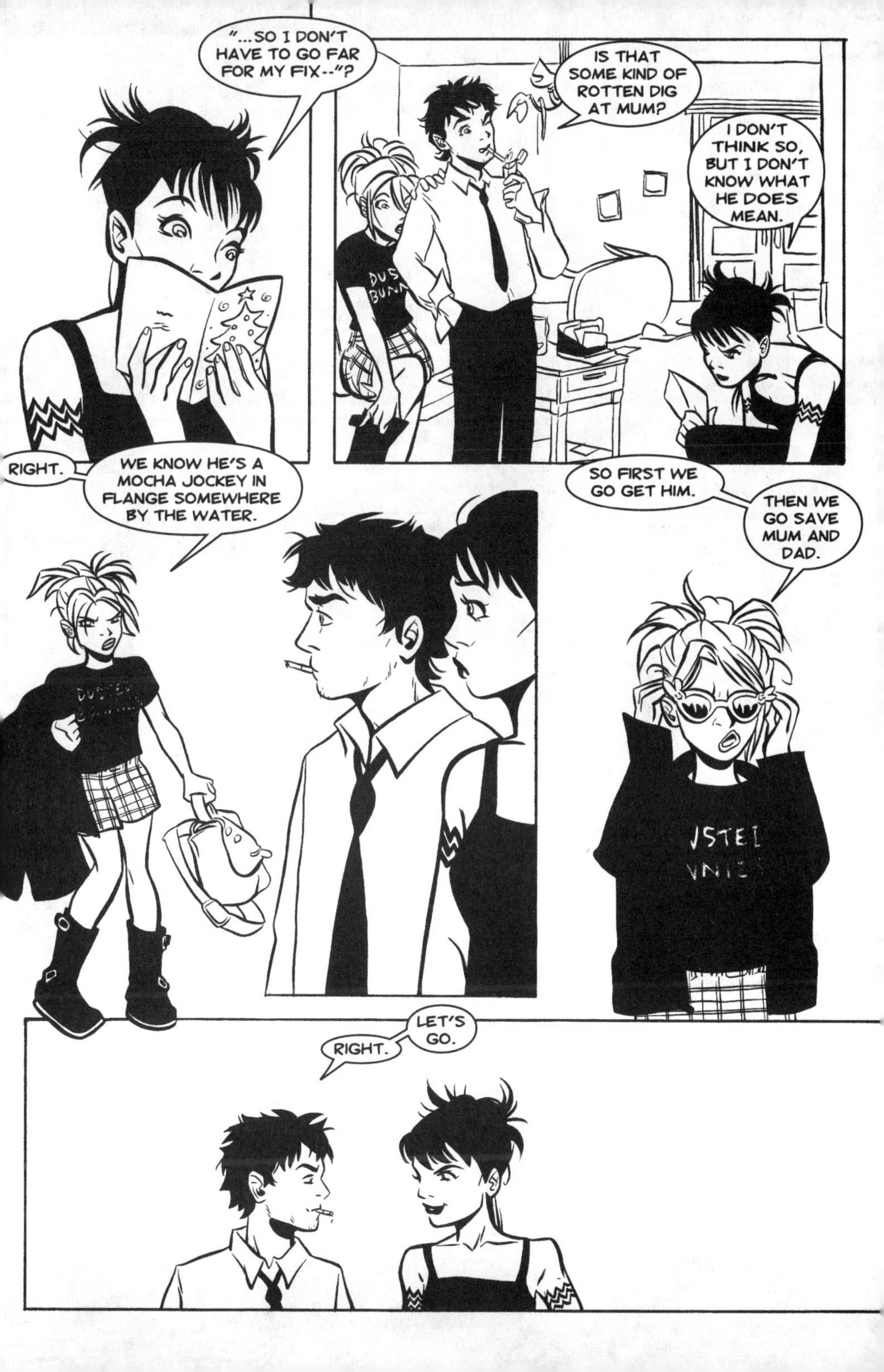
"...SO I DON'T HAVE TO GO FAR FOR MY FIX--"?
IS THAT SOME KIND OF ROTTEN DIG AT MUM?
I DON'T THINK SO, BUT I DON'T KNOW WHAT HE DOES MEAN.
DUS BUNN
RIGHT.
WE KNOW HE'S A MOCHA JOCKEY IN FLANGE SOMEWHERE BY THE WATER.
SO FIRST WE GO GET HIM.
THEN WE GO SAVE MUM AND DAD.
USTEI VNIES
RIGHT.
LET'S GO.

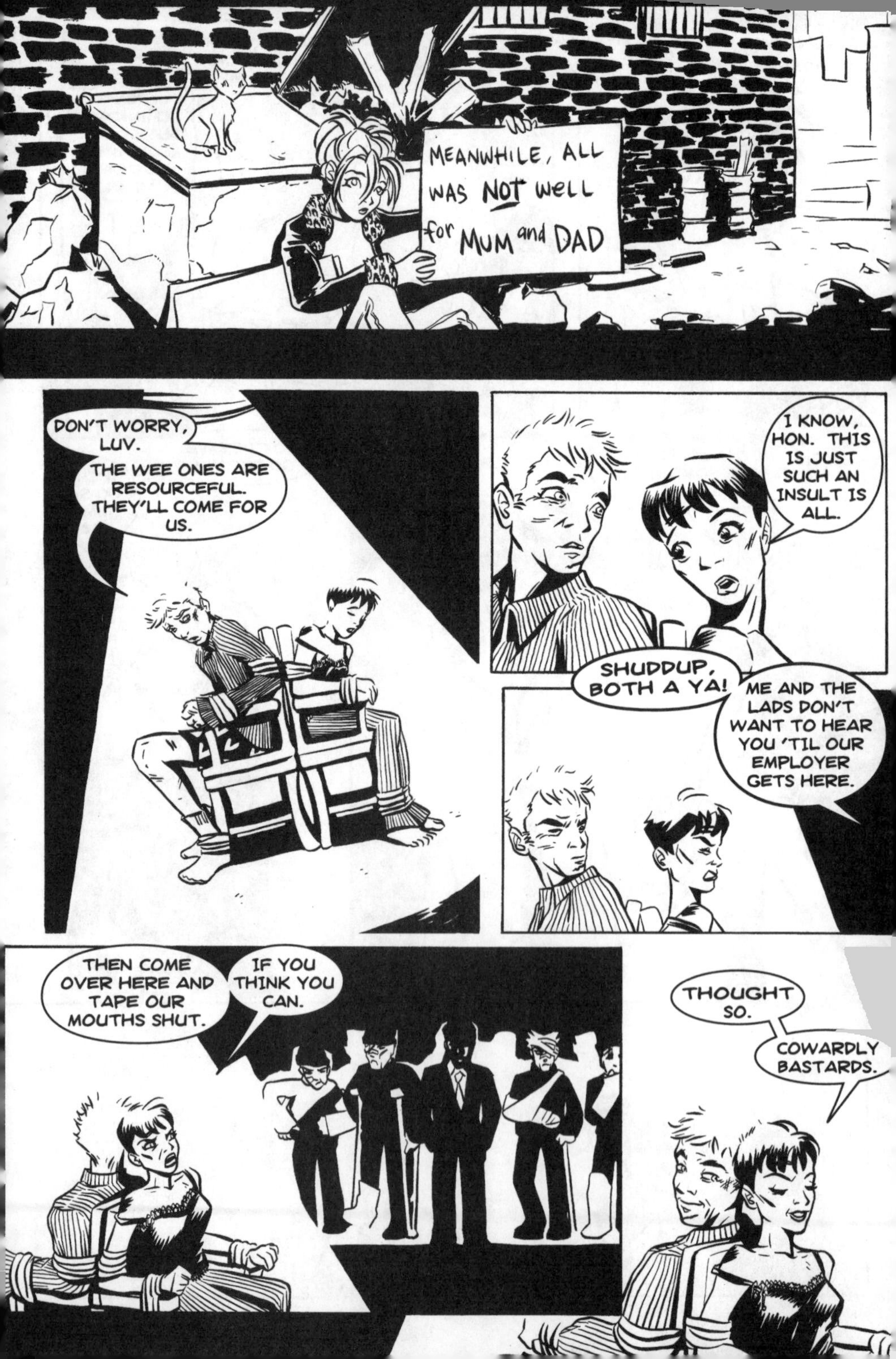
MEANWHILE, ALL WAS NOT WELL for MUM and DAD
DON'T WORRY, LUV.
THE WEE ONES ARE RESOURCEFUL. THEY'LL COME FOR US.
I KNOW, HON. THIS IS JUST SUCH AN INSULT IS ALL.
SHUDDUP, BOTH A YA!
ME AND THE LADS DON'T WANT TO HEAR YOU 'TIL OUR EMPLOYER GETS HERE.
THEN COME OVER HERE AND TAPE OUR MOUTHS SHUT.
IF YOU THINK YOU CAN.
THOUGHT SO.
COWARDLY BASTARDS.

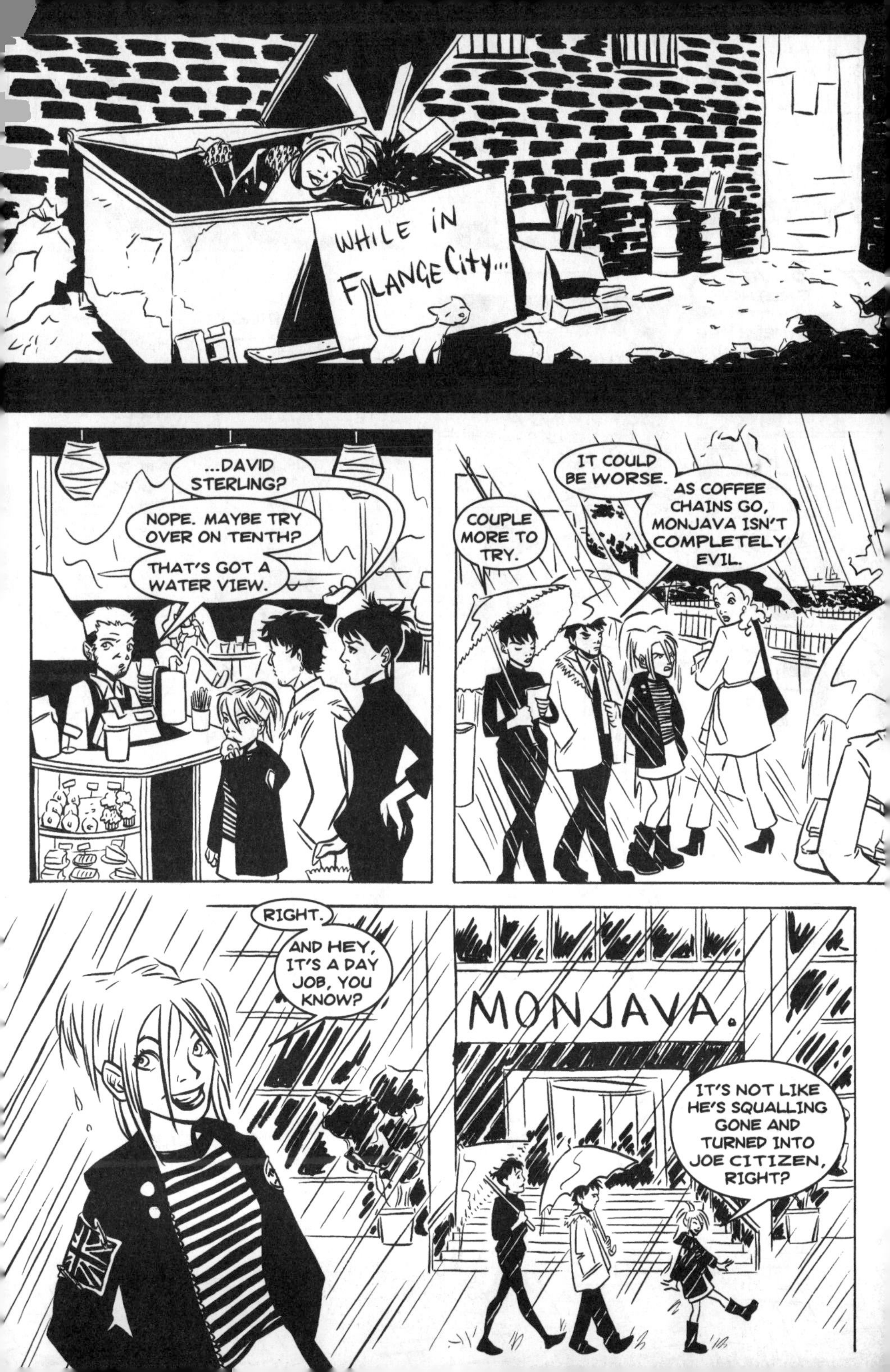
WHILE IN FLANGE CITY...
...DAVID STERLING?
NOPE. MAYBE TRY OVER ON TENTH?
THAT'S GOT A WATER VIEW.
COUPLE MORE TO TRY.
IT COULD BE WORSE.
AS COFFEE CHAINS GO, MONJAVA ISN'T COMPLETELY EVIL.
RIGHT.
AND HEY, IT'S A DAY JOB, YOU KNOW?
MONJAVA.
IT'S NOT LIKE HE'S SQUALLING GONE AND TURNED INTO JOE CITIZEN, RIGHT?

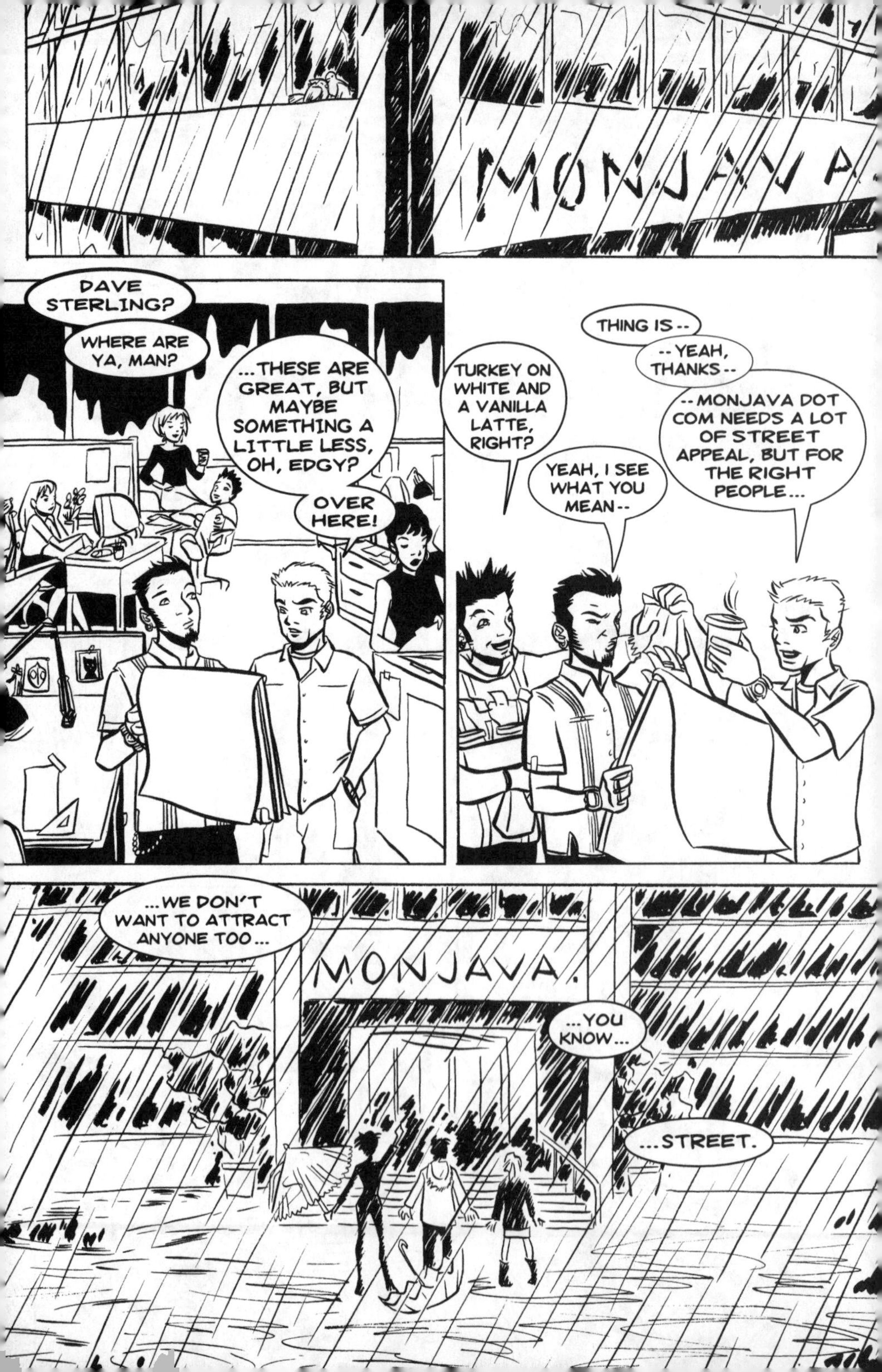
MONJAVA
DAVE STERLING?
WHERE ARE YA, MAN?
...THESE ARE GREAT, BUT MAYBE SOMETHING A LITTLE LESS, OH, EDGY?
OVER HERE!
TURKEY ON WHITE AND A VANILLA LATTE, RIGHT?
THING IS --
YEAH, I SEE WHAT YOU MEAN --
-- YEAH, THANKS --
-- MONJAVA DOT COM NEEDS A LOT OF STREET APPEAL, BUT FOR THE RIGHT PEOPLE...
...WE DON'T WANT TO ATTRACT ANYONE TOO...
MONJAVA.
...YOU KNOW...
...STREET.

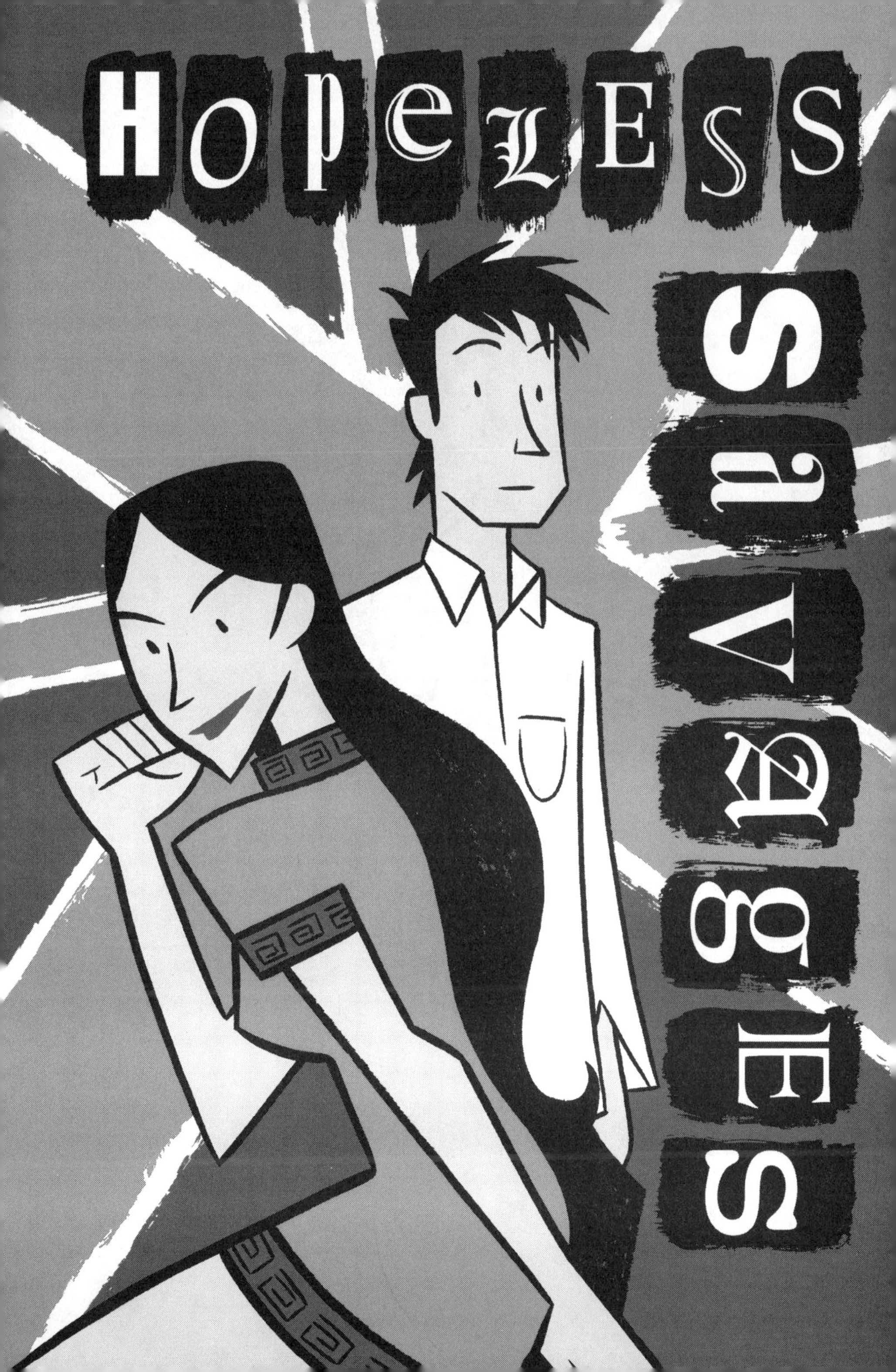
HopeLEss
SaVAgEs

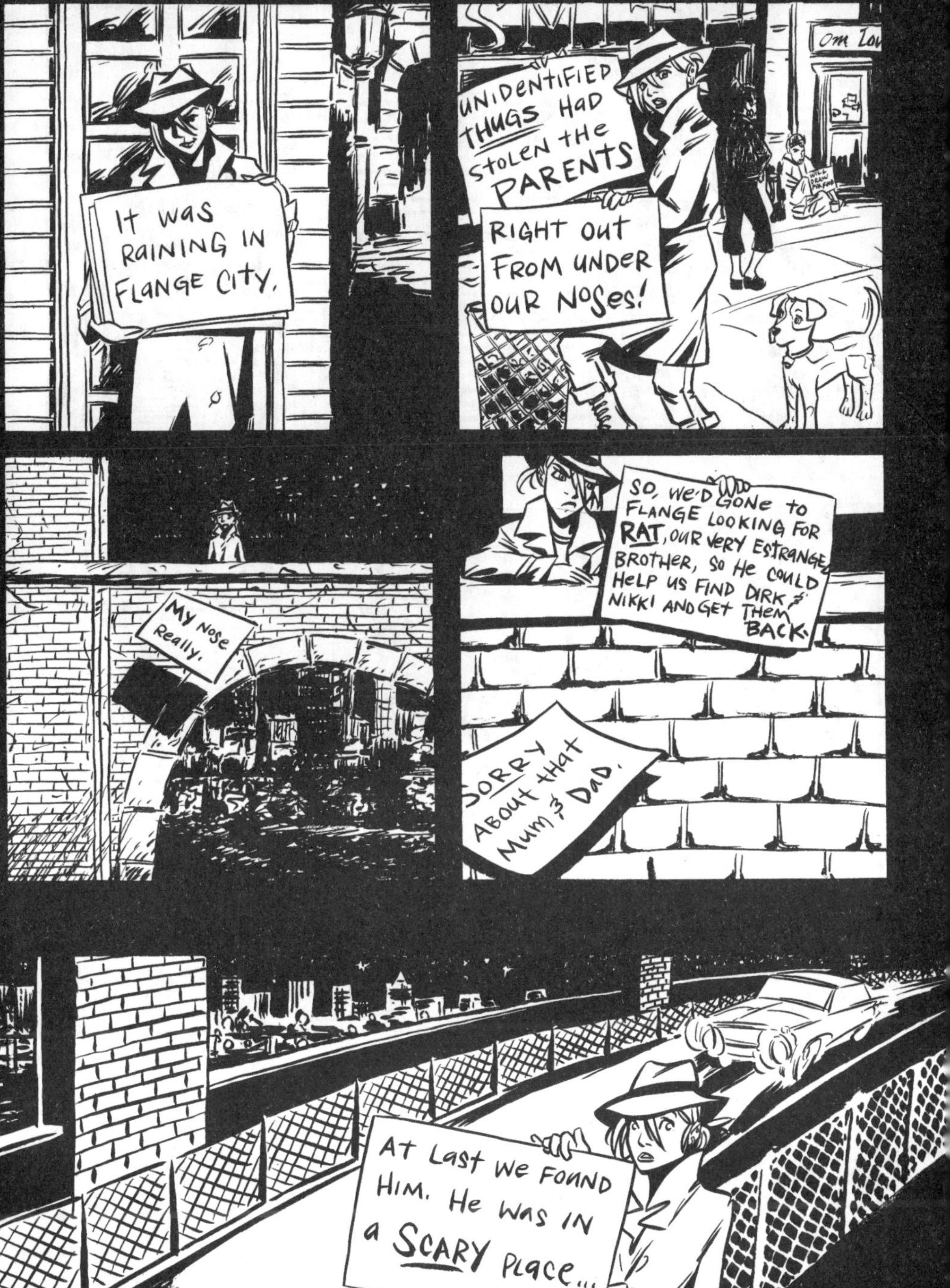
It was RAINING IN FLANGE City.
UNIDENTIFIED THUGS HAD STOLEN THE PARENTS
RIGHT OUT FROM UNDER OUR NOSES!
My Nose Really.
SO, WE'D GONE TO FLANGE LOOKING FOR RAT, OUR VERY ESTRANGED BROTHER, SO HE COULD HELP US FIND DIRK & NIKKI AND GET THEM BACK.
SORRY About that Mum & Dad.
At Last we FOUND HIM. He was IN a SCARY place...

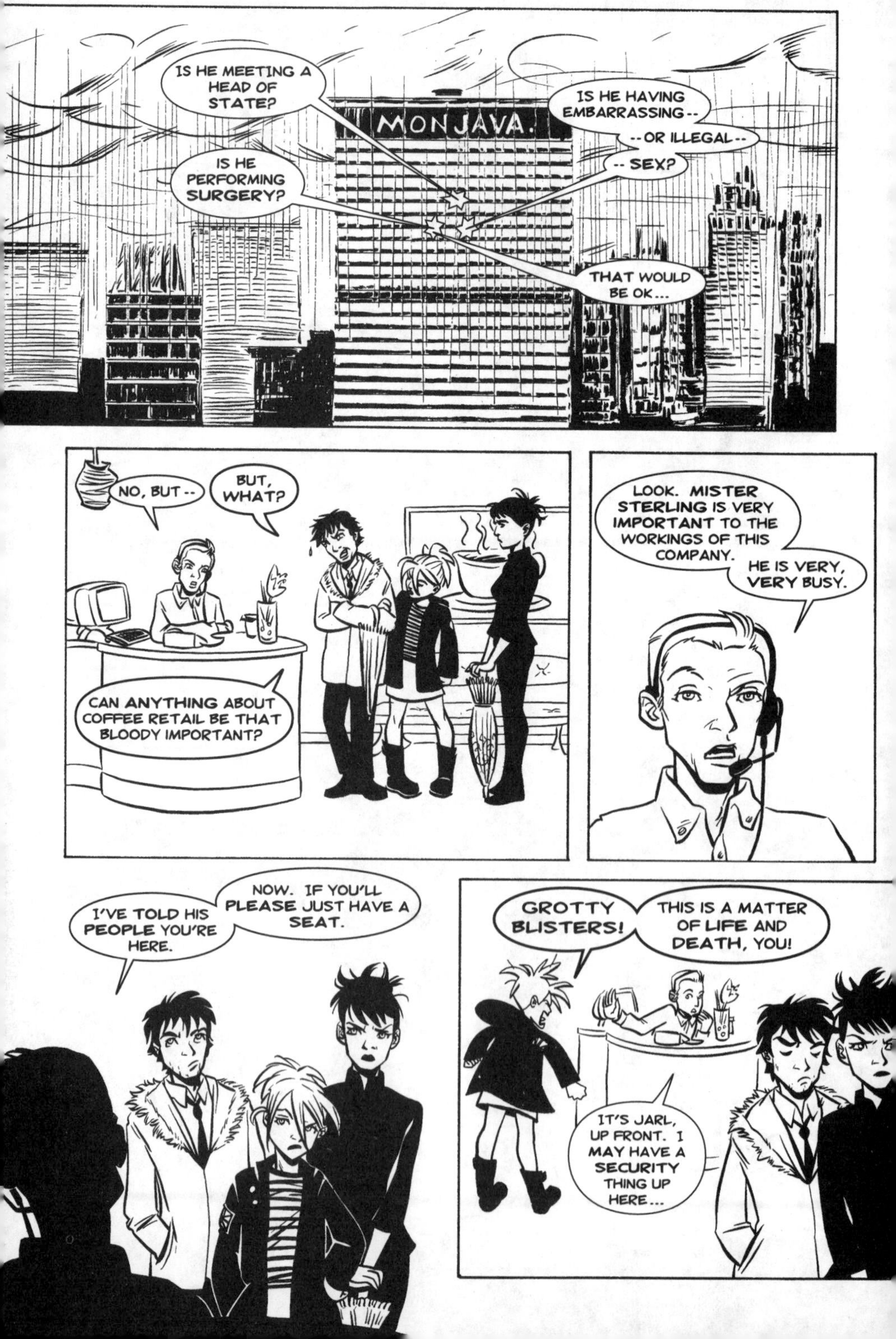

IS HE MEETING A HEAD OF STATE?
MONJAVA.
IS HE HAVING EMBARRASSING --
-- OR ILLEGAL --
-- SEX?
IS HE PERFORMING SURGERY?
THAT WOULD BE OK...
NO, BUT --
BUT, WHAT?
CAN ANYTHING ABOUT COFFEE RETAIL BE THAT BLOODY IMPORTANT?
LOOK. MISTER STERLING IS VERY IMPORTANT TO THE WORKINGS OF THIS COMPANY.
HE IS VERY, VERY BUSY.
I'VE TOLD HIS PEOPLE YOU'RE HERE.
NOW. IF YOU'LL PLEASE JUST HAVE A SEAT.
GROTTY BLISTERS!
THIS IS A MATTER OF LIFE AND DEATH, YOU!
IT'S JARL, UP FRONT. I MAY HAVE A SECURITY THING UP HERE...

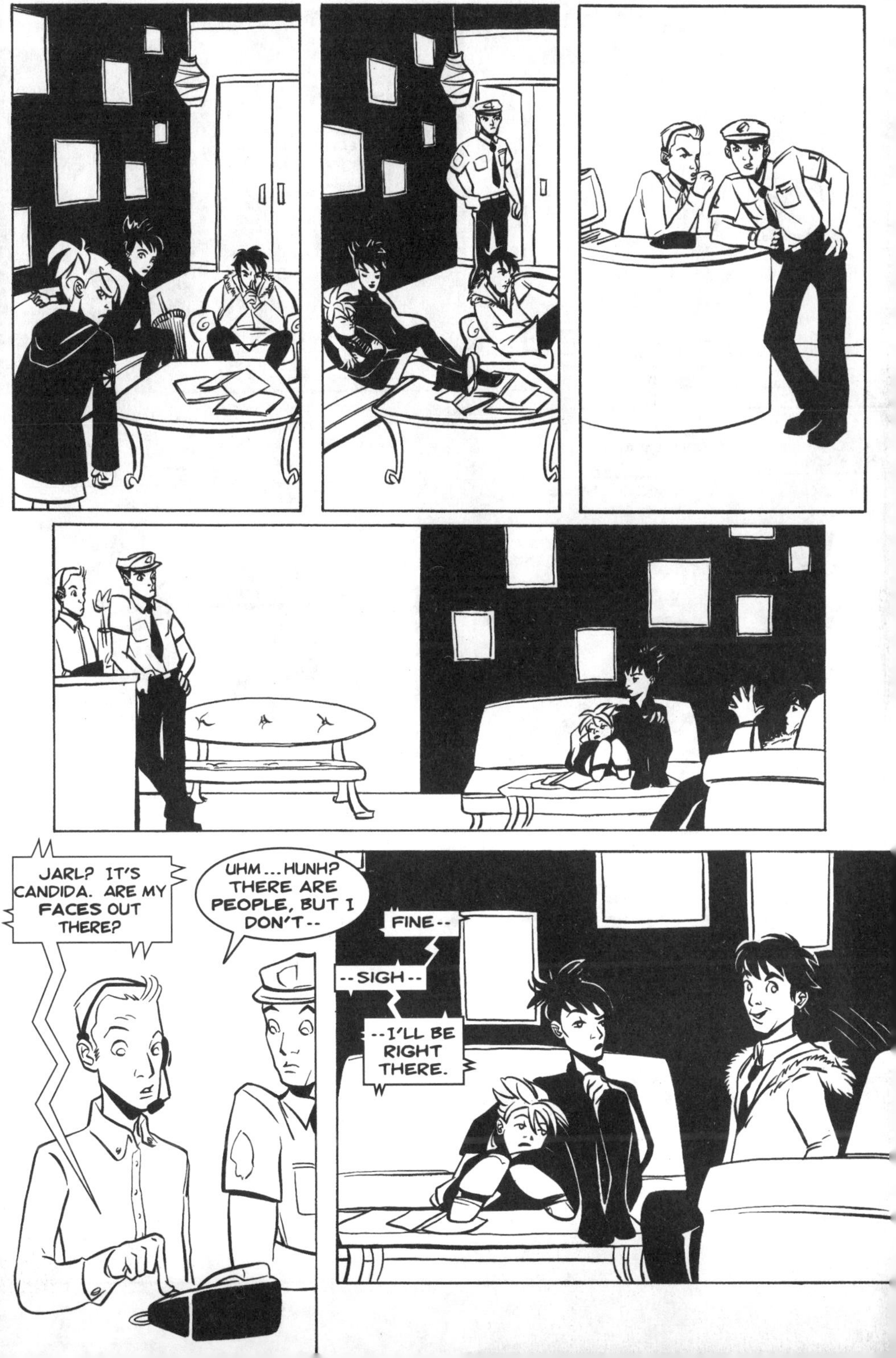
JARL? IT'S CANDIDA. ARE MY FACES OUT THERE?
UHM... HUNH? THERE ARE PEOPLE, BUT I DON'T--
FINE--
--SIGH--
--I'LL BE RIGHT THERE.

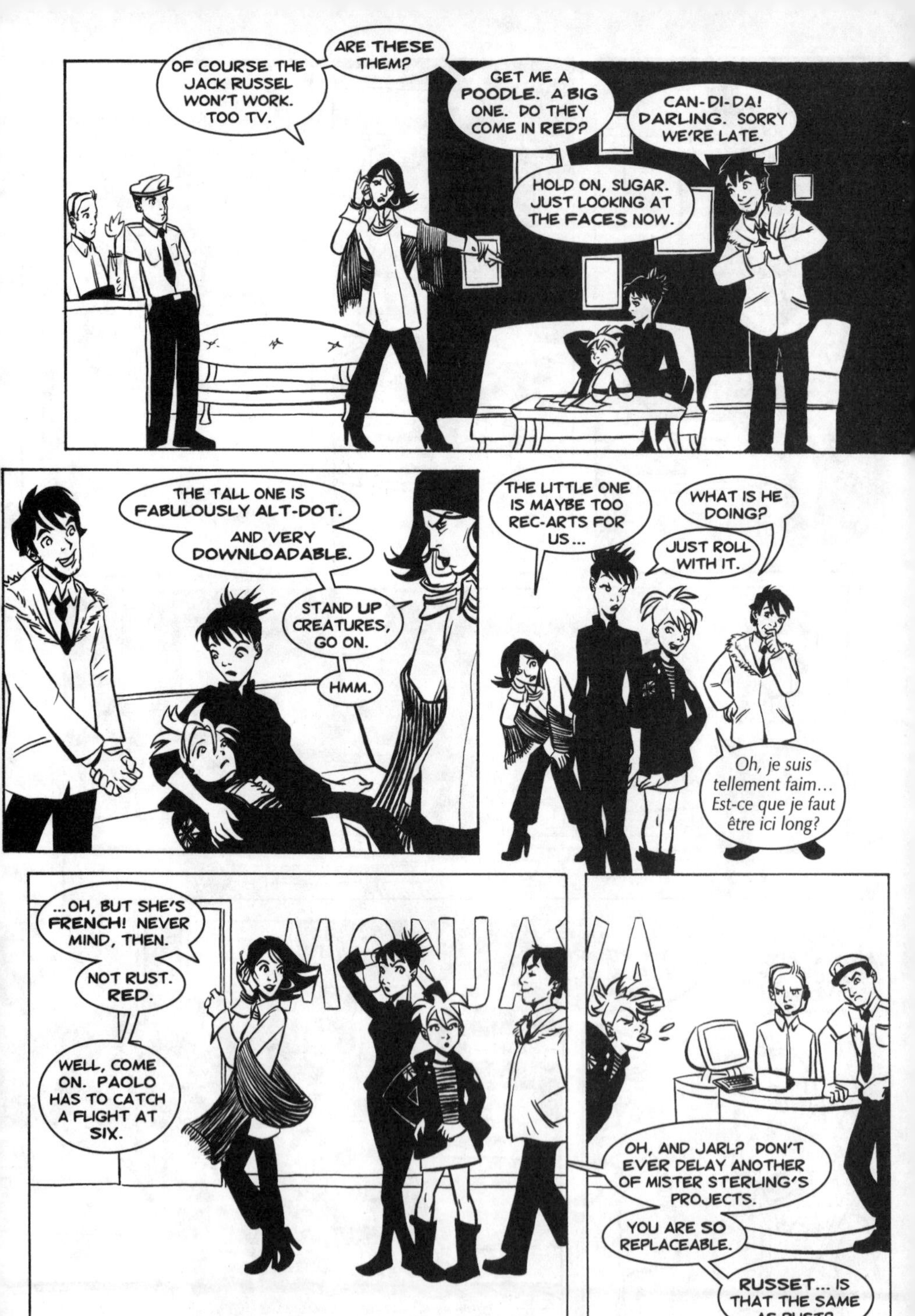
OF COURSE THE JACK RUSSEL WON'T WORK. TOO TV.
ARE THESE THEM?
GET ME A POODLE. A BIG ONE. DO THEY COME IN RED?
CAN-DI-DA! DARLING. SORRY WE'RE LATE.
HOLD ON, SUGAR. JUST LOOKING AT THE FACES NOW.
THE TALL ONE IS FABULOUSLY ALT-DOT.
AND VERY DOWNLOADABLE.
STAND UP CREATURES, GO ON.
HMM.
THE LITTLE ONE IS MAYBE TOO REC-ARTS FOR US...
WHAT IS HE DOING?
JUST ROLL WITH IT.
Oh, je suis tellement faim… Est-ce que je faut être ici long?
...OH, BUT SHE'S FRENCH! NEVER MIND, THEN.
NOT RUST. RED.
WELL, COME ON. PAOLO HAS TO CATCH A FLIGHT AT SIX.
OH, AND JARL? DON'T EVER DELAY ANOTHER OF MISTER STERLING'S PROJECTS.
YOU ARE SO REPLACEABLE.
RUSSET... IS THAT THE SAME AS RUST?

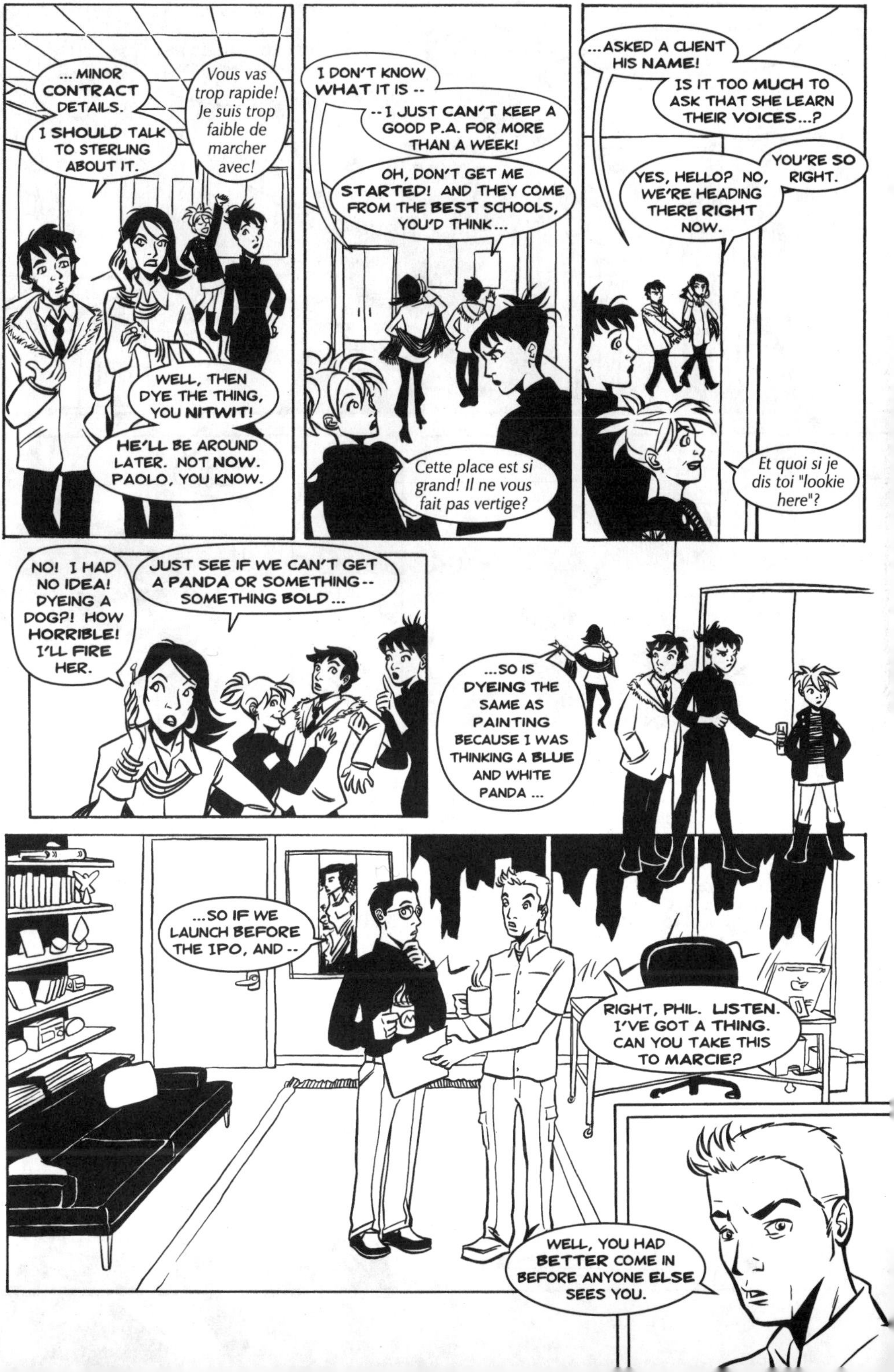
... MINOR CONTRACT DETAILS.
I SHOULD TALK TO STERLING ABOUT IT.
Vous vas trop rapide! Je suis trop faible de marcher avec!
WELL, THEN DYE THE THING, YOU NITWIT!
HE'LL BE AROUND LATER. NOT NOW. PAOLO, YOU KNOW.
I DON'T KNOW WHAT IT IS --
-- I JUST CAN'T KEEP A GOOD P.A. FOR MORE THAN A WEEK!
OH, DON'T GET ME STARTED! AND THEY COME FROM THE BEST SCHOOLS, YOU'D THINK...
Cette place est si grand! Il ne vous fait pas vertige?
...ASKED A CLIENT HIS NAME!
IS IT TOO MUCH TO ASK THAT SHE LEARN THEIR VOICES...?
YES, HELLO? NO, WE'RE HEADING THERE RIGHT NOW.
YOU'RE SO RIGHT.
Et quoi si je dis toi "lookie here"?
NO! I HAD NO IDEA! DYEING A DOG?! HOW HORRIBLE! I'LL FIRE HER.
JUST SEE IF WE CAN'T GET A PANDA OR SOMETHING -- SOMETHING BOLD...
...SO IS DYEING THE SAME AS PAINTING BECAUSE I WAS THINKING A BLUE AND WHITE PANDA ...
...SO IF WE LAUNCH BEFORE THE IPO, AND --
RIGHT, PHIL. LISTEN. I'VE GOT A THING. CAN YOU TAKE THIS TO MARCIE?
WELL, YOU HAD BETTER COME IN BEFORE ANYONE ELSE SEES YOU.

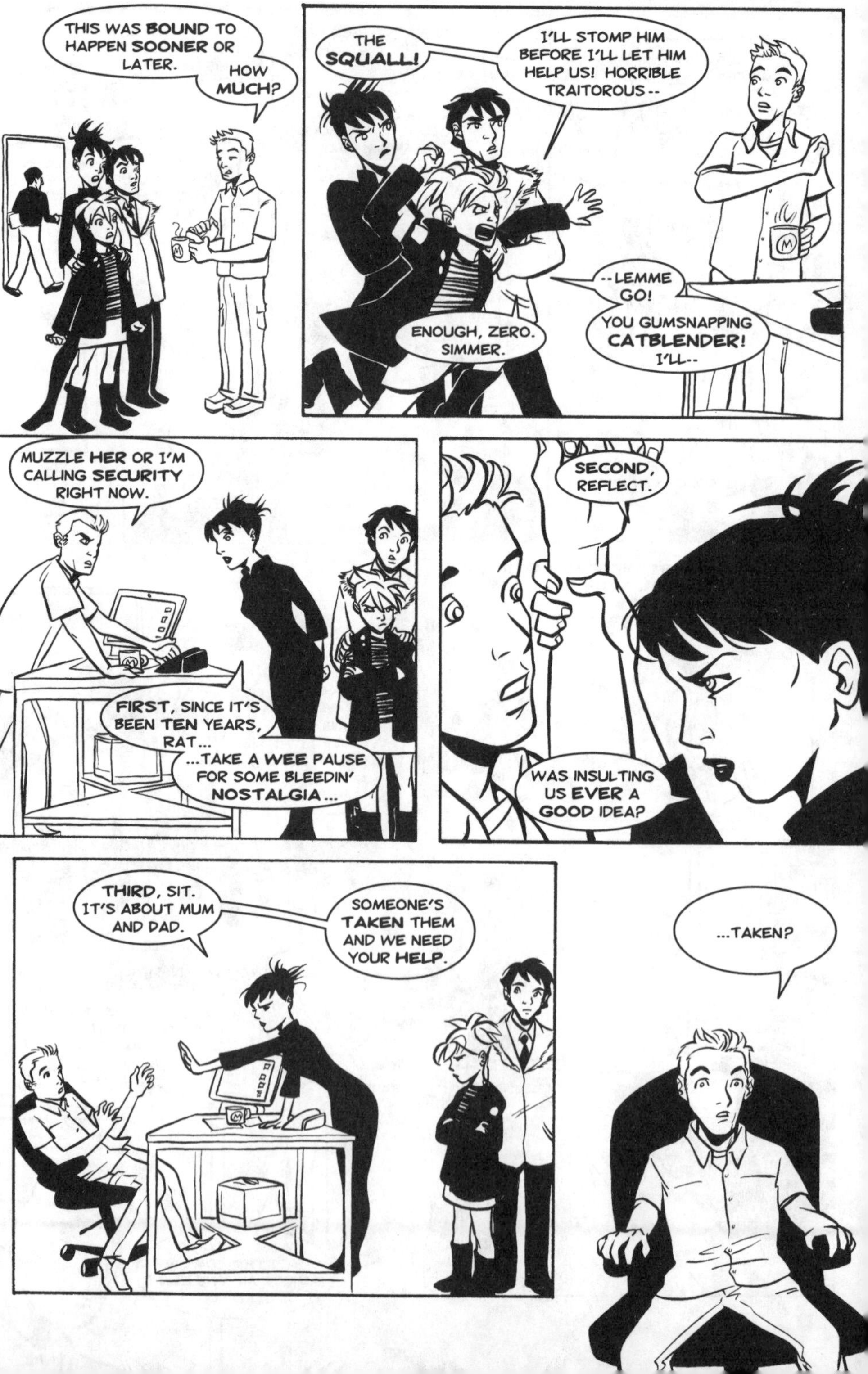

THIS WAS BOUND TO HAPPEN SOONER OR LATER.
HOW MUCH?
THE SQUALL!
I'LL STOMP HIM BEFORE I'LL LET HIM HELP US! HORRIBLE TRAITOROUS --
--LEMME GO!
YOU GUMSNAPPING CATBLENDER! I'LL--
ENOUGH, ZERO. SIMMER.
MUZZLE HER OR I'M CALLING SECURITY RIGHT NOW.
FIRST, SINCE IT'S BEEN TEN YEARS, RAT...
...TAKE A WEE PAUSE FOR SOME BLEEDIN' NOSTALGIA...
SECOND, REFLECT.
WAS INSULTING US EVER A GOOD IDEA?
THIRD, SIT. IT'S ABOUT MUM AND DAD.
SOMEONE'S TAKEN THEM AND WE NEED YOUR HELP.
...TAKEN?

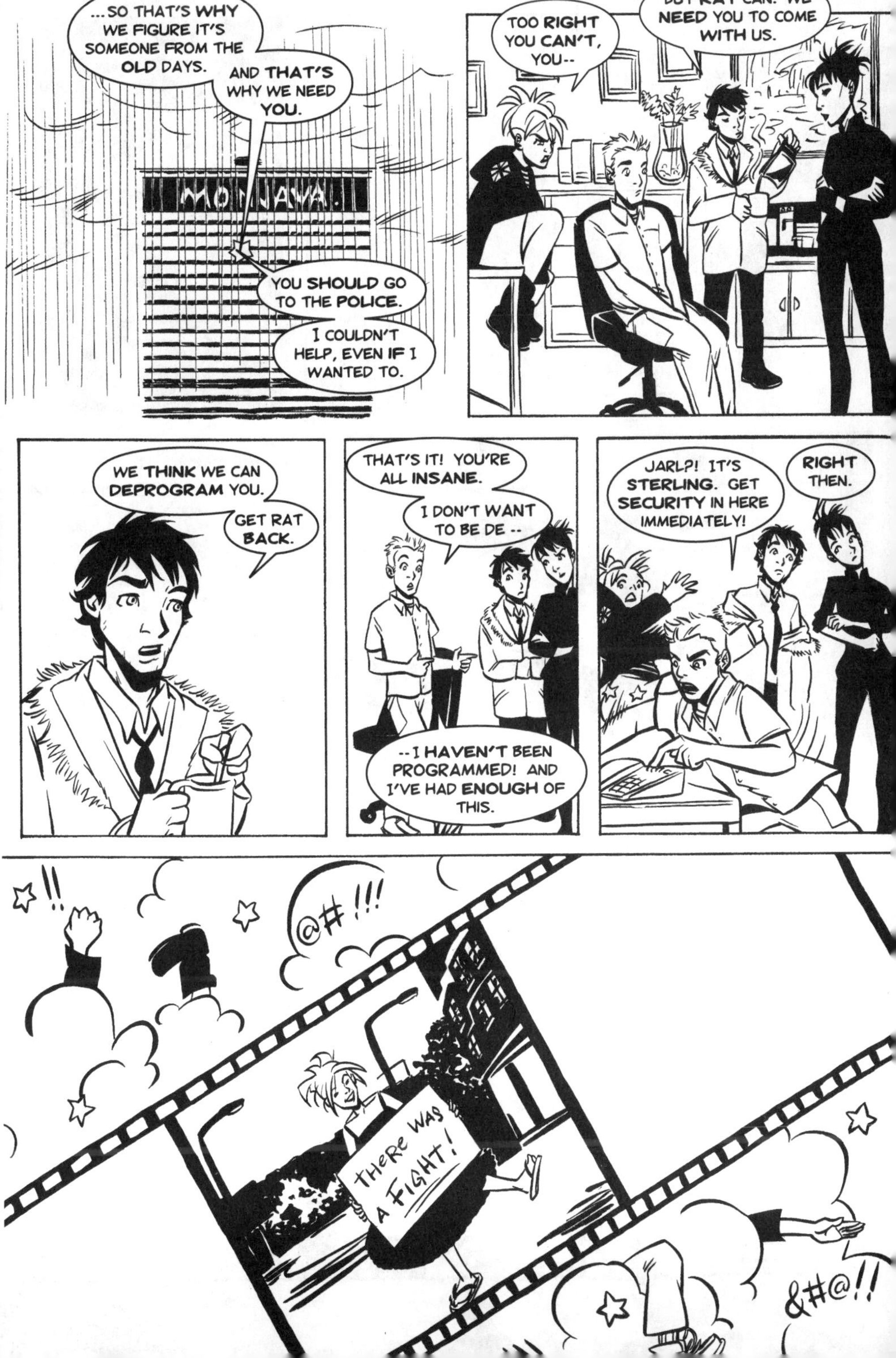
...SO THAT'S WHY WE FIGURE IT'S SOMEONE FROM THE OLD DAYS.
AND THAT'S WHY WE NEED YOU.
YOU SHOULD GO TO THE POLICE.
I COULDN'T HELP, EVEN IF I WANTED TO.
MONJAVA.
TOO RIGHT YOU CAN'T, YOU--
BUT RAT CAN. WE NEED YOU TO COME WITH US.
WE THINK WE CAN DEPROGRAM YOU.
GET RAT BACK.
THAT'S IT! YOU'RE ALL INSANE.
I DON'T WANT TO BE DE --
--I HAVEN'T BEEN PROGRAMMED! AND I'VE HAD ENOUGH OF THIS.
JARL?! IT'S STERLING. GET SECURITY IN HERE IMMEDIATELY!
RIGHT THEN.
!!
@# !!!
THERE WAS A FIGHT!
&#@!!

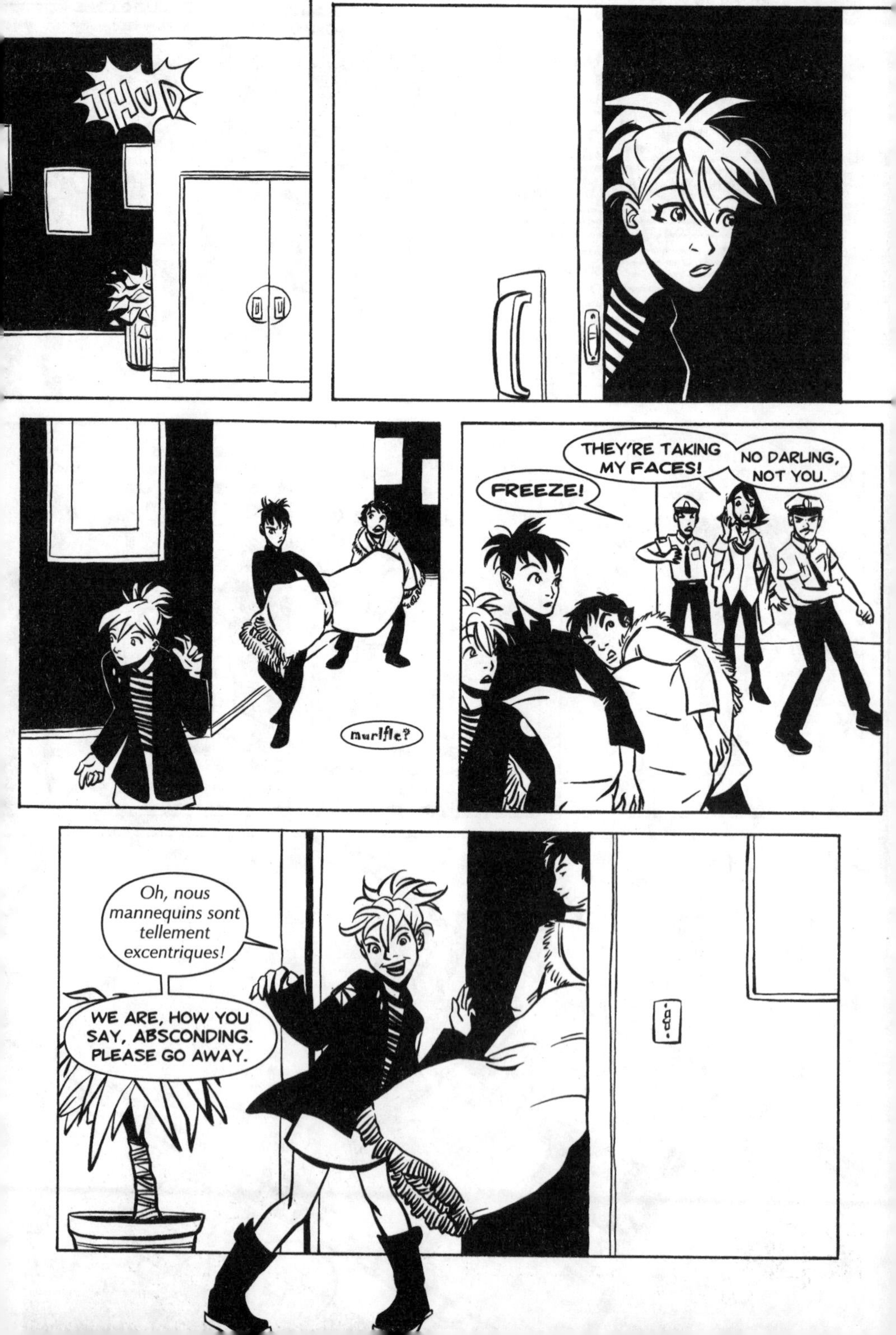
THUD
murlfle?
FREEZE!
THEY'RE TAKING MY FACES!
NO DARLING, NOT YOU.
Oh, nous mannequins sont tellement excentriques!
WE ARE, HOW YOU SAY, ABSCONDING. PLEASE GO AWAY.

HUNH?

SLAM!

STAIRS

THEY'VE GOT MISTER STERLING'S CARPET!

EXIT

I SAID FREEZE!

TO THE ELEVATOR! AFTER THEM!

EXIT

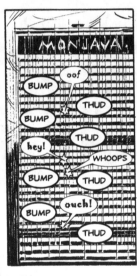

MONJAVAL

BUMP

oof!

THUD

BUMP

THUD

hey!

WHOOPS

BUMP

THUD

BUMP

ouch!

THUD

JUST TELL PAOLO I'LL BE THERE IN A MINUTE.

THEY HAVE TO COME OUT EVENTUALLY. THERE'S NO OTHER EXIT.

WELL, ACTUALLY, MISS...

M LEVEL L

FIRE EXIT

IDIOTS! I WORK WITH IDIOTS!

I SAID FREEZE!

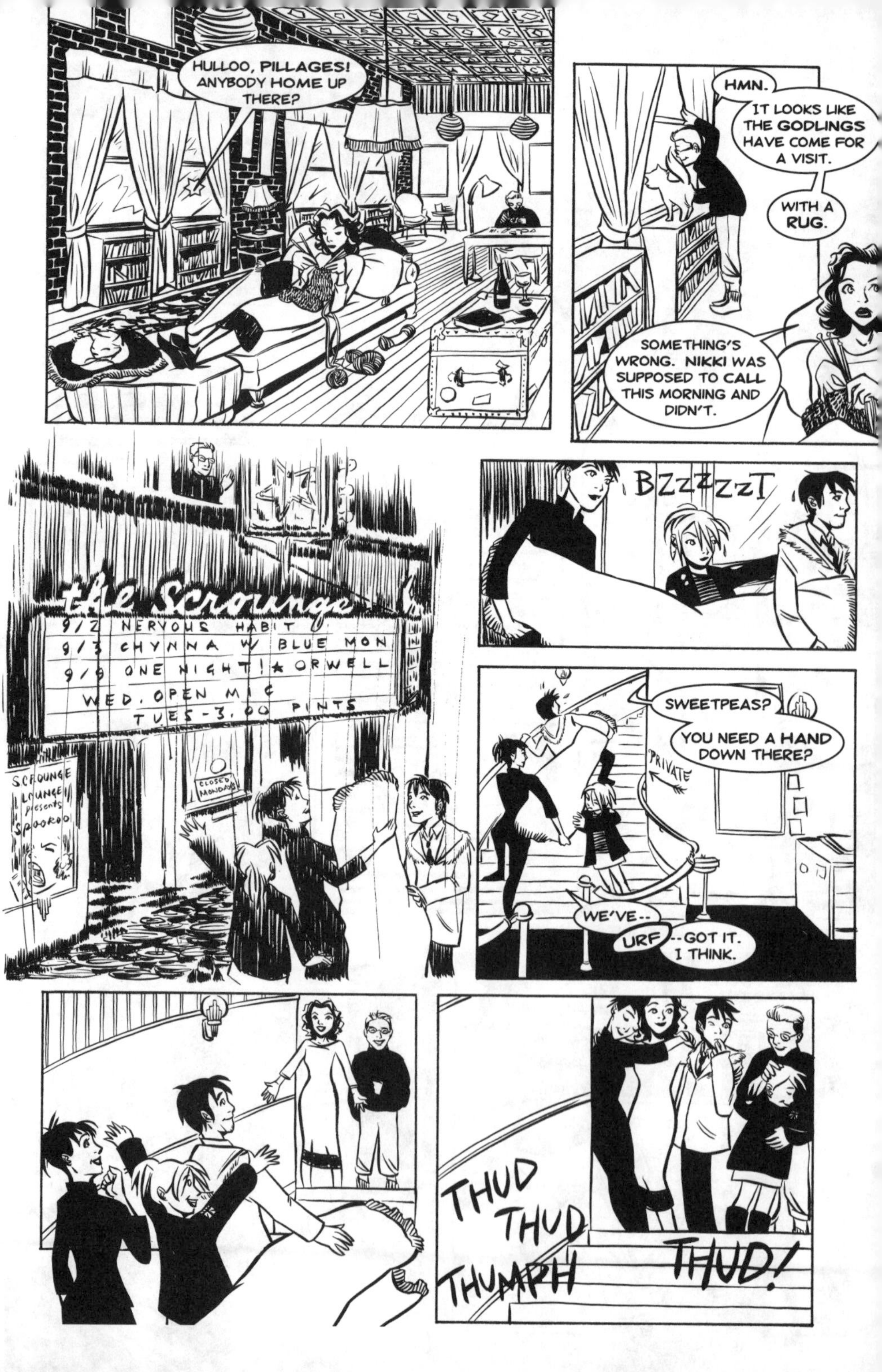
HULLOO, PILLAGES! ANYBODY HOME UP THERE?
HMN.
IT LOOKS LIKE THE GODLINGS HAVE COME FOR A VISIT.
WITH A RUG.
SOMETHING'S WRONG. NIKKI WAS SUPPOSED TO CALL THIS MORNING AND DIDN'T.
the Scrounge
9/2 NERVOUS HABIT
9/3 CHYNNA W BLUE MON
9/9 ONE NIGHT! ★ ORWELL
WED. OPEN MIC
TUES-3.00 PINTS
CLOSED MONDAYS
SCROUNGE LOUNGE presents
BZZZZZT
SWEETPEAS?
YOU NEED A HAND DOWN THERE?
PRIVATE
WE'VE--
URF
--GOT IT. I THINK.
THUD
THUD
THUMPH
THUD!

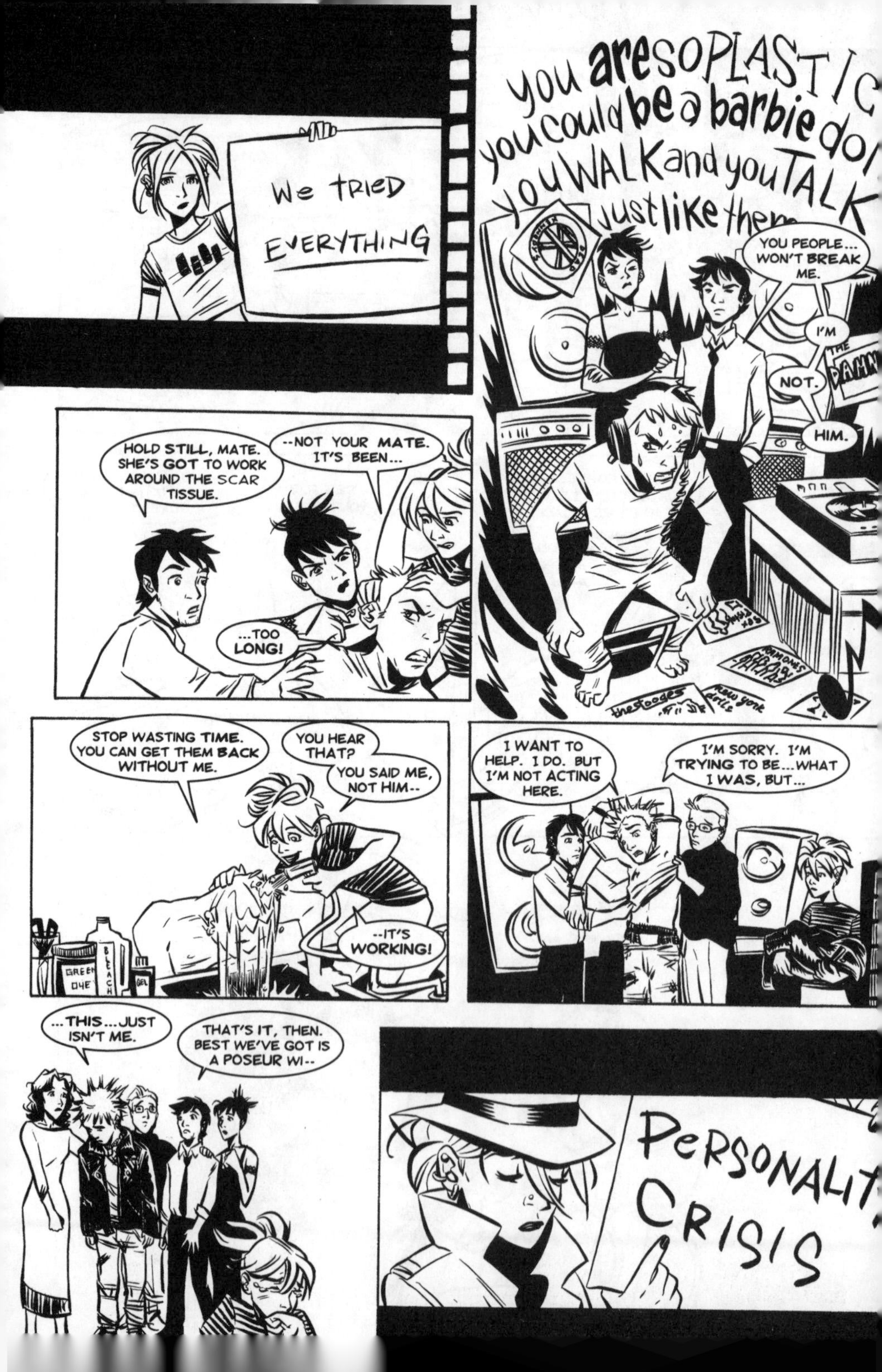

We TRIED EVERYTHING
you are so PLASTIC you could be a barbie doll you WALK and you TALK just like them
YOU PEOPLE... WON'T BREAK ME.
I'M
NOT.
HIM.
HOLD STILL, MATE. SHE'S GOT TO WORK AROUND THE SCAR TISSUE.
--NOT YOUR MATE. IT'S BEEN...
...TOO LONG!
RAMONES
the stooges
new york dolls
STOP WASTING TIME. YOU CAN GET THEM BACK WITHOUT ME.
YOU HEAR THAT?
YOU SAID ME, NOT HIM--
--IT'S WORKING!
GREEN DYE
BLEACH
GEL
I WANT TO HELP. I DO. BUT I'M NOT ACTING HERE.
I'M SORRY. I'M TRYING TO BE...WHAT I WAS, BUT...
...THIS...JUST ISN'T ME.
THAT'S IT, THEN. BEST WE'VE GOT IS A POSEUR WI--
PERSONALITY CRISIS

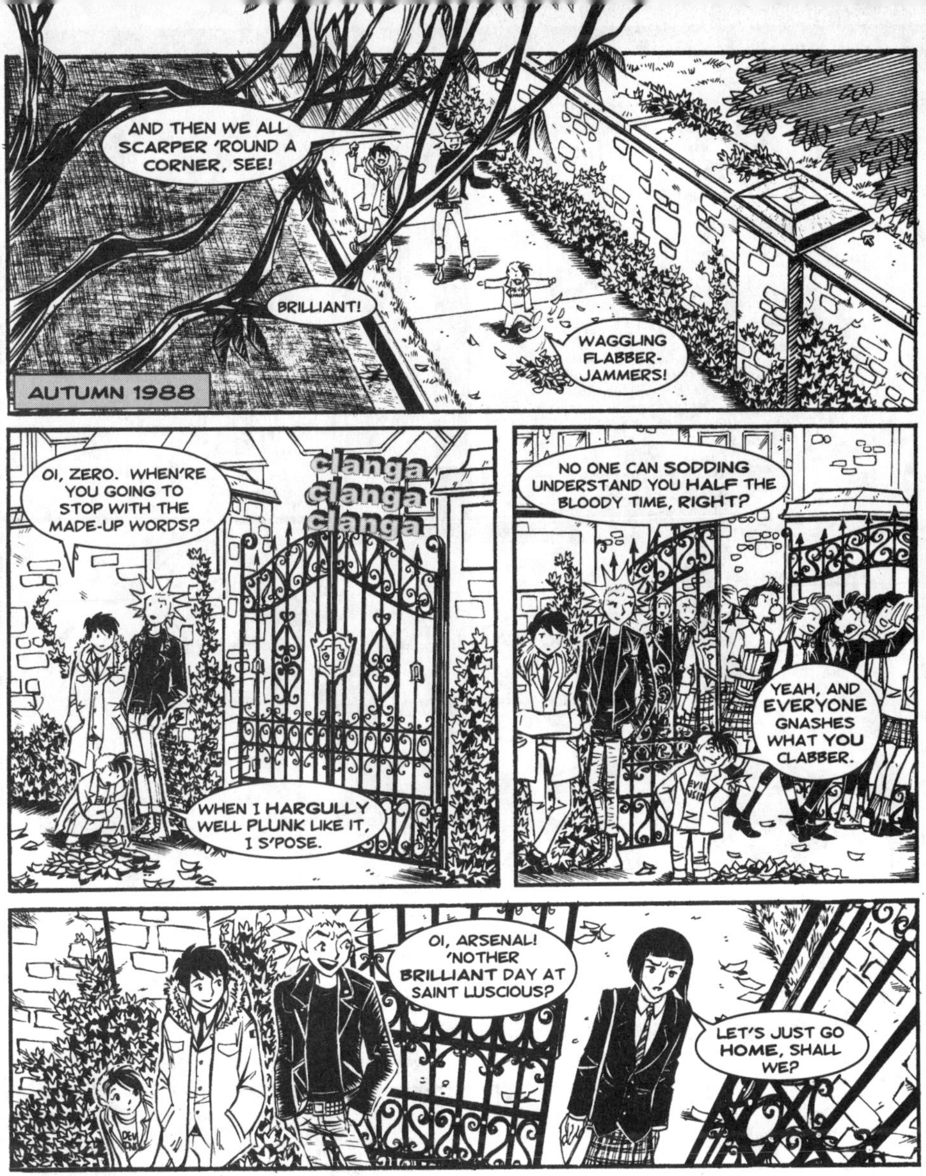
AND THEN WE ALL SCARPER 'ROUND A CORNER, SEE!
BRILLIANT!
WAGGLING FLABBER-JAMMERS!
AUTUMN 1988
clanga clanga clanga
OI, ZERO. WHEN'RE YOU GOING TO STOP WITH THE MADE-UP WORDS?
WHEN I HARGULLY WELL PLUNK LIKE IT, I S'POSE.
NO ONE CAN SODDING UNDERSTAND YOU HALF THE BLOODY TIME, RIGHT?
YEAH, AND EVERYONE GNASHES WHAT YOU CLABBER.
OI, ARSENAL! 'NOTHER BRILLIANT DAY AT SAINT LUSCIOUS?
LET'S JUST GO HOME, SHALL WE?

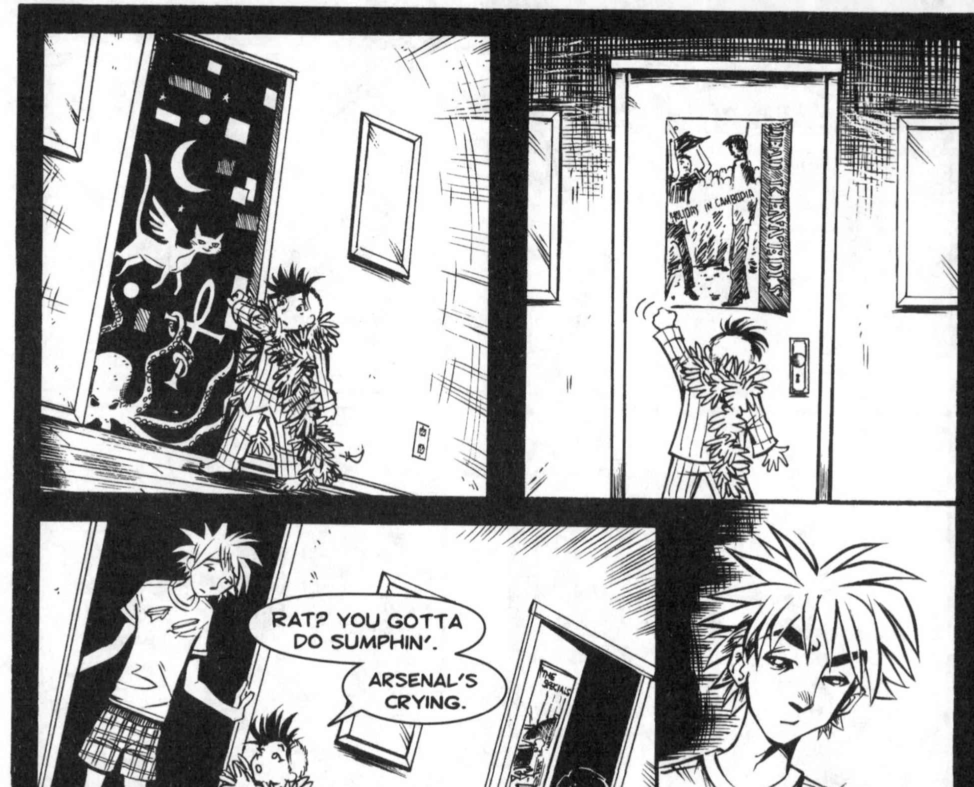
HOLIDAY IN CAMBODIA
RAT? YOU GOTTA DO SUMPHIN'.
ARSENAL'S CRYING.
THE SPECIALS
PiL

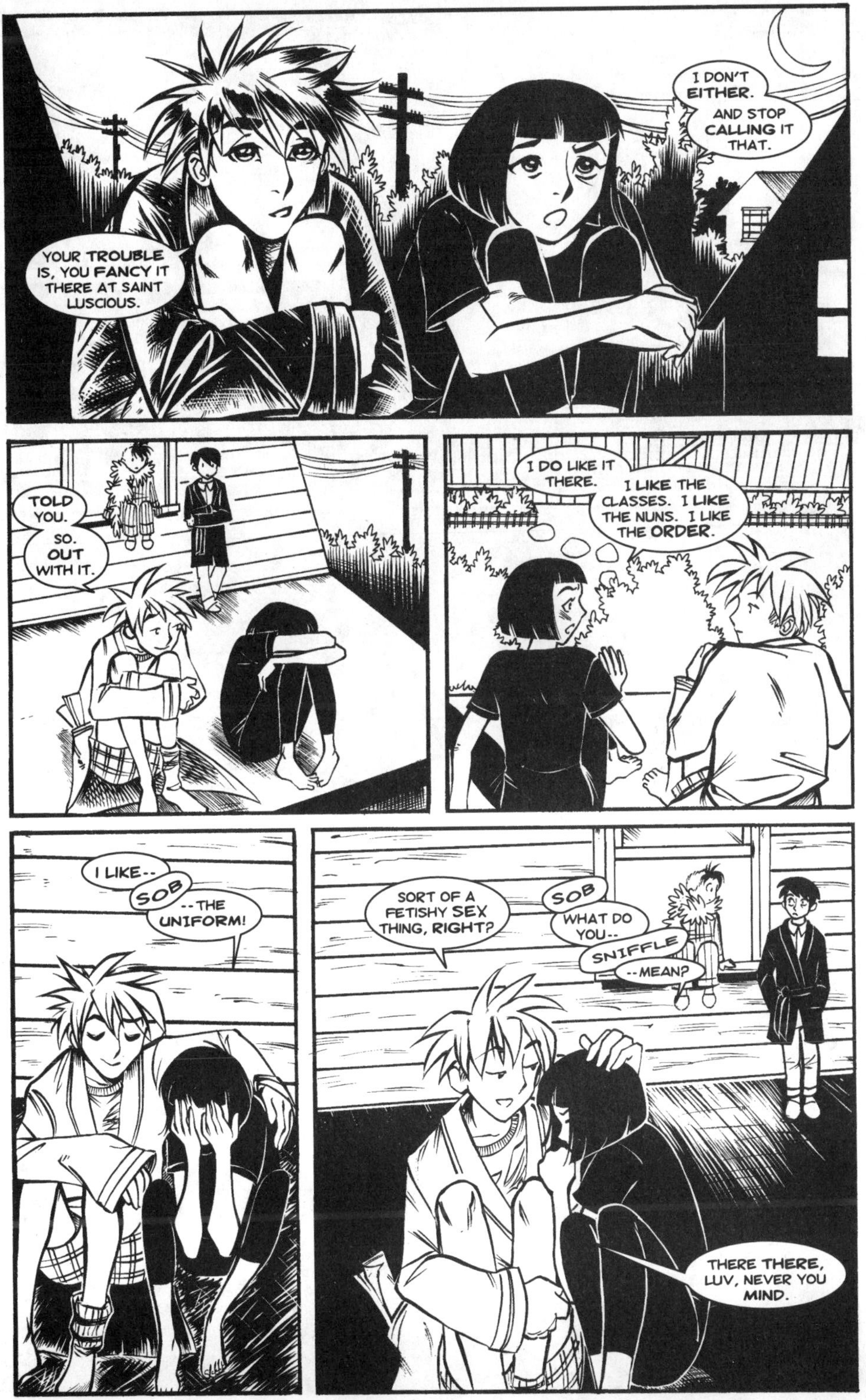
YOUR TROUBLE IS, YOU FANCY IT THERE AT SAINT LUSCIOUS.
I DON'T EITHER.
AND STOP CALLING IT THAT.
TOLD YOU.
SO. OUT WITH IT.
I DO LIKE IT THERE.
I LIKE THE CLASSES. I LIKE THE NUNS. I LIKE THE ORDER.
I LIKE--
SOB
--THE UNIFORM!
SORT OF A FETISHY SEX THING, RIGHT?
SOB
WHAT DO YOU--
SNIFFLE
--MEAN?
THERE THERE, LUV, NEVER YOU MIND.

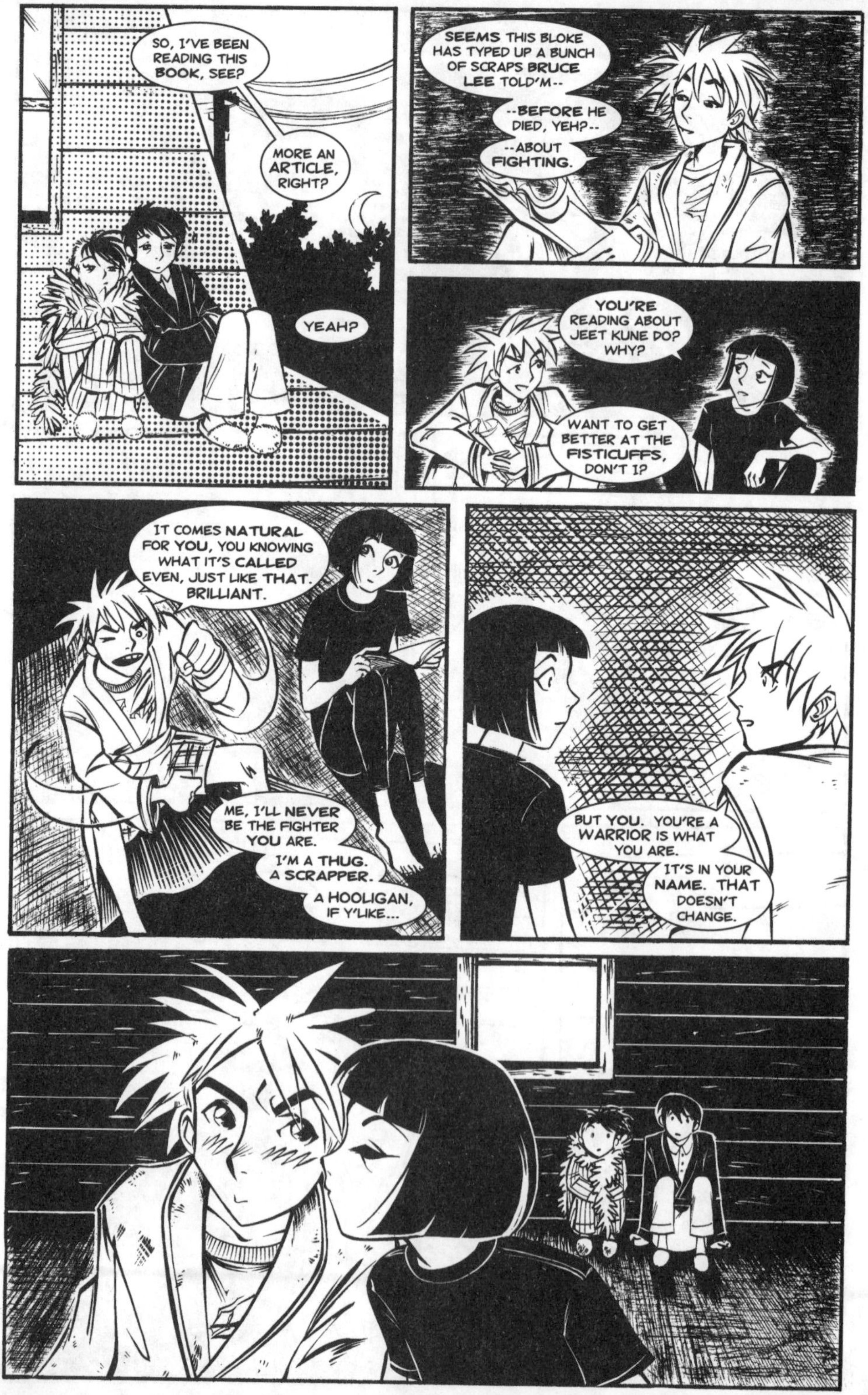
SO, I'VE BEEN READING THIS BOOK, SEE?
MORE AN ARTICLE, RIGHT?
YEAH?
SEEMS THIS BLOKE HAS TYPED UP A BUNCH OF SCRAPS BRUCE LEE TOLD'M--
--BEFORE HE DIED, YEH?--
--ABOUT FIGHTING.
YOU'RE READING ABOUT JEET KUNE DO? WHY?
WANT TO GET BETTER AT THE FISTICUFFS, DON'T I?
IT COMES NATURAL FOR YOU, YOU KNOWING WHAT IT'S CALLED EVEN, JUST LIKE THAT. BRILLIANT.
ME, I'LL NEVER BE THE FIGHTER YOU ARE.
I'M A THUG. A SCRAPPER.
A HOOLIGAN, IF Y'LIKE...
BUT YOU. YOU'RE A WARRIOR IS WHAT YOU ARE.
IT'S IN YOUR NAME. THAT DOESN'T CHANGE.

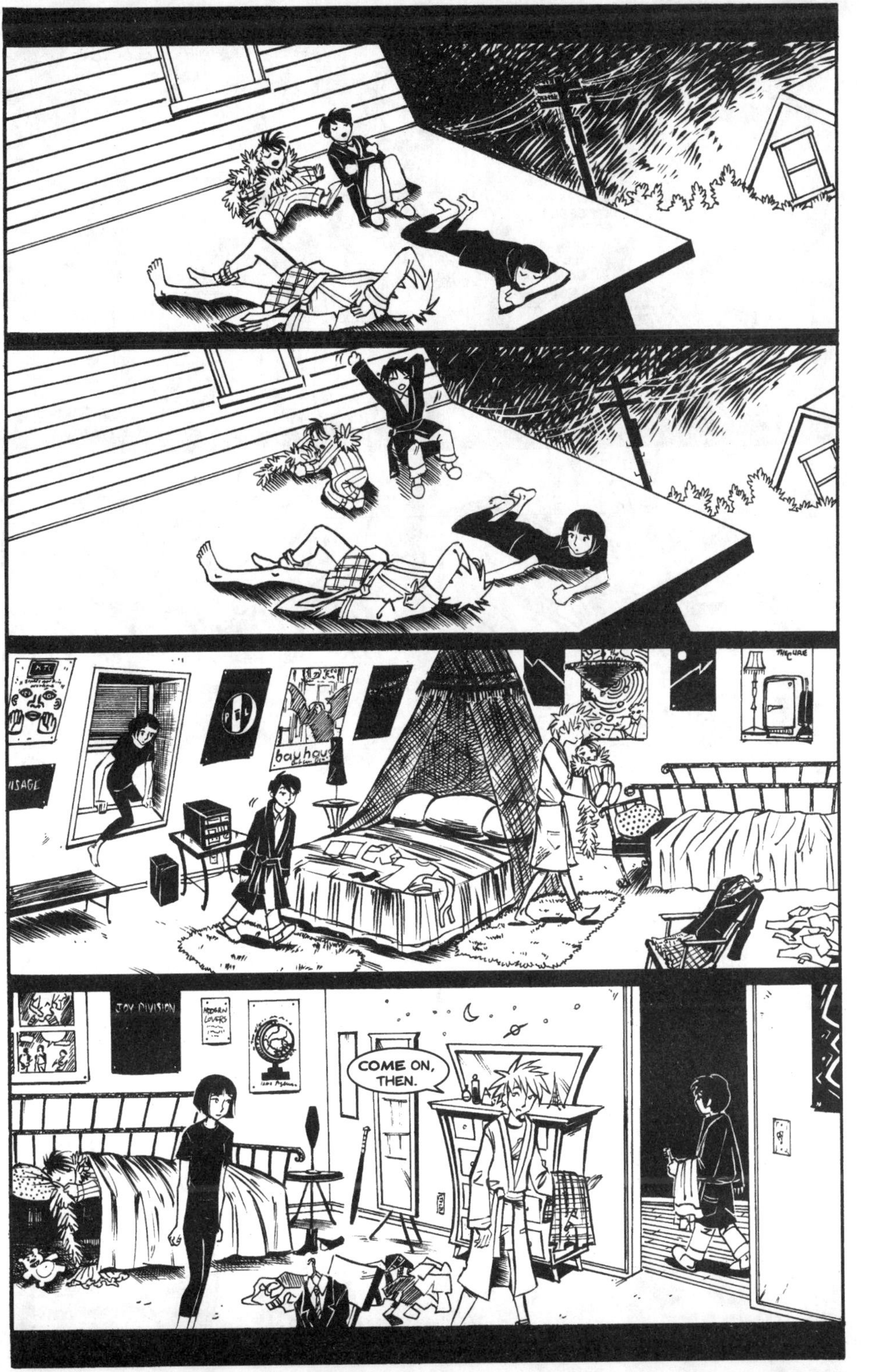
bauhaus
JOY DIVISION
MODERN LOVERS
COME ON, THEN.

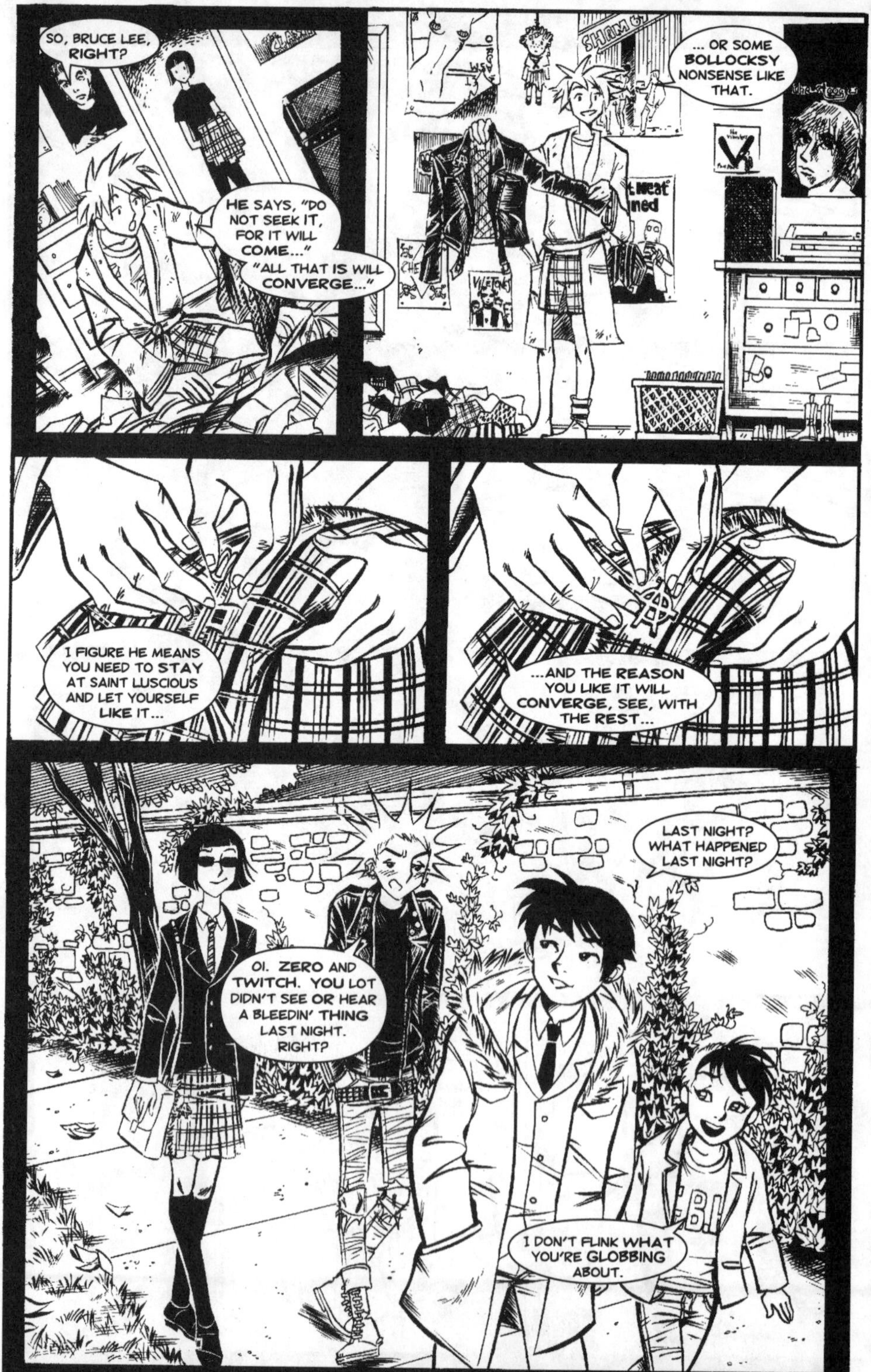
SO, BRUCE LEE, RIGHT?
HE SAYS, "DO NOT SEEK IT, FOR IT WILL COME..."
"ALL THAT IS WILL CONVERGE..."
... OR SOME BOLLOCKSY NONSENSE LIKE THAT.
I FIGURE HE MEANS YOU NEED TO STAY AT SAINT LUSCIOUS AND LET YOURSELF LIKE IT...
...AND THE REASON YOU LIKE IT WILL CONVERGE, SEE, WITH THE REST...
LAST NIGHT? WHAT HAPPENED LAST NIGHT?
OI. ZERO AND TWITCH. YOU LOT DIDN'T SEE OR HEAR A BLEEDIN' THING LAST NIGHT. RIGHT?
I DON'T FLINK WHAT YOU'RE GLOBBING ABOUT.

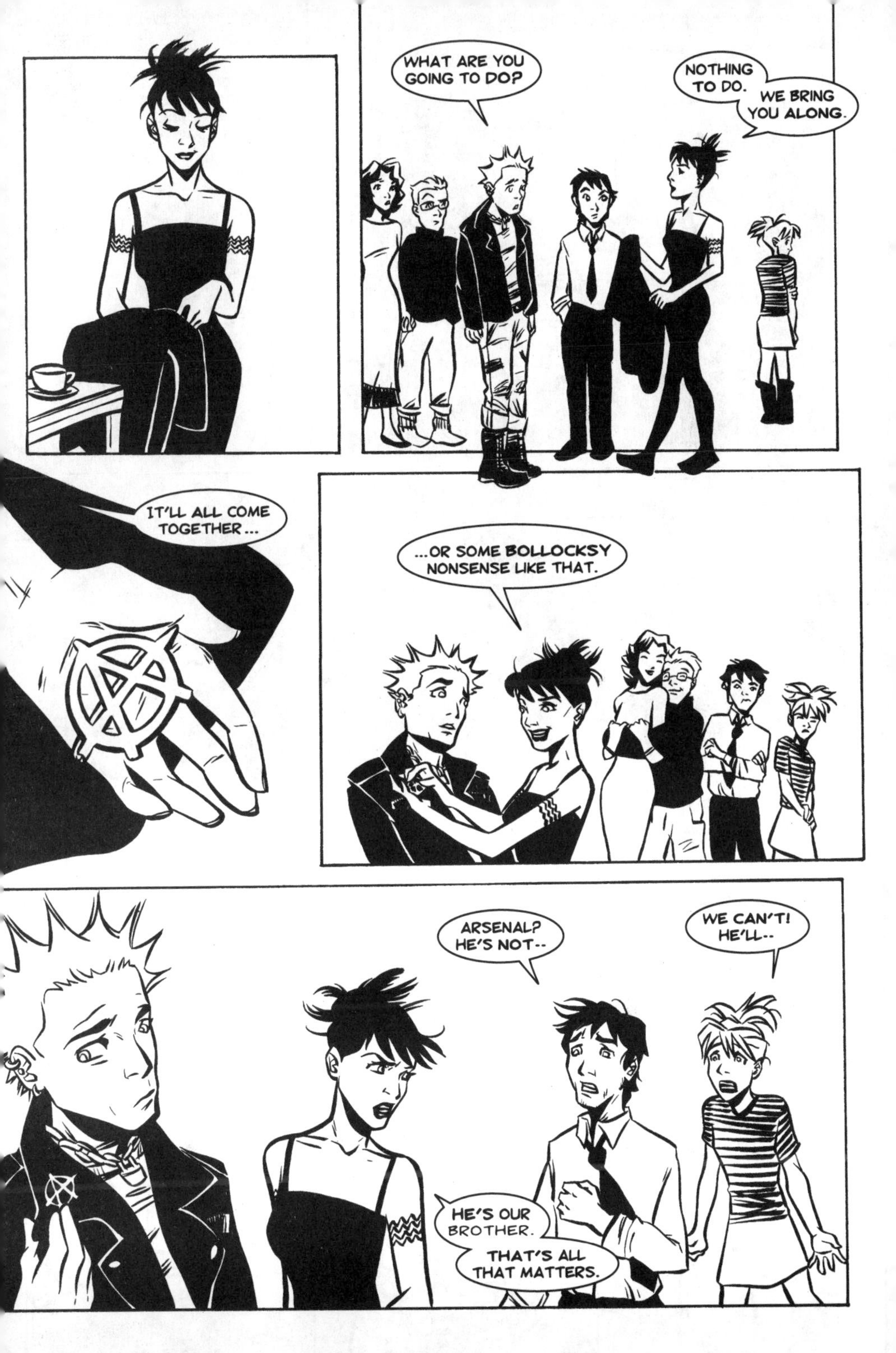
WHAT ARE YOU GOING TO DO?
NOTHING TO DO.
WE BRING YOU ALONG.
IT'LL ALL COME TOGETHER...
...OR SOME BOLLOCKSY NONSENSE LIKE THAT.
ARSENAL? HE'S NOT--
WE CAN'T! HE'LL--
HE'S OUR BROTHER.
THAT'S ALL THAT MATTERS.

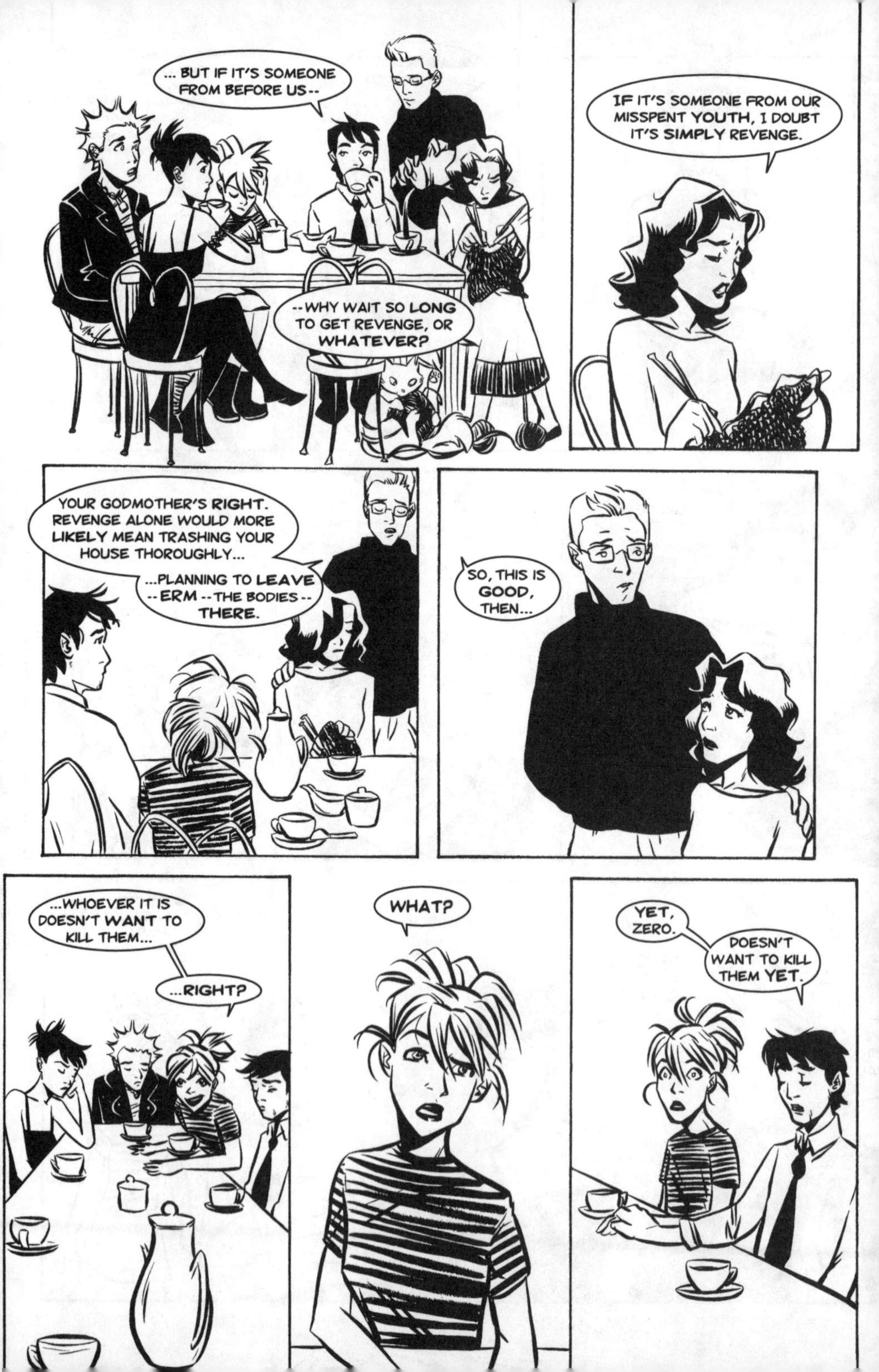

... BUT IF IT'S SOMEONE FROM BEFORE US --
-- WHY WAIT SO LONG TO GET REVENGE, OR WHATEVER?
IF IT'S SOMEONE FROM OUR MISSPENT YOUTH, I DOUBT IT'S SIMPLY REVENGE.
YOUR GODMOTHER'S RIGHT. REVENGE ALONE WOULD MORE LIKELY MEAN TRASHING YOUR HOUSE THOROUGHLY...
...PLANNING TO LEAVE -- ERM -- THE BODIES -- THERE.
SO, THIS IS GOOD, THEN...
...WHOEVER IT IS DOESN'T WANT TO KILL THEM...
...RIGHT?
WHAT?
YET, ZERO.
DOESN'T WANT TO KILL THEM YET.

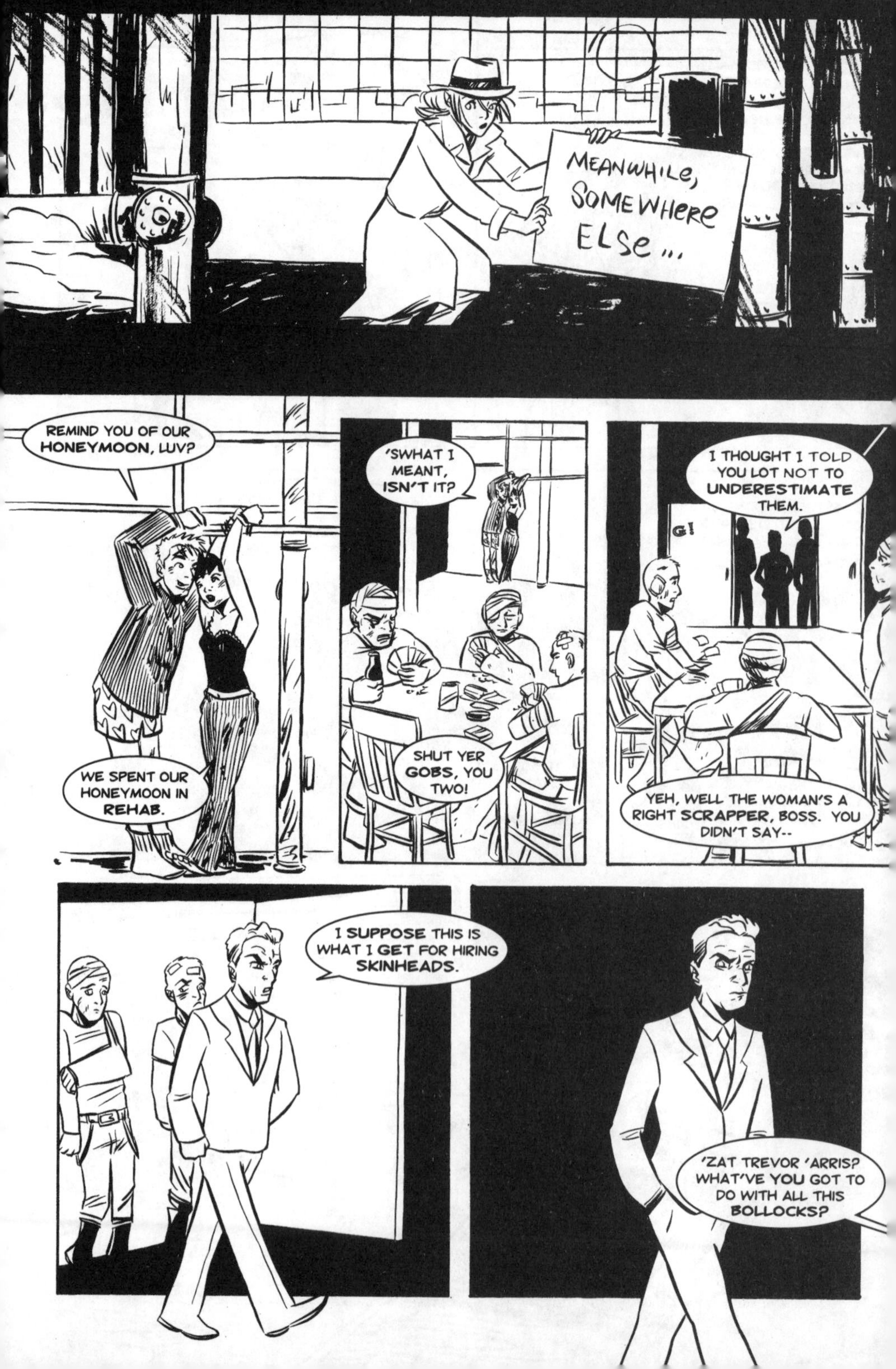
MEANWHILE, SOMEWHERE ELSE...
REMIND YOU OF OUR HONEYMOON, LUV?
WE SPENT OUR HONEYMOON IN REHAB.
'SWHAT I MEANT, ISN'T IT?
SHUT YER GOBS, YOU TWO!
I THOUGHT I TOLD YOU LOT NOT TO UNDERESTIMATE THEM.
G!
YEH, WELL THE WOMAN'S A RIGHT SCRAPPER, BOSS. YOU DIDN'T SAY--
I SUPPOSE THIS IS WHAT I GET FOR HIRING SKINHEADS.
'ZAT TREVOR 'ARRIS? WHAT'VE YOU GOT TO DO WITH ALL THIS BOLLOCKS?

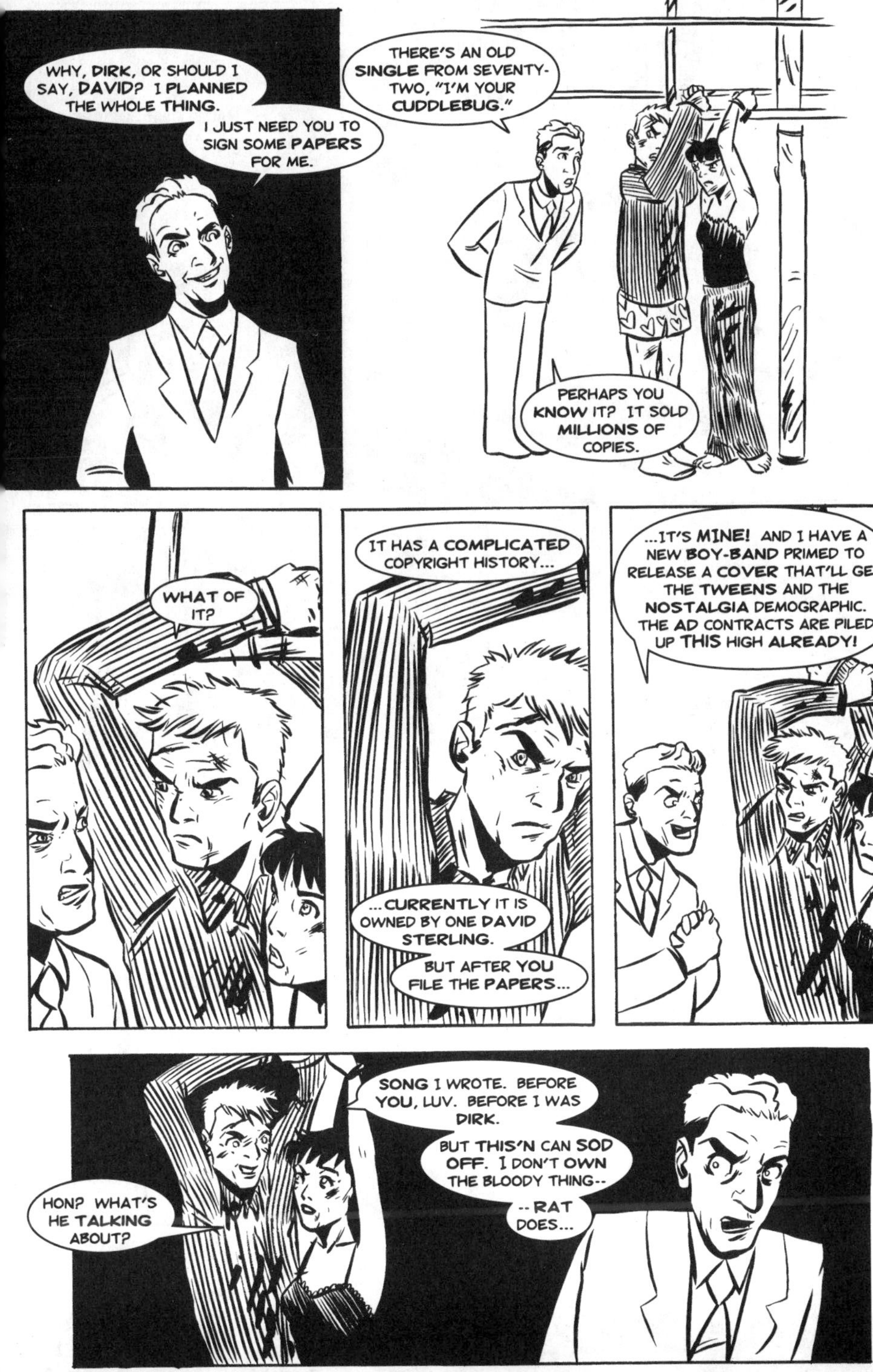
WHY, DIRK, OR SHOULD I SAY, DAVID? I PLANNED THE WHOLE THING.
I JUST NEED YOU TO SIGN SOME PAPERS FOR ME.
THERE'S AN OLD SINGLE FROM SEVENTY-TWO, "I'M YOUR CUDDLEBUG."
PERHAPS YOU KNOW IT? IT SOLD MILLIONS OF COPIES.
WHAT OF IT?
IT HAS A COMPLICATED COPYRIGHT HISTORY...
...CURRENTLY IT IS OWNED BY ONE DAVID STERLING.
BUT AFTER YOU FILE THE PAPERS...
...IT'S MINE! AND I HAVE A NEW BOY-BAND PRIMED TO RELEASE A COVER THAT'LL GET THE TWEENS AND THE NOSTALGIA DEMOGRAPHIC. THE AD CONTRACTS ARE PILED UP THIS HIGH ALREADY!
SONG I WROTE. BEFORE YOU, LUV. BEFORE I WAS DIRK.
BUT THIS'N CAN SOD OFF. I DON'T OWN THE BLOODY THING--
--RAT DOES...
HON? WHAT'S HE TALKING ABOUT?

...AND I CAN PROMISE HE'LL HAVE **NOTHING** TO DO WITH THIS **MESS.**

HEY, **RAT?** YOU REMEMBER MUCH ABOUT WEEJ?

HE HAD A **REP** FOR BEING HONEST WITH THE **BANDS** HE HANDLED, WHICH WAS **RARE.**

HE MANAGED NIKKI AND DIRK UNTIL JUST BEFORE TWITCH WAS BORN.

INTRODUCED THEM, I THINK.

SINATRA AND SPIGOT ARE **RIGHT.** HE'LL KNOW WHAT THIS IS ABOUT IF ANYONE DOES.

...UNDER CONTROL. THEY JUST GOT HERE.

RELAX.

I'LL TAKE CARE OF IT.

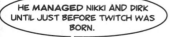

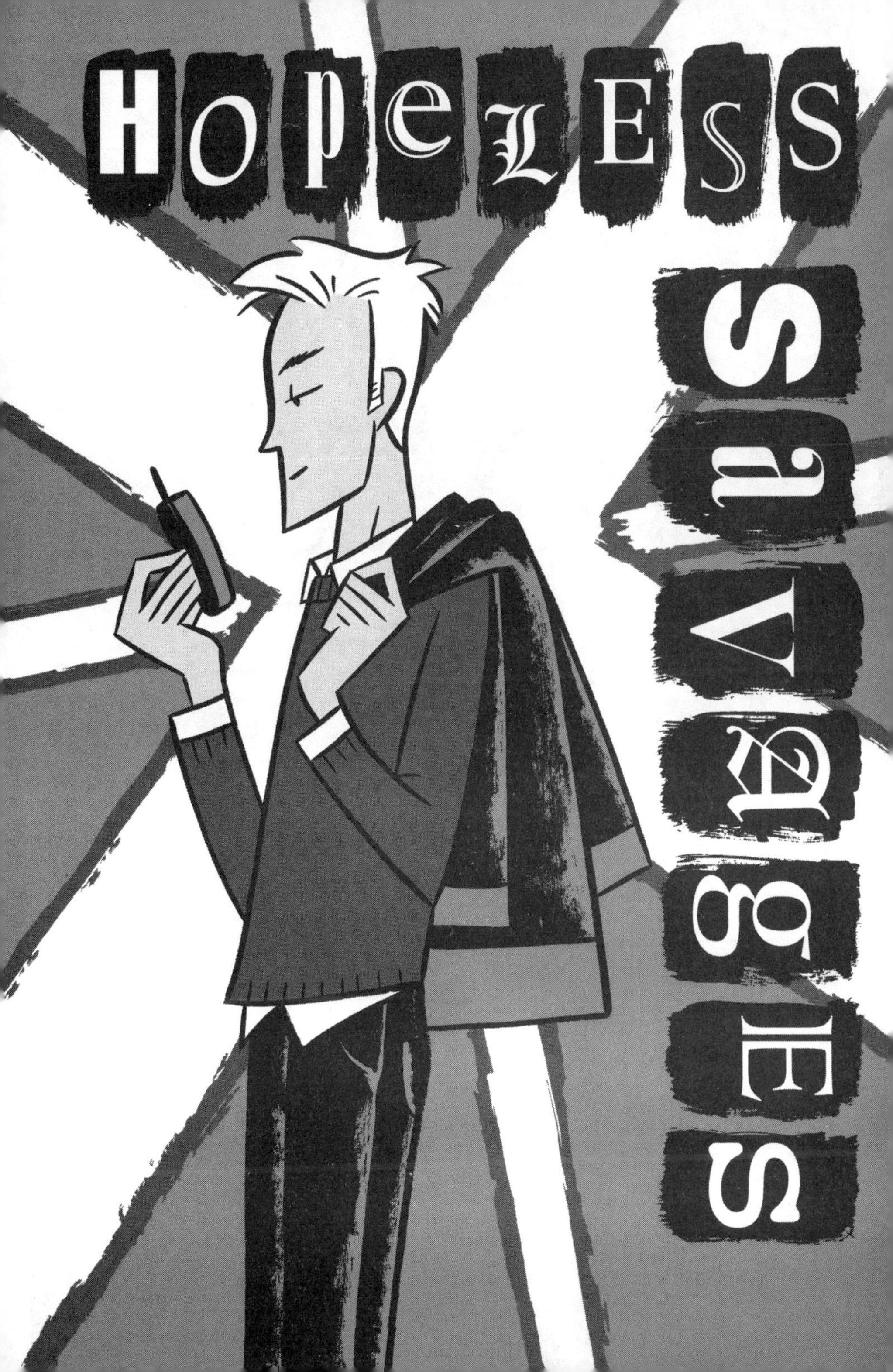
Hopeless
Savages

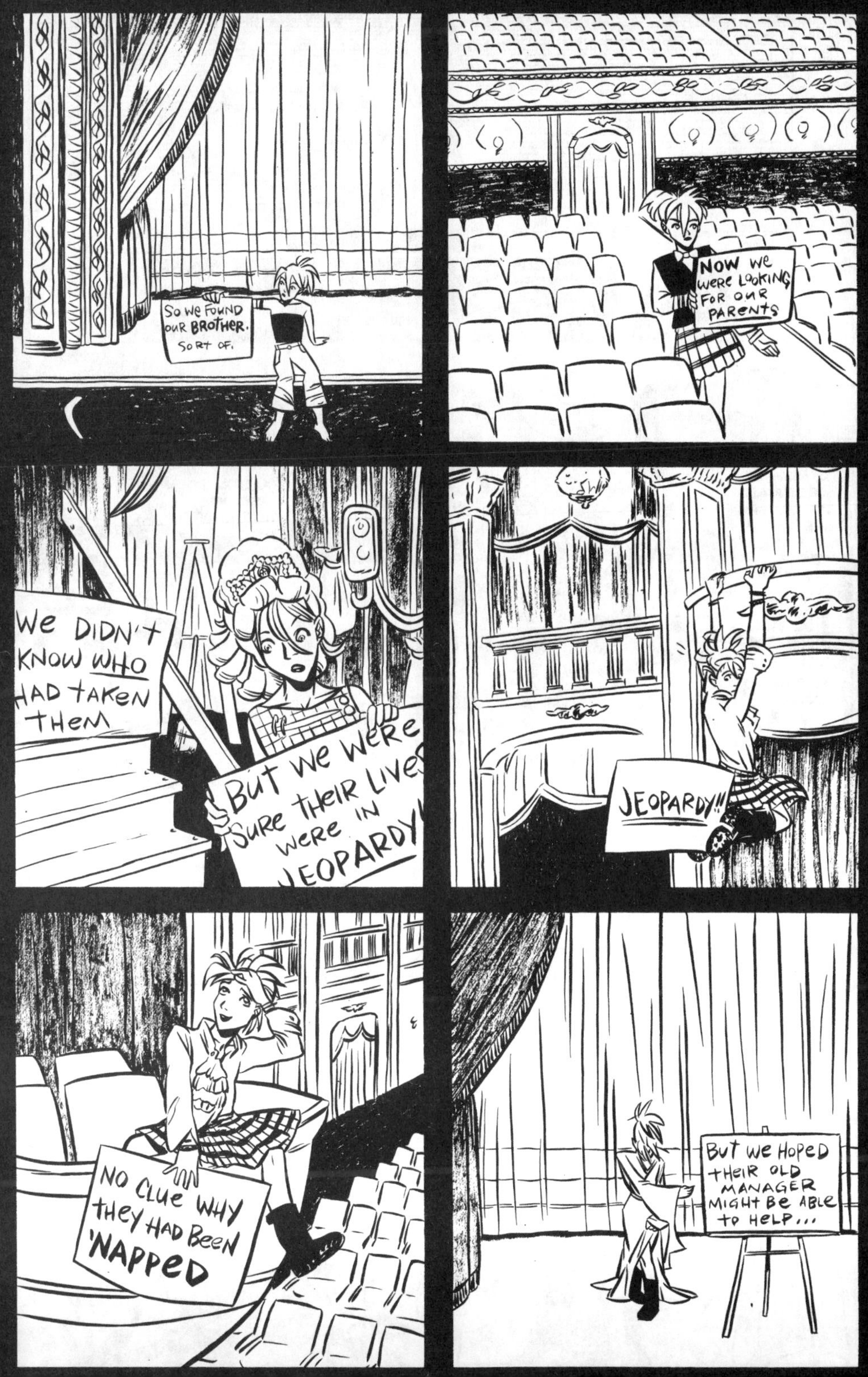

So we found our BROTHER. Sort of.
NOW we were looking for our parents
We didn't know WHO had taken them
But we were sure their lives were in JEOPARDY!
JEOPARDY!!
No clue why they had been 'NAPPED
But we hoped their old manager might be able to help...

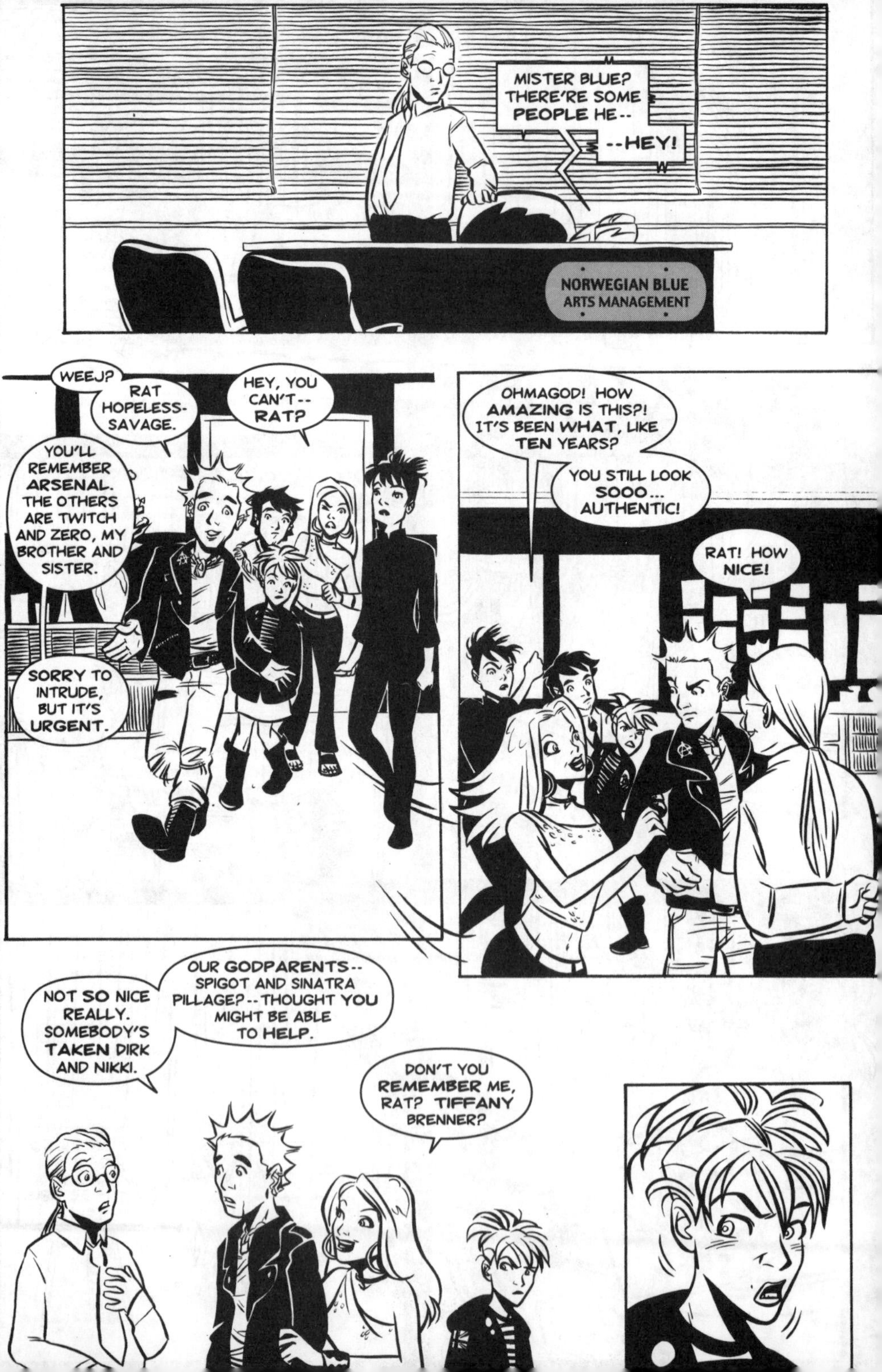
MISTER BLUE? THERE'RE SOME PEOPLE HE--
--HEY!
NORWEGIAN BLUE ARTS MANAGEMENT
WEEJ?
RAT HOPELESS-SAVAGE.
HEY, YOU CAN'T-- RAT?
YOU'LL REMEMBER ARSENAL. THE OTHERS ARE TWITCH AND ZERO, MY BROTHER AND SISTER.
SORRY TO INTRUDE, BUT IT'S URGENT.
OHMAGOD! HOW AMAZING IS THIS?! IT'S BEEN WHAT, LIKE TEN YEARS?
YOU STILL LOOK SOOO... AUTHENTIC!
RAT! HOW NICE!
NOT SO NICE REALLY. SOMEBODY'S TAKEN DIRK AND NIKKI.
OUR GODPARENTS-- SPIGOT AND SINATRA PILLAGE?--THOUGHT YOU MIGHT BE ABLE TO HELP.
DON'T YOU REMEMBER ME, RAT? TIFFANY BRENNER?

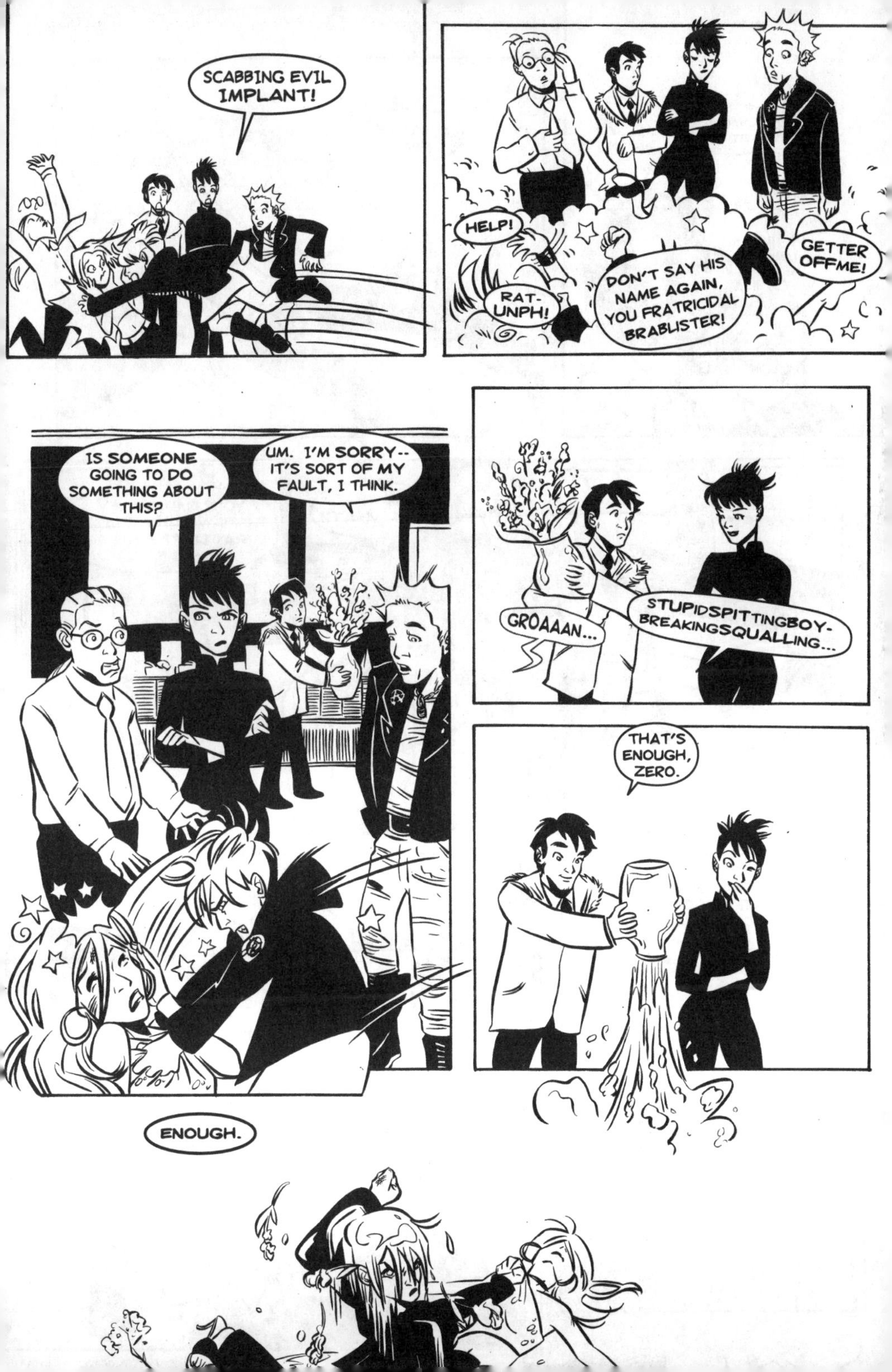
SCABBING EVIL IMPLANT!
HELP!
RAT-UNPH!
DON'T SAY HIS NAME AGAIN, YOU FRATRICIDAL BRABLISTER!
GETTER OFFME!
IS SOMEONE GOING TO DO SOMETHING ABOUT THIS?
UM. I'M SORRY-- IT'S SORT OF MY FAULT, I THINK.
GROAAAN...
STUPIDSPITTINGBOY-BREAKINGSQUALLING...
THAT'S ENOUGH, ZERO.
ENOUGH.

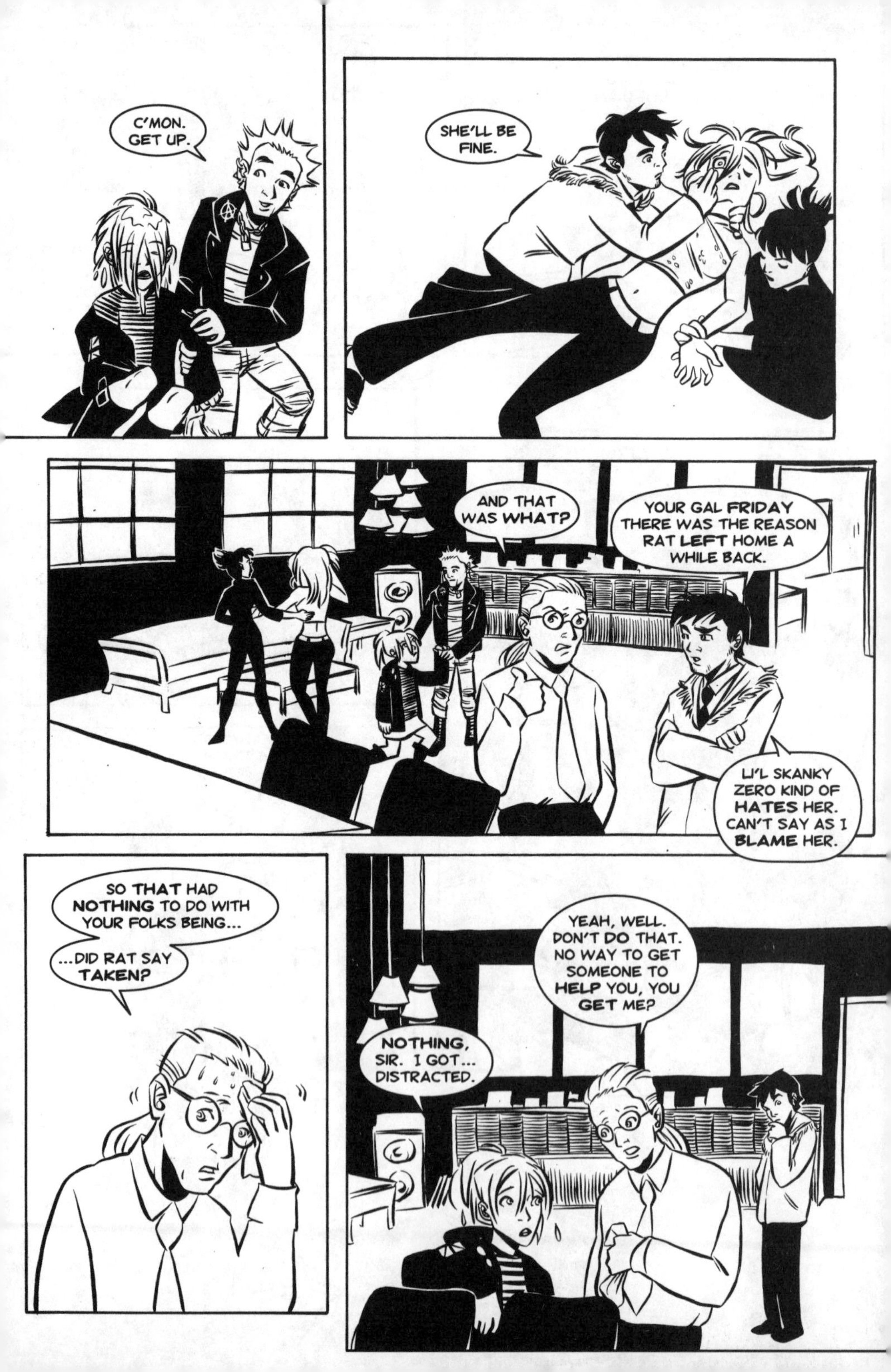
C'MON. GET UP.
SHE'LL BE FINE.
AND THAT WAS WHAT?
YOUR GAL FRIDAY THERE WAS THE REASON RAT LEFT HOME A WHILE BACK.
LI'L SKANKY ZERO KIND OF HATES HER. CAN'T SAY AS I BLAME HER.
SO THAT HAD NOTHING TO DO WITH YOUR FOLKS BEING...
...DID RAT SAY TAKEN?
YEAH, WELL. DON'T DO THAT. NO WAY TO GET SOMEONE TO HELP YOU, YOU GET ME?
NOTHING, SIR. I GOT... DISTRACTED.

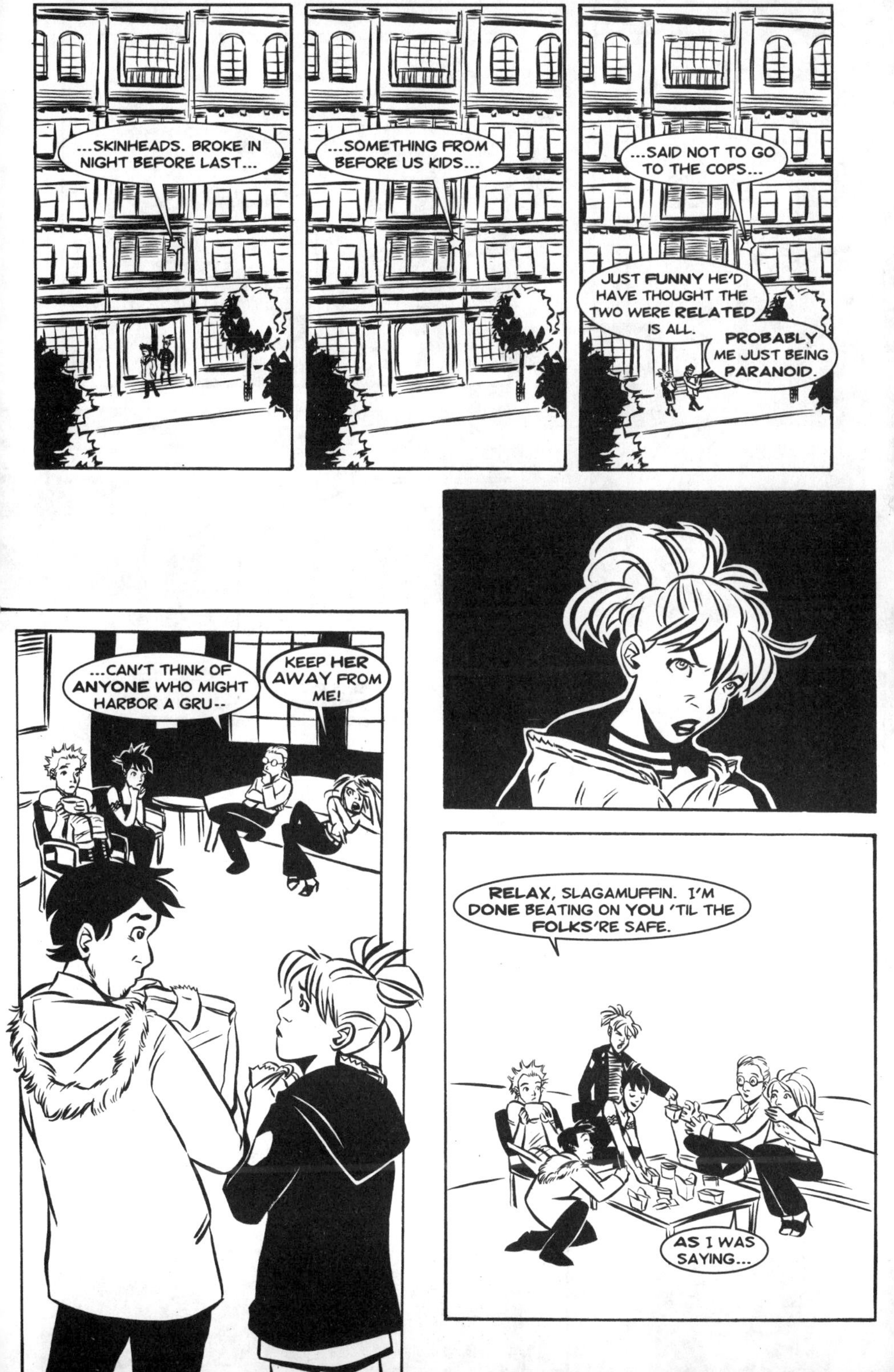

...SKINHEADS. BROKE IN NIGHT BEFORE LAST...
...SOMETHING FROM BEFORE US KIDS...
...SAID NOT TO GO TO THE COPS...
JUST FUNNY HE'D HAVE THOUGHT THE TWO WERE RELATED IS ALL.
PROBABLY ME JUST BEING PARANOID.
...CAN'T THINK OF ANYONE WHO MIGHT HARBOR A GRU--
KEEP HER AWAY FROM ME!
RELAX, SLAGAMUFFIN. I'M DONE BEATING ON YOU 'TIL THE FOLKS'RE SAFE.
AS I WAS SAYING...

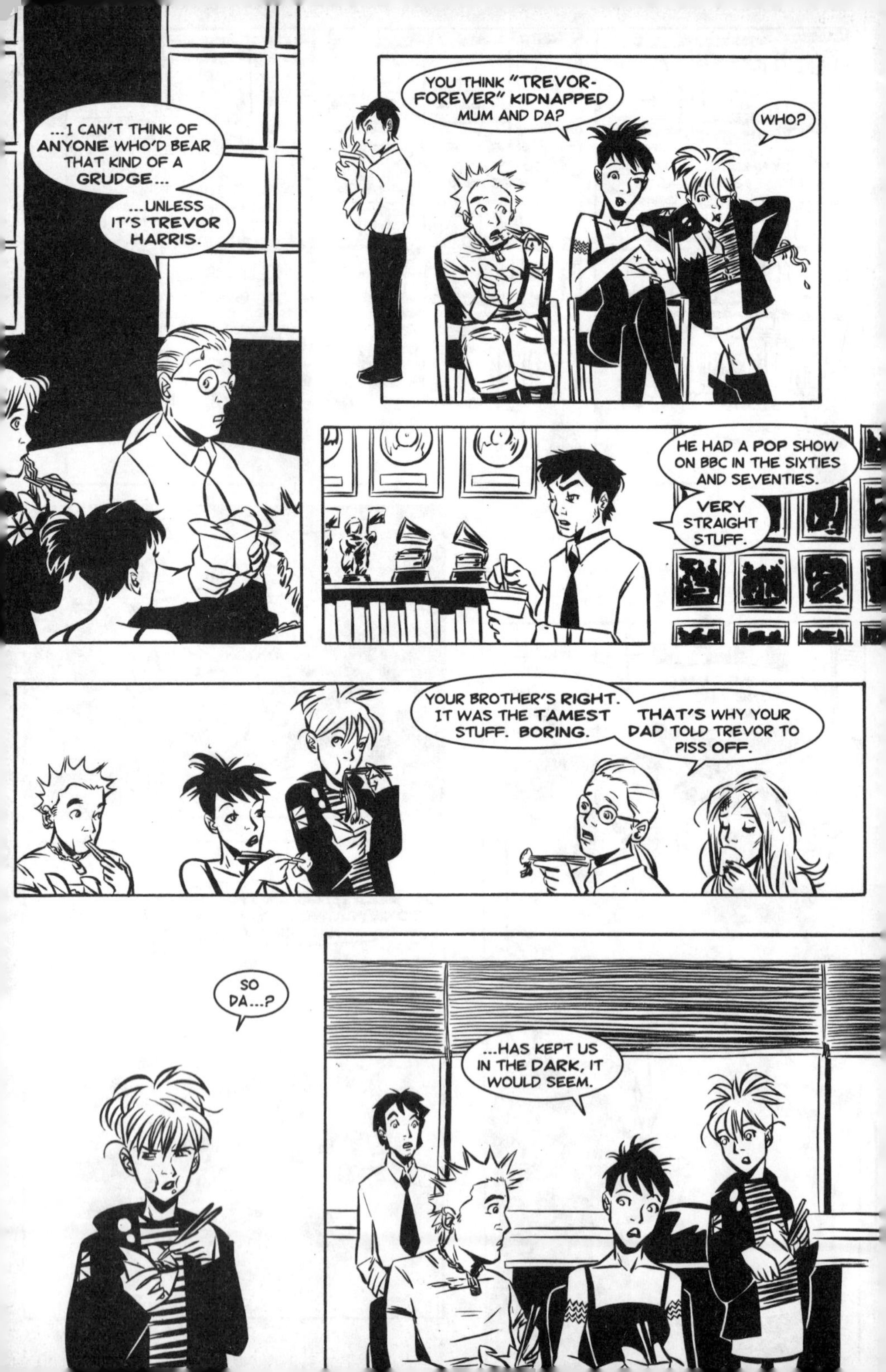

...I CAN'T THINK OF ANYONE WHO'D BEAR THAT KIND OF A GRUDGE...
...UNLESS IT'S TREVOR HARRIS.
YOU THINK "TREVOR-FOREVER" KIDNAPPED MUM AND DA?
WHO?
HE HAD A POP SHOW ON BBC IN THE SIXTIES AND SEVENTIES.
VERY STRAIGHT STUFF.
YOUR BROTHER'S RIGHT. IT WAS THE TAMEST STUFF. BORING.
THAT'S WHY YOUR DAD TOLD TREVOR TO PISS OFF.
SO DA...?
...HAS KEPT US IN THE DARK, IT WOULD SEEM.

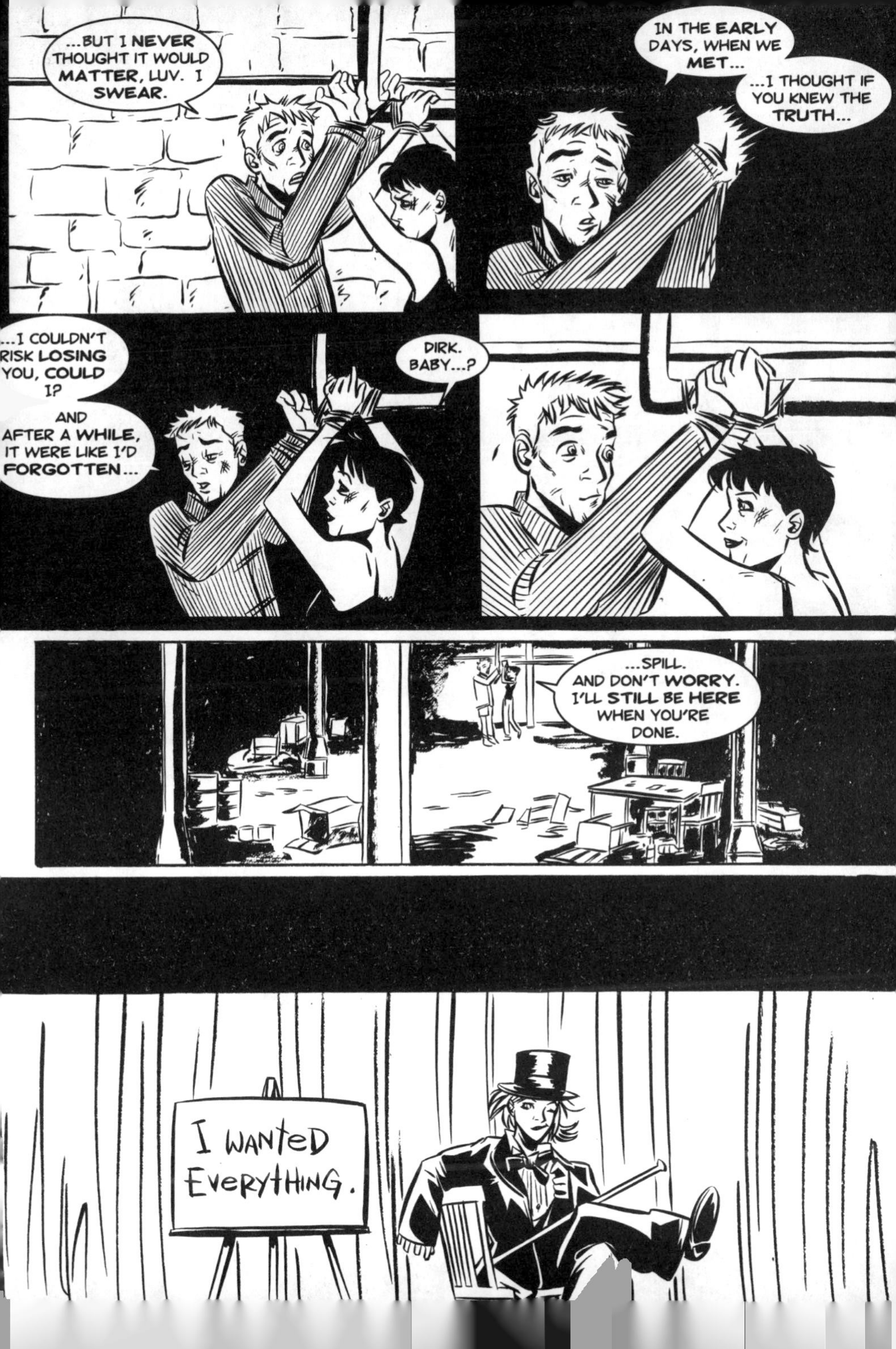
...BUT I NEVER THOUGHT IT WOULD MATTER, LUV. I SWEAR.
IN THE EARLY DAYS, WHEN WE MET...
...I THOUGHT IF YOU KNEW THE TRUTH...
...I COULDN'T RISK LOSING YOU, COULD I?
AND AFTER A WHILE, IT WERE LIKE I'D FORGOTTEN...
DIRK. BABY...?
...SPILL. AND DON'T WORRY. I'LL STILL BE HERE WHEN YOU'RE DONE.
I WANTED EVERYTHING.

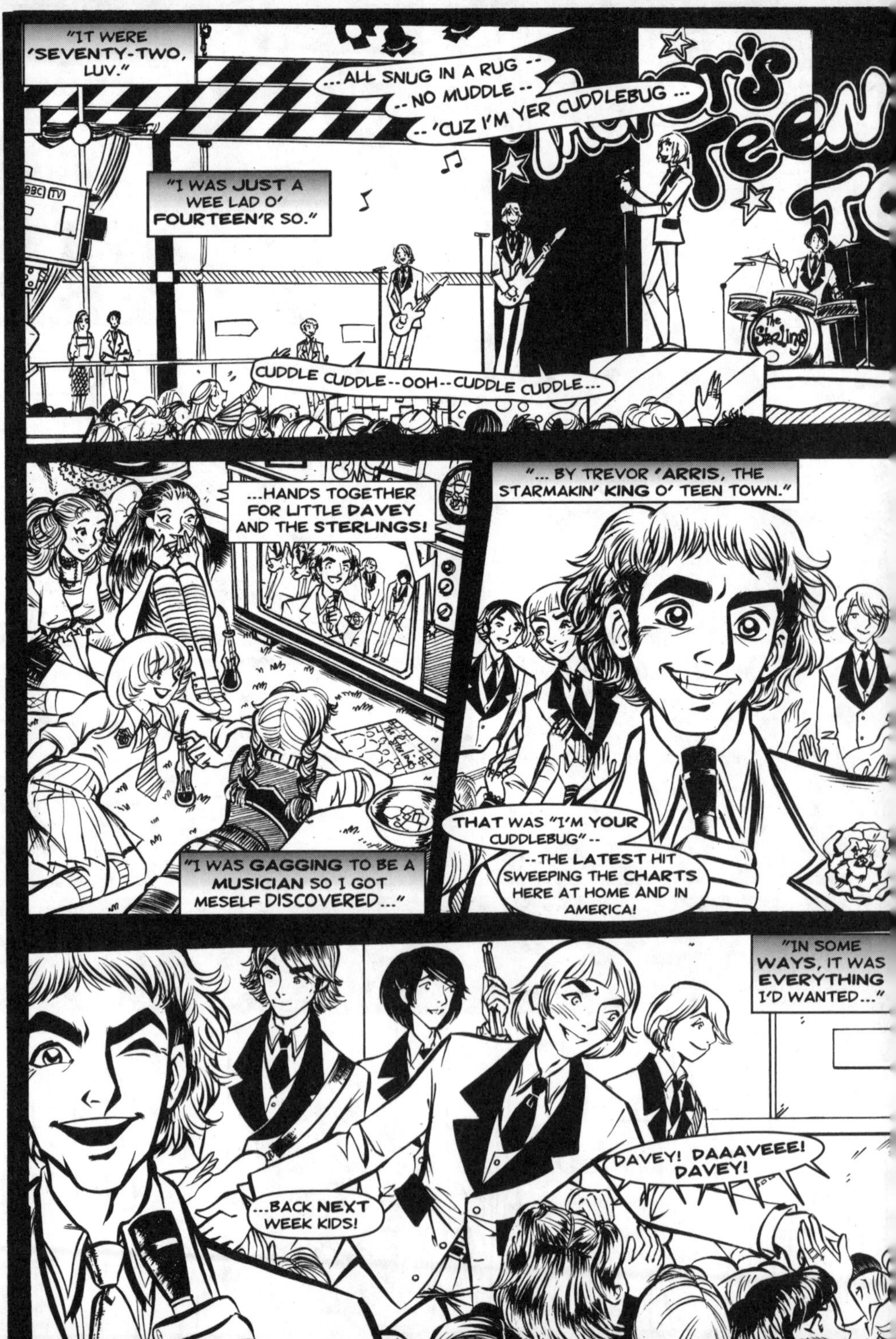
"IT WERE 'SEVENTY-TWO, LUV."
...ALL SNUG IN A RUG --
-- NO MUDDLE --
-- 'CUZ I'M YER CUDDLEBUG ...
"I WAS JUST A WEE LAD O' FOURTEEN'R SO."
BBC TV
THE STERLINGS
CUDDLE CUDDLE--OOH--CUDDLE CUDDLE...
...HANDS TOGETHER FOR LITTLE DAVEY AND THE STERLINGS!
"I WAS GAGGING TO BE A MUSICIAN SO I GOT MESELF DISCOVERED..."
"... BY TREVOR 'ARRIS, THE STARMAKIN' KING O' TEEN TOWN."
THAT WAS "I'M YOUR CUDDLEBUG" --
--THE LATEST HIT SWEEPING THE CHARTS HERE AT HOME AND IN AMERICA!
"IN SOME WAYS, IT WAS EVERYTHING I'D WANTED..."
...BACK NEXT WEEK KIDS!
DAVEY! DAAAVEEE! DAVEY!

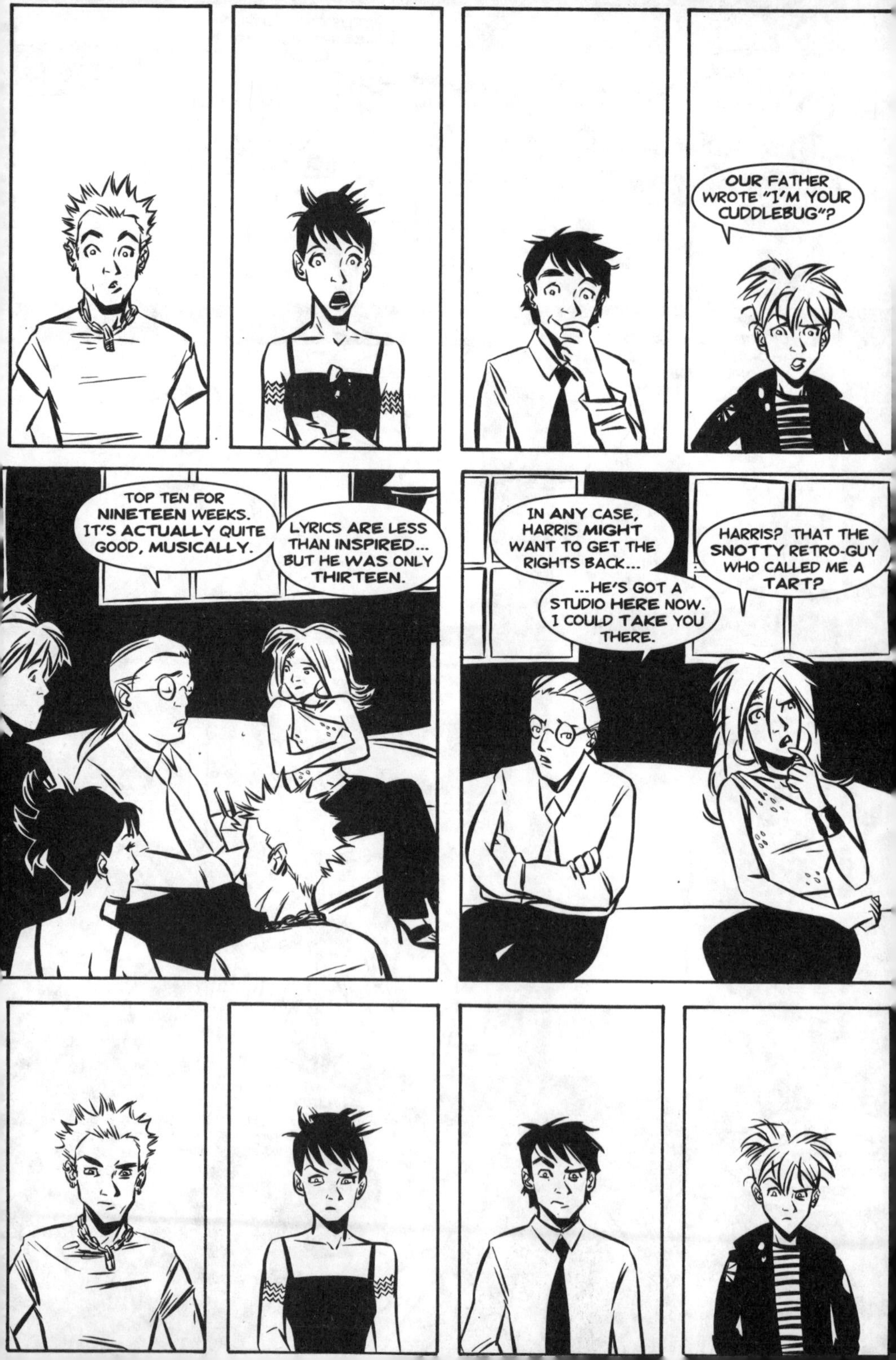
OUR FATHER WROTE "I'M YOUR CUDDLEBUG"?
TOP TEN FOR NINETEEN WEEKS. IT'S ACTUALLY QUITE GOOD, MUSICALLY.
LYRICS ARE LESS THAN INSPIRED... BUT HE WAS ONLY THIRTEEN.
IN ANY CASE, HARRIS MIGHT WANT TO GET THE RIGHTS BACK...
...HE'S GOT A STUDIO HERE NOW. I COULD TAKE YOU THERE.
HARRIS? THAT THE SNOTTY RETRO-GUY WHO CALLED ME A TART?

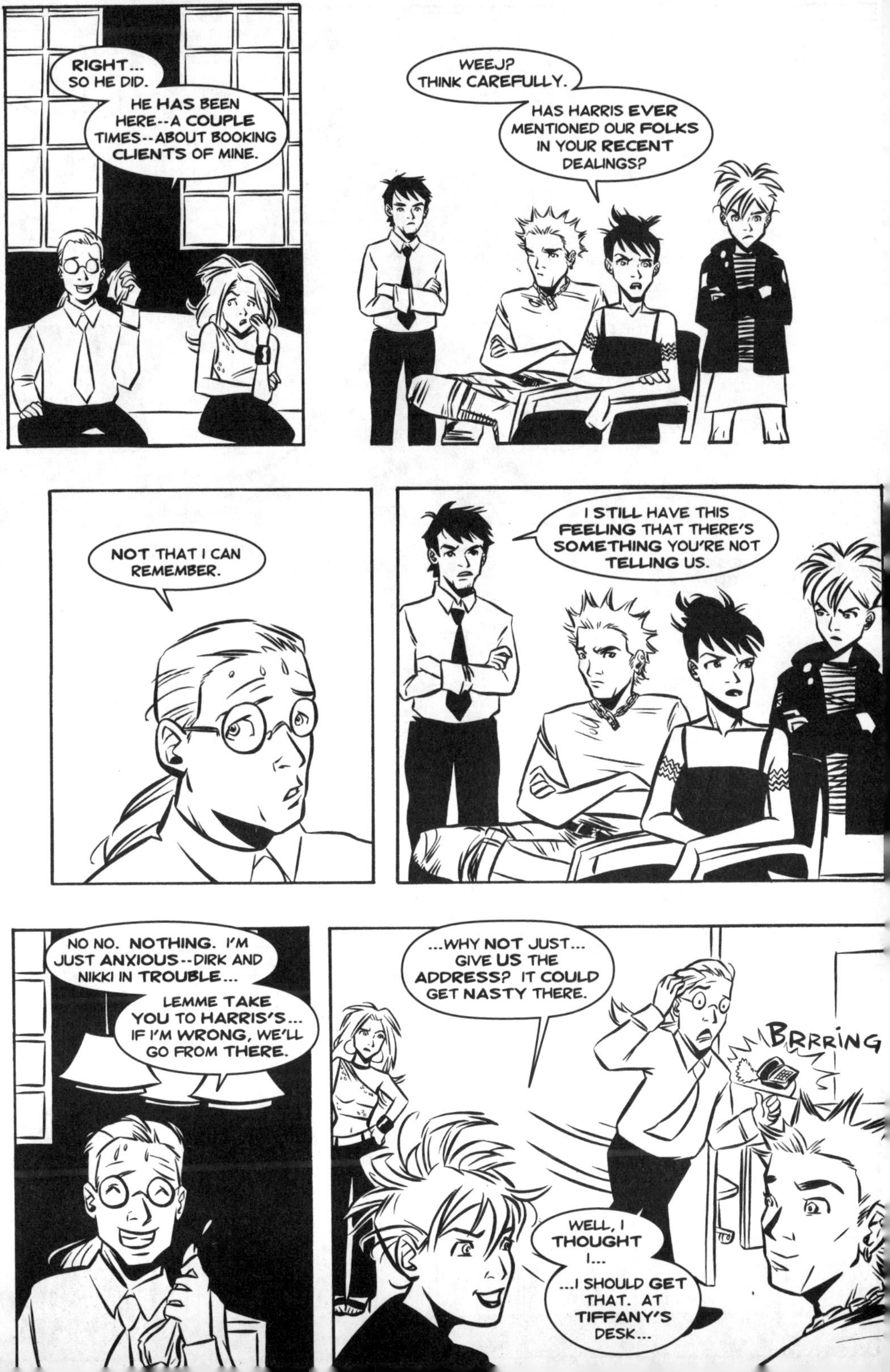
RIGHT... SO HE DID.
HE HAS BEEN HERE--A COUPLE TIMES--ABOUT BOOKING CLIENTS OF MINE.
WEEJ? THINK CAREFULLY.
HAS HARRIS EVER MENTIONED OUR FOLKS IN YOUR RECENT DEALINGS?
NOT THAT I CAN REMEMBER.
I STILL HAVE THIS FEELING THAT THERE'S SOMETHING YOU'RE NOT TELLING US.
NO NO. NOTHING. I'M JUST ANXIOUS--DIRK AND NIKKI IN TROUBLE...
LEMME TAKE YOU TO HARRIS'S... IF I'M WRONG, WE'LL GO FROM THERE.
...WHY NOT JUST... GIVE US THE ADDRESS? IT COULD GET NASTY THERE.
BRRRING
WELL, I THOUGHT I...
...I SHOULD GET THAT. AT TIFFANY'S DESK...

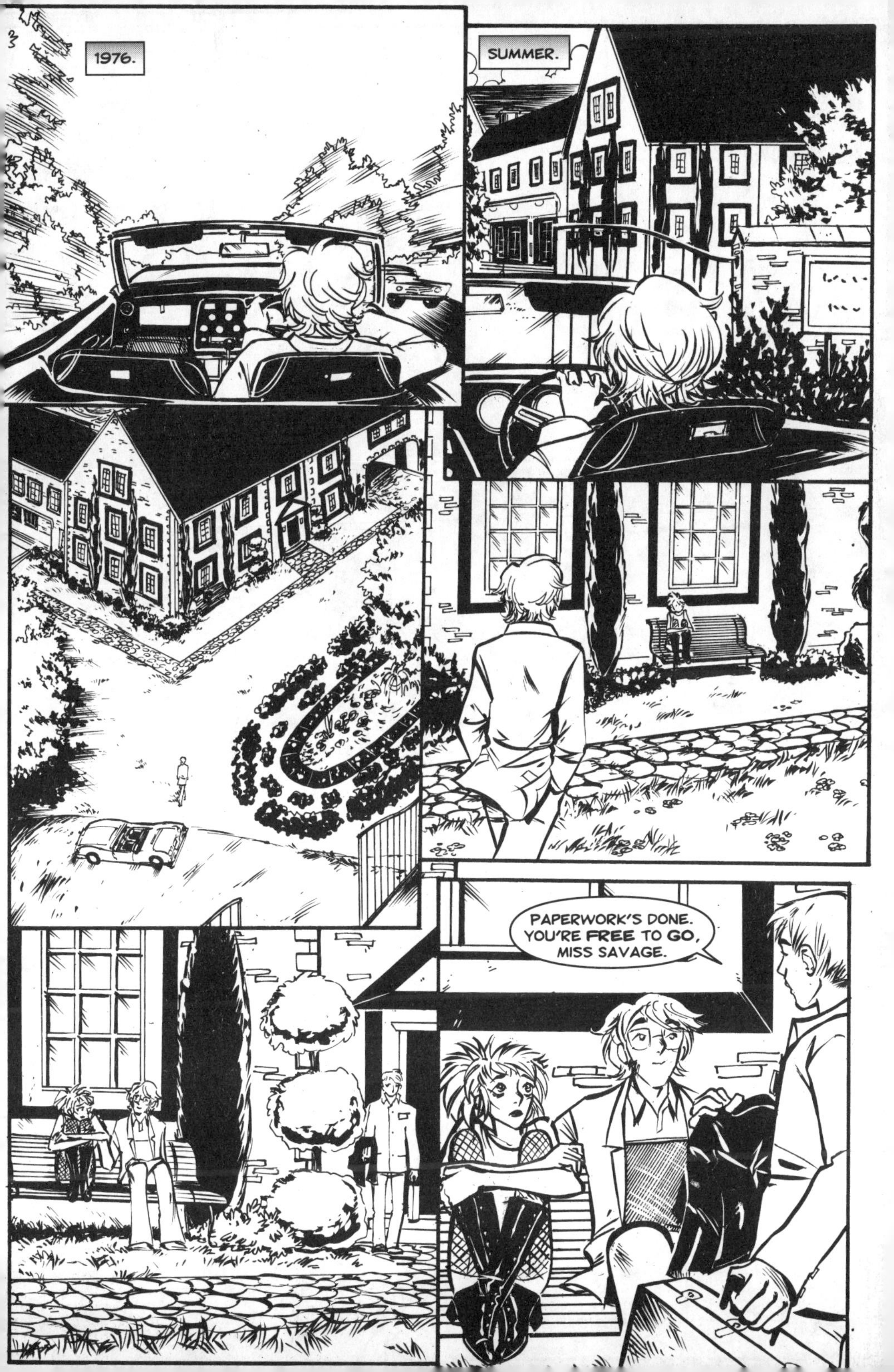
1976.
SUMMER.
PAPERWORK'S DONE. YOU'RE **FREE** TO **GO**, MISS SAVAGE.

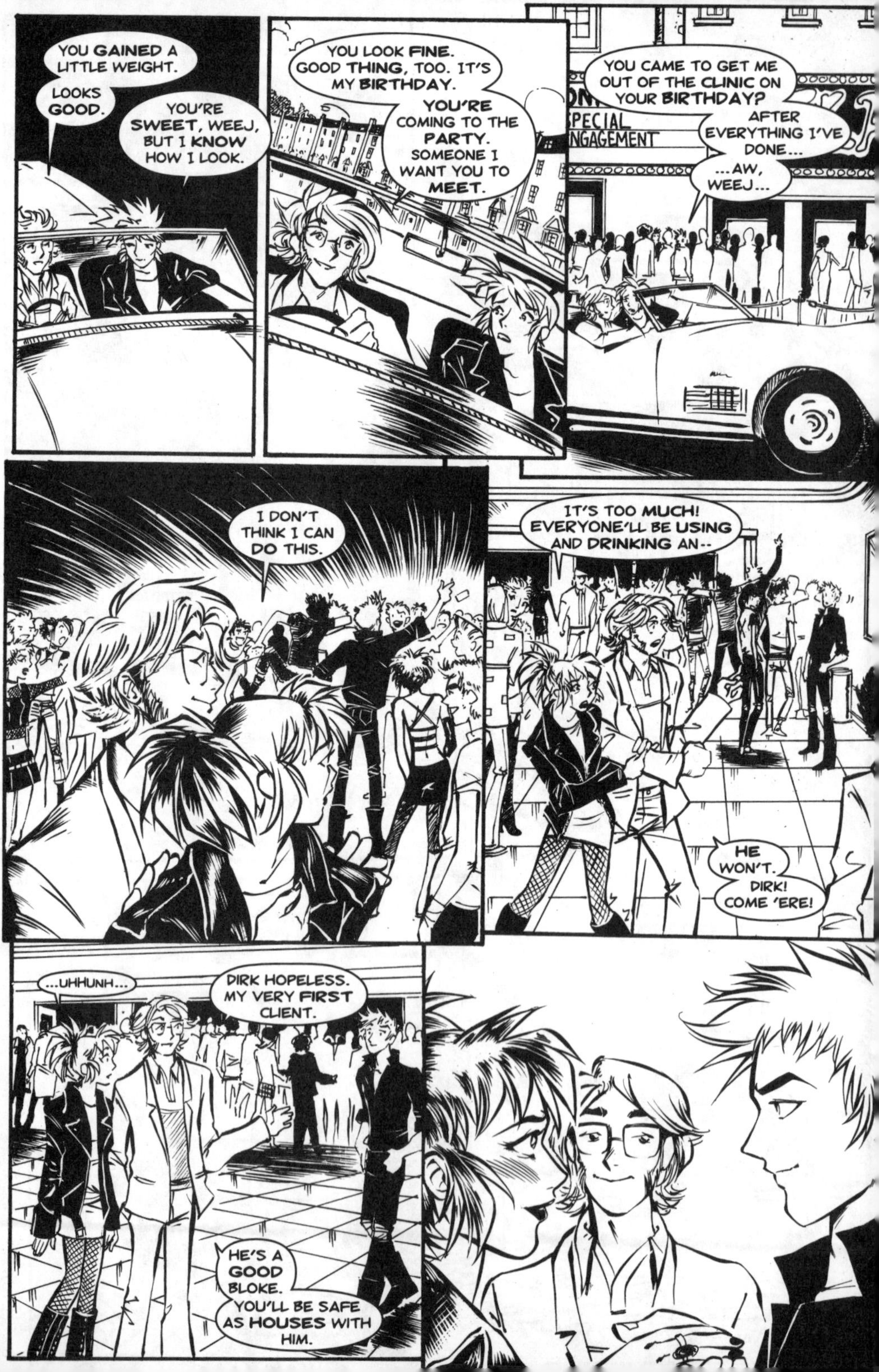

YOU GAINED A LITTLE WEIGHT.
LOOKS GOOD.
YOU'RE SWEET, WEEJ, BUT I KNOW HOW I LOOK.
YOU LOOK FINE. GOOD THING, TOO. IT'S MY BIRTHDAY.
YOU'RE COMING TO THE PARTY. SOMEONE I WANT YOU TO MEET.
YOU CAME TO GET ME OUT OF THE CLINIC ON YOUR BIRTHDAY?
AFTER EVERYTHING I'VE DONE...
...AW, WEEJ...
I DON'T THINK I CAN DO THIS.
IT'S TOO MUCH! EVERYONE'LL BE USING AND DRINKING AN--
HE WON'T.
DIRK! COME 'ERE!
...UHHUNH...
DIRK HOPELESS. MY VERY FIRST CLIENT.
HE'S A GOOD BLOKE.
YOU'LL BE SAFE AS HOUSES WITH HIM.

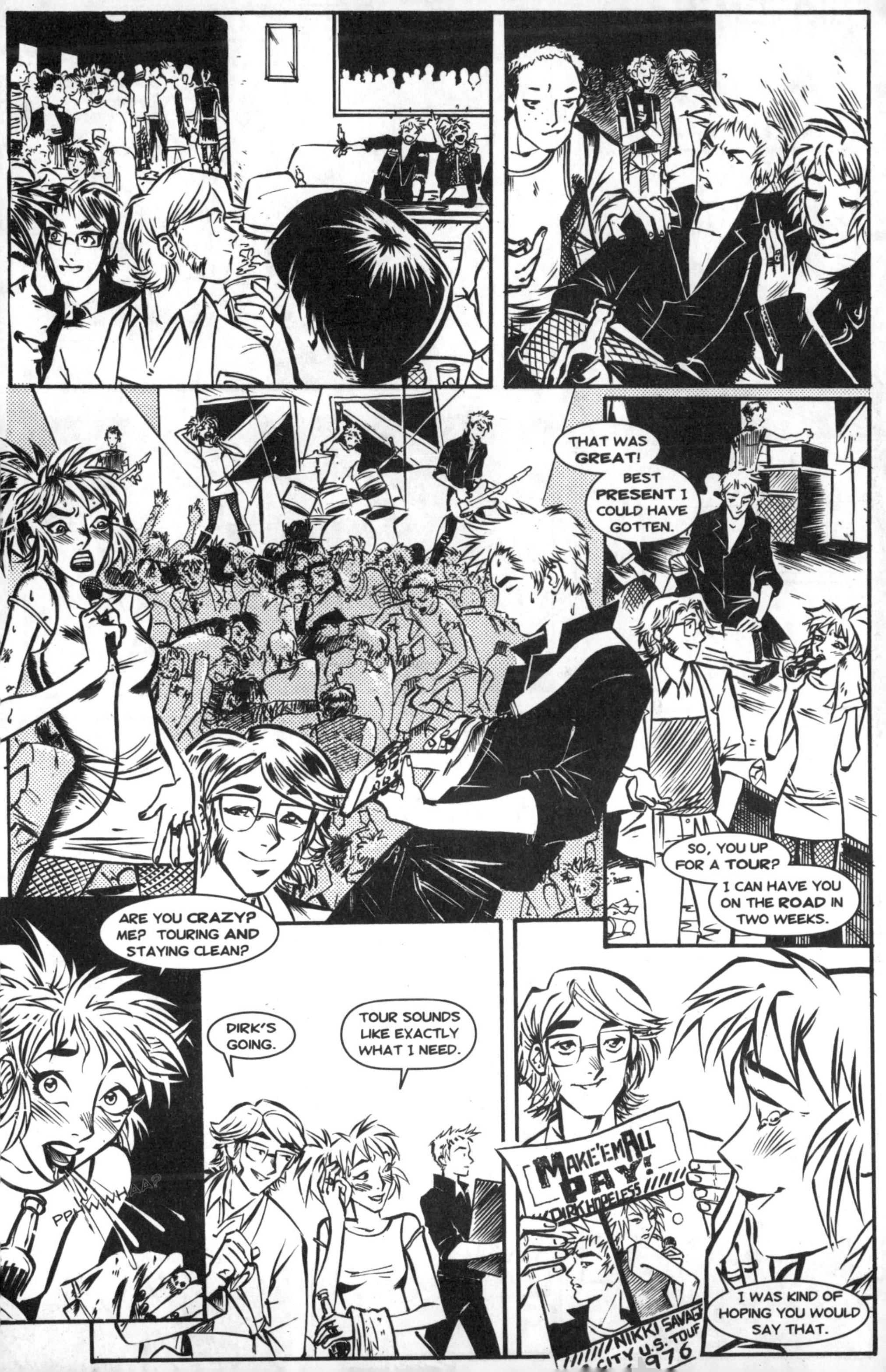
THAT WAS GREAT!
BEST PRESENT I COULD HAVE GOTTEN.
SO, YOU UP FOR A TOUR?
I CAN HAVE YOU ON THE ROAD IN TWO WEEKS.
ARE YOU CRAZY? ME? TOURING AND STAYING CLEAN?
PPHWWHAA?
DIRK'S GOING.
TOUR SOUNDS LIKE EXACTLY WHAT I NEED.
MAKE'EM ALL PAY!
DIRK HOPELESS
I WAS KIND OF HOPING YOU WOULD SAY THAT.

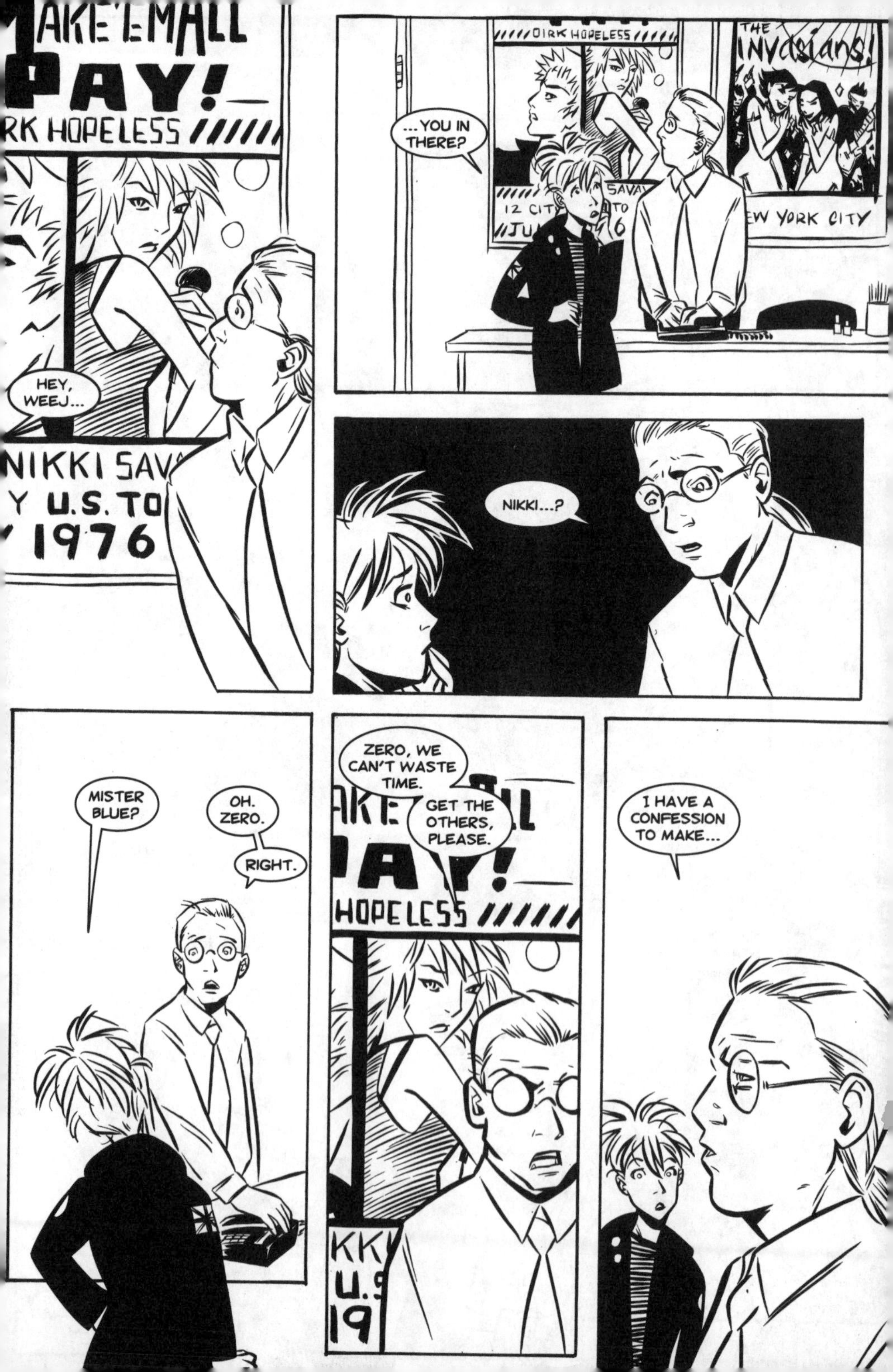
AKE 'EM ALL PAY!
RK HOPELESS
NIKKI SAVA
Y U.S. TO
1976
HEY, WEEJ...
DIRK HOPELESS
THE INVASIANS!
12 CITY
SAVA
TO
6
JU
EW YORK CITY
...YOU IN THERE?
NIKKI...?
MISTER BLUE?
OH. ZERO.
RIGHT.
ZERO, WE CAN'T WASTE TIME.
GET THE OTHERS, PLEASE.
I HAVE A CONFESSION TO MAKE...

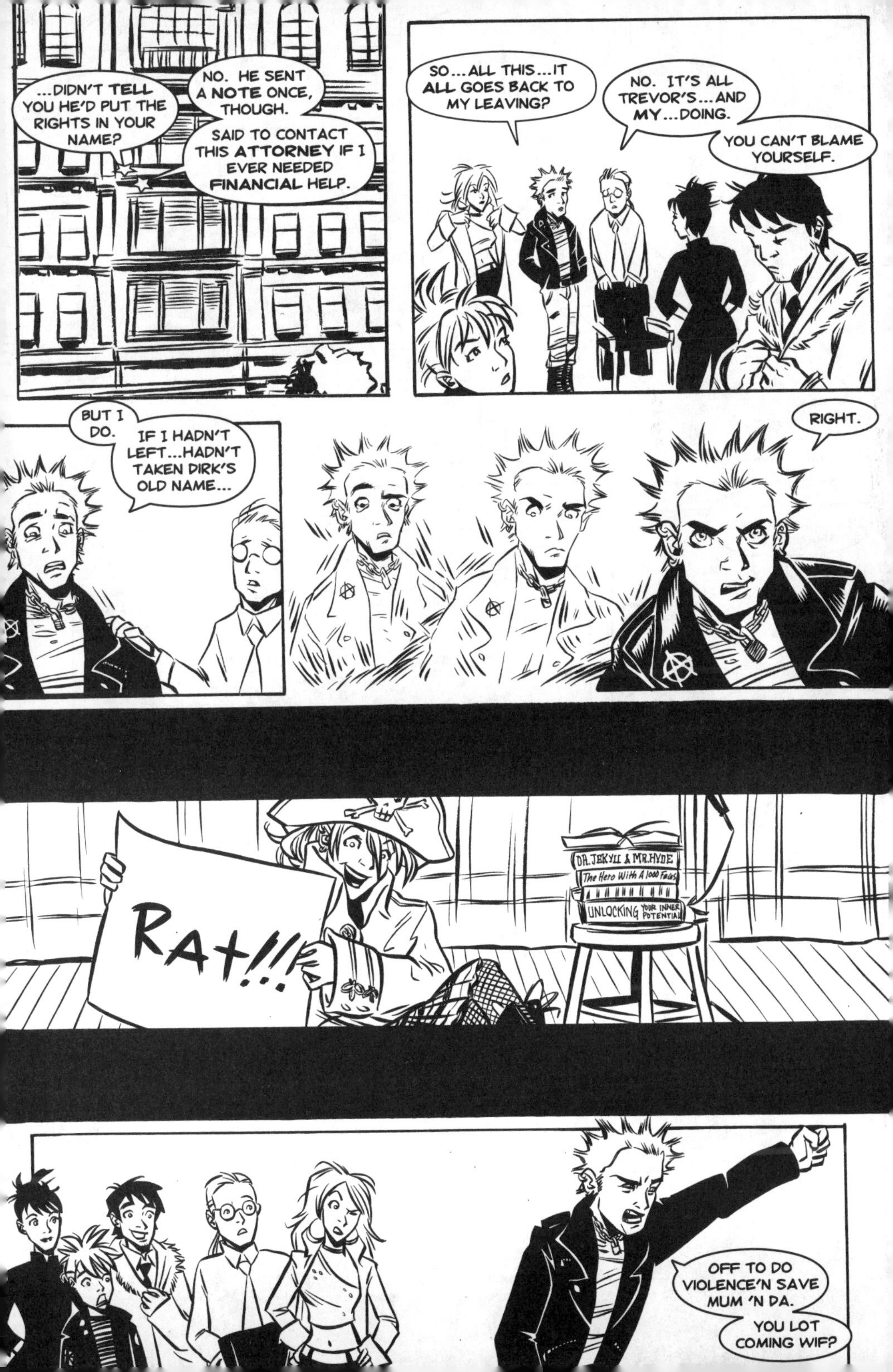
...DIDN'T TELL YOU HE'D PUT THE RIGHTS IN YOUR NAME?
NO. HE SENT A NOTE ONCE, THOUGH.
SAID TO CONTACT THIS ATTORNEY IF I EVER NEEDED FINANCIAL HELP.
SO... ALL THIS... IT ALL GOES BACK TO MY LEAVING?
NO. IT'S ALL TREVOR'S... AND MY... DOING.
YOU CAN'T BLAME YOURSELF.
BUT I DO.
IF I HADN'T LEFT... HADN'T TAKEN DIRK'S OLD NAME...
RIGHT.
RAT!!!
DR. JEKYLL & MR. HYDE
The Hero With A 1000 Faces
UNLOCKING YOUR INNER POTENTIAL
OFF TO DO VIOLENCE'N SAVE MUM 'N DA.
YOU LOT COMING WIF?

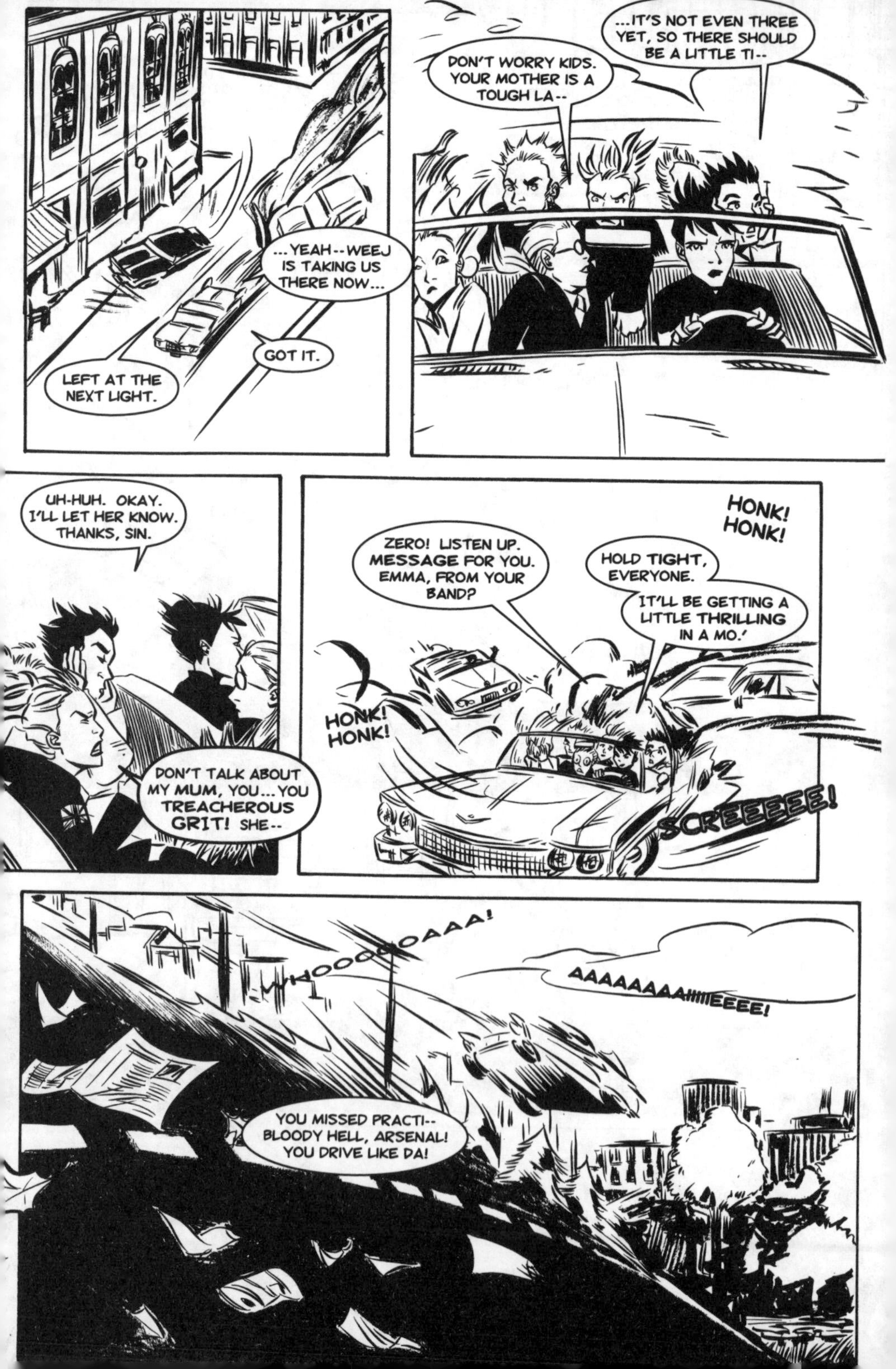
...YEAH--WEEJ IS TAKING US THERE NOW...
LEFT AT THE NEXT LIGHT.
GOT IT.
DON'T WORRY KIDS. YOUR MOTHER IS A TOUGH LA--
...IT'S NOT EVEN THREE YET, SO THERE SHOULD BE A LITTLE TI--
UH-HUH. OKAY. I'LL LET HER KNOW. THANKS, SIN.
DON'T TALK ABOUT MY MUM, YOU... YOU TREACHEROUS GRIT! SHE--
HONK! HONK!
ZERO! LISTEN UP. MESSAGE FOR YOU. EMMA, FROM YOUR BAND?
HOLD TIGHT, EVERYONE.
IT'LL BE GETTING A LITTLE THRILLING IN A MO.'
HONK! HONK!
SCREEEEEE!
WHOOOOOOAAAA!
AAAAAAAAIIIIIEEEE!
YOU MISSED PRACTI-- BLOODY HELL, ARSENAL! YOU DRIVE LIKE DA!

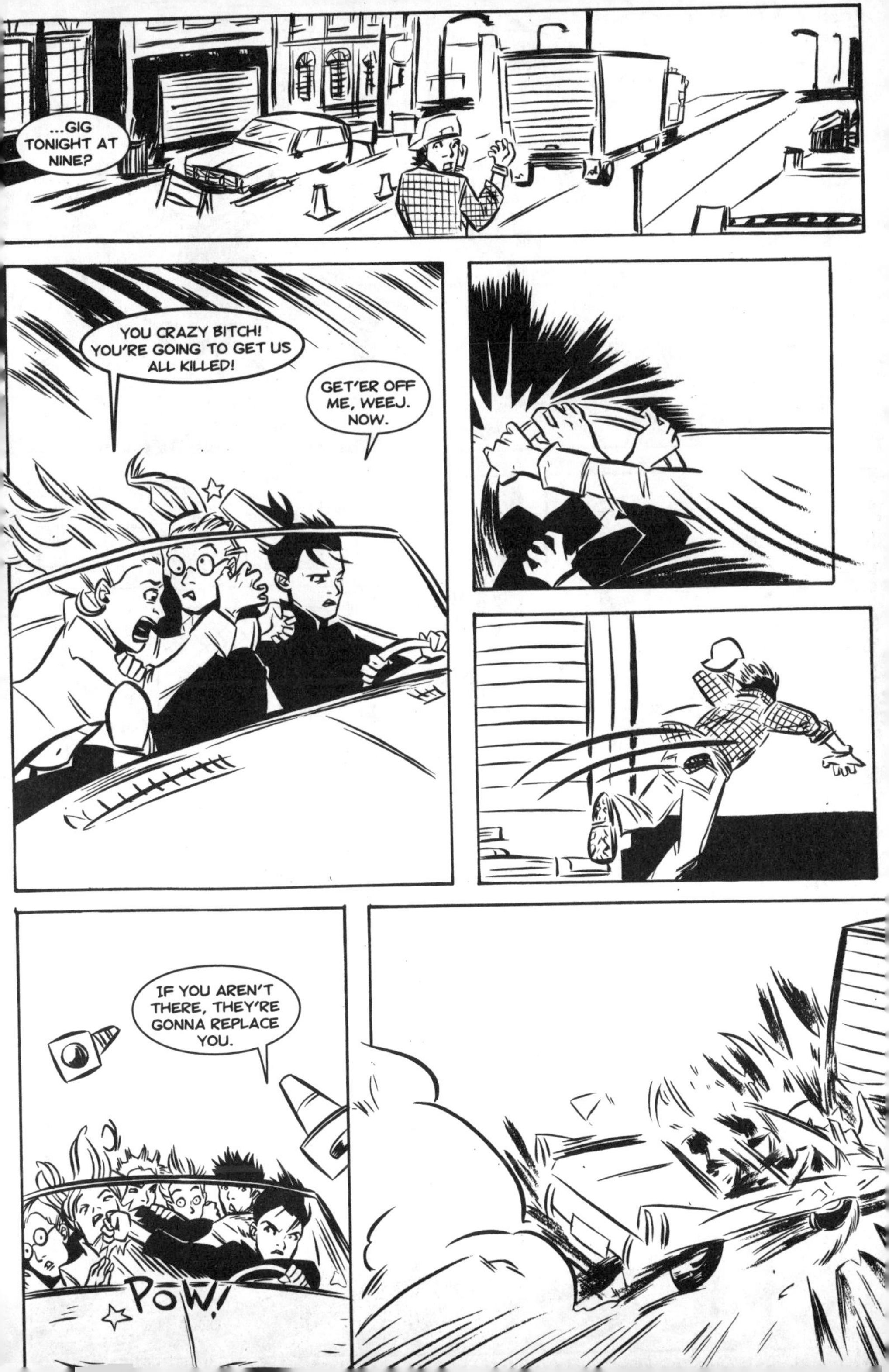
...GIG TONIGHT AT NINE?
YOU CRAZY BITCH! YOU'RE GOING TO GET US ALL KILLED!
GET'ER OFF ME, WEEJ. NOW.
IF YOU AREN'T THERE, THEY'RE GONNA REPLACE YOU.
POW!

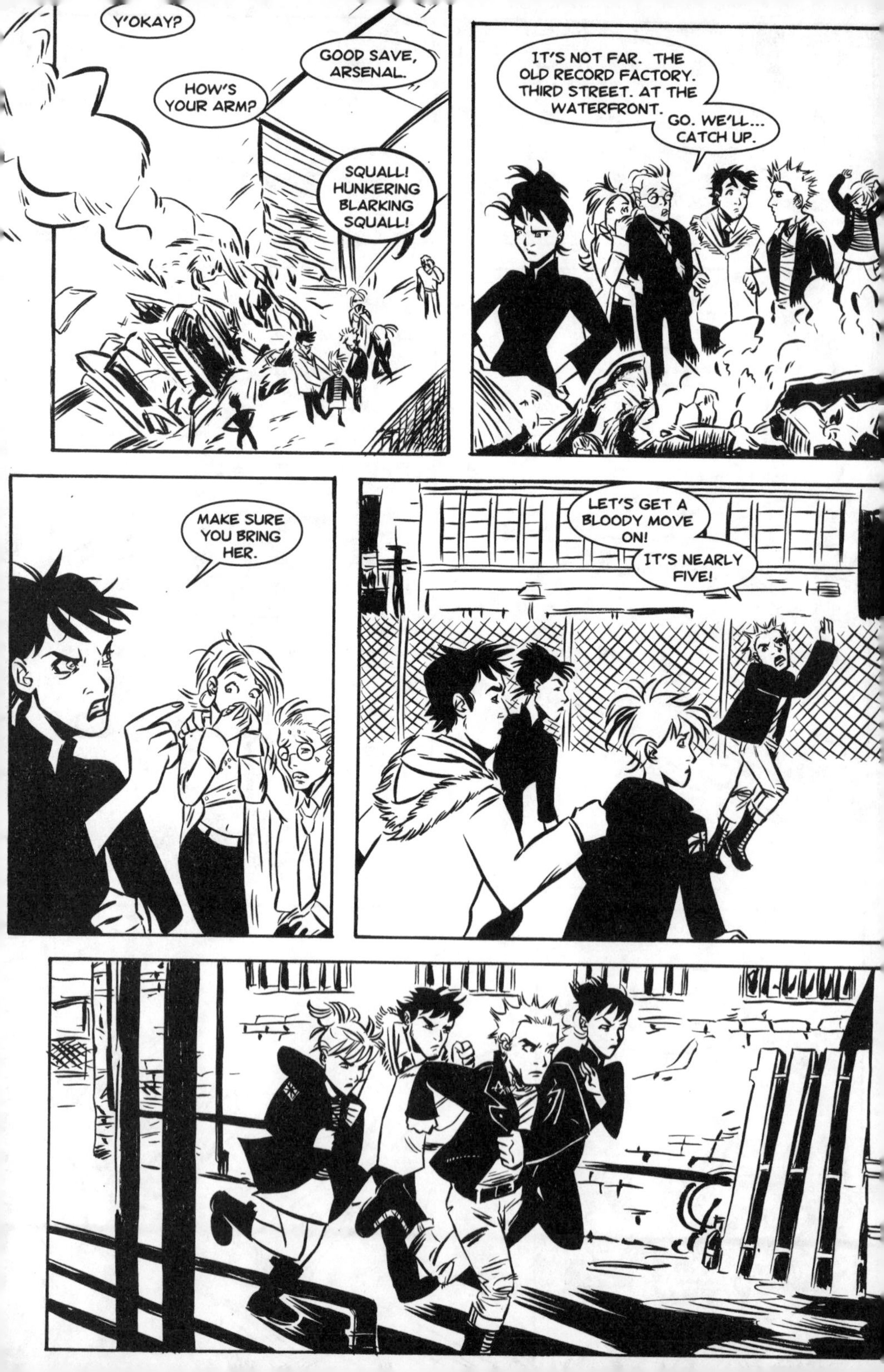

Y'OKAY?
HOW'S YOUR ARM?
GOOD SAVE, ARSENAL.
SQUALL! HUNKERING BLARKING SQUALL!
IT'S NOT FAR. THE OLD RECORD FACTORY. THIRD STREET. AT THE WATERFRONT.
GO. WE'LL... CATCH UP.
MAKE SURE YOU BRING HER.
LET'S GET A BLOODY MOVE ON!
IT'S NEARLY FIVE!

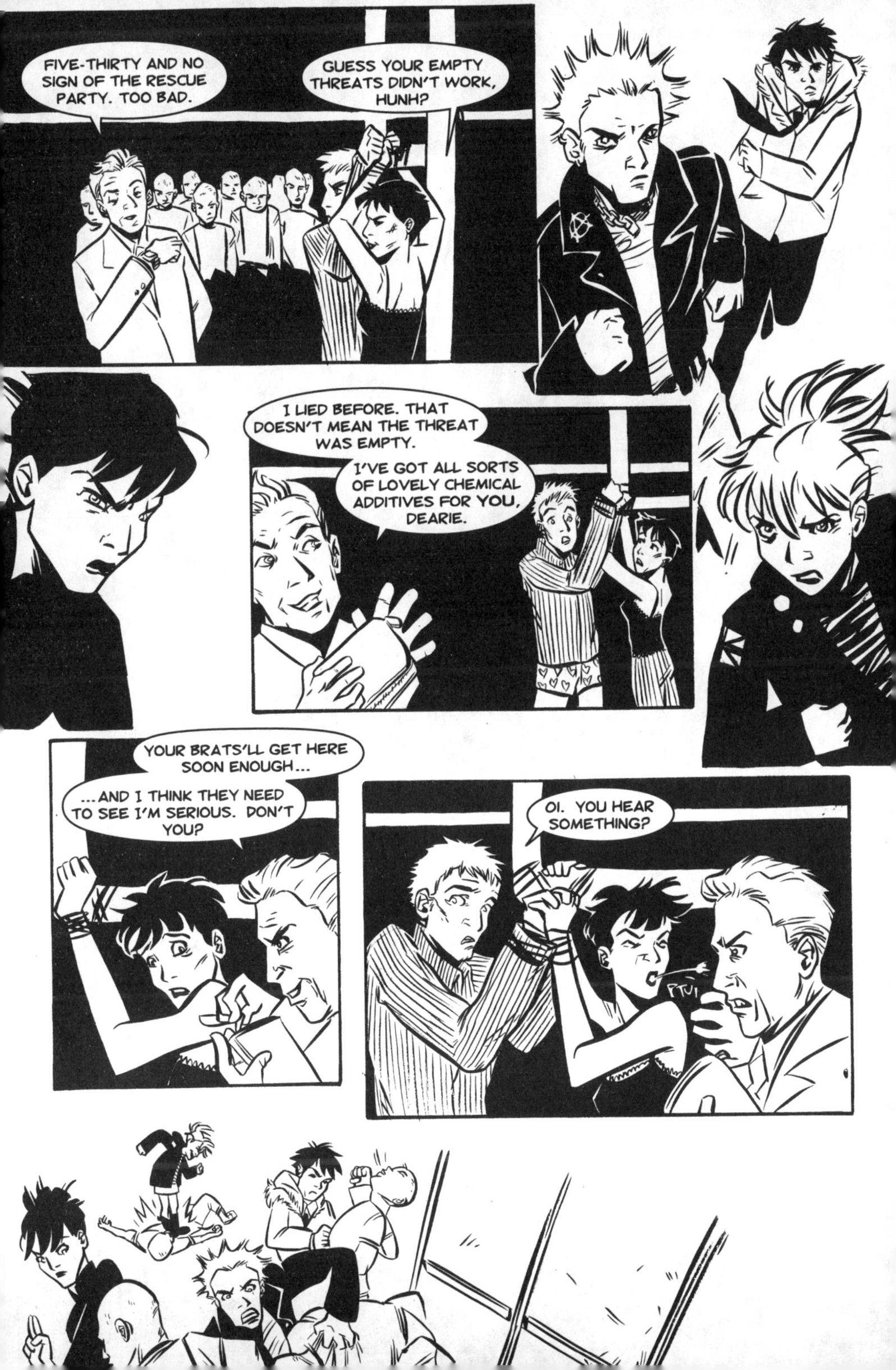
FIVE-THIRTY AND NO SIGN OF THE RESCUE PARTY. TOO BAD.
GUESS YOUR EMPTY THREATS DIDN'T WORK, HUNH?
I LIED BEFORE. THAT DOESN'T MEAN THE THREAT WAS EMPTY.
I'VE GOT ALL SORTS OF LOVELY CHEMICAL ADDITIVES FOR YOU, DEARIE.
YOUR BRATS'LL GET HERE SOON ENOUGH...
...AND I THINK THEY NEED TO SEE I'M SERIOUS. DON'T YOU?
OI. YOU HEAR SOMETHING?
PTUI

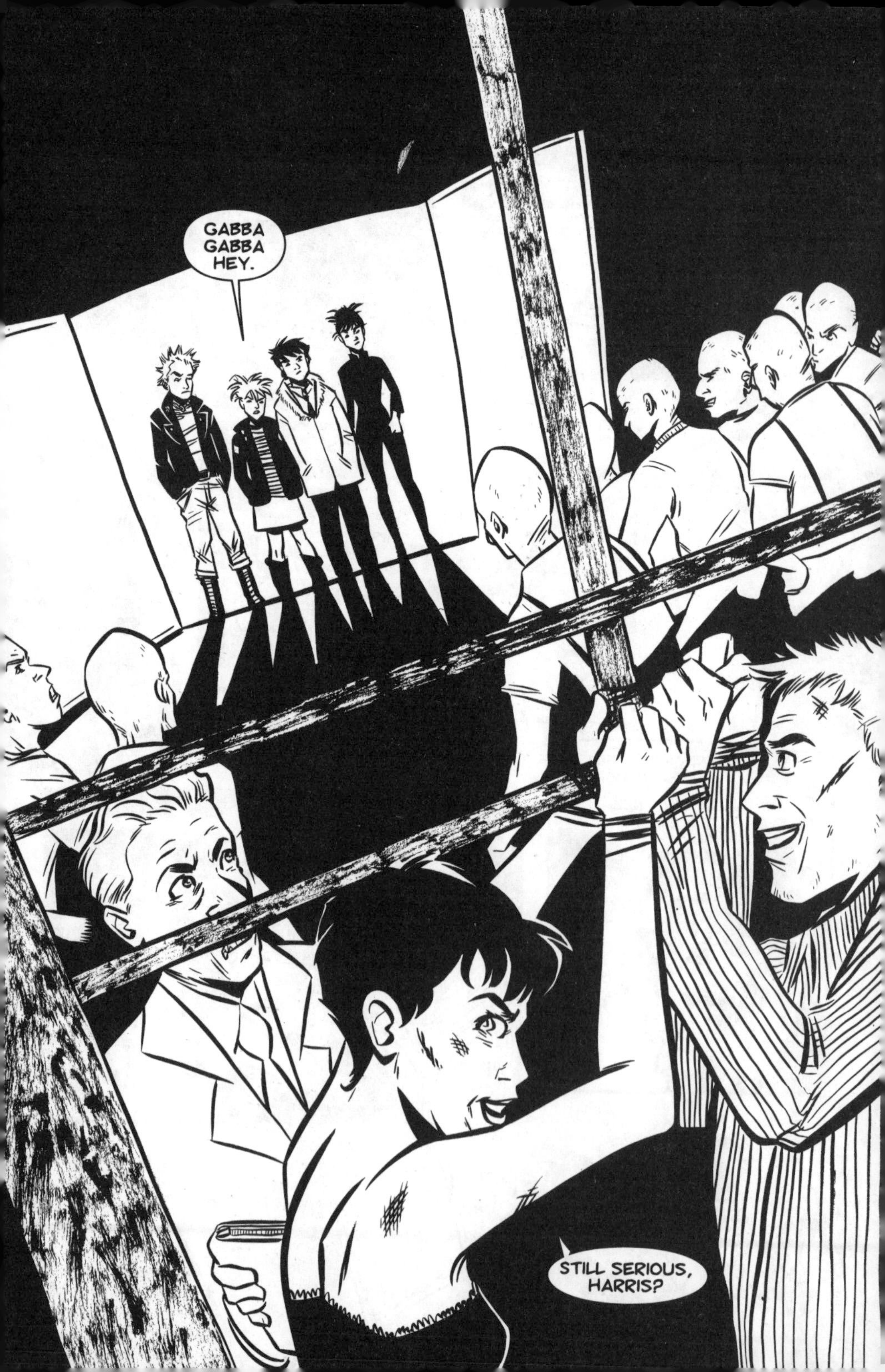
GABBA GABBA HEY.
STILL SERIOUS, HARRIS?

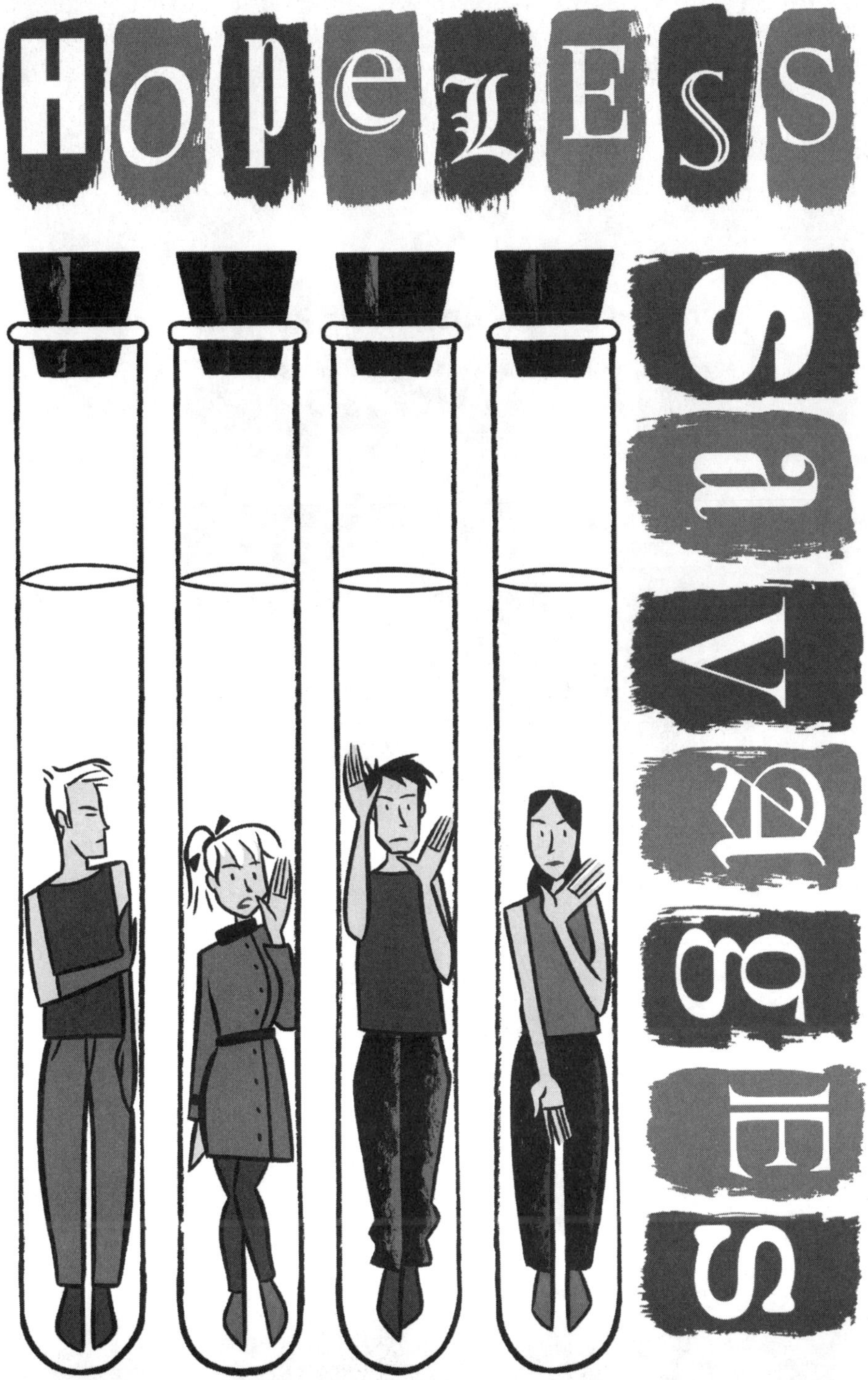
HOPELESS
SAVAGES

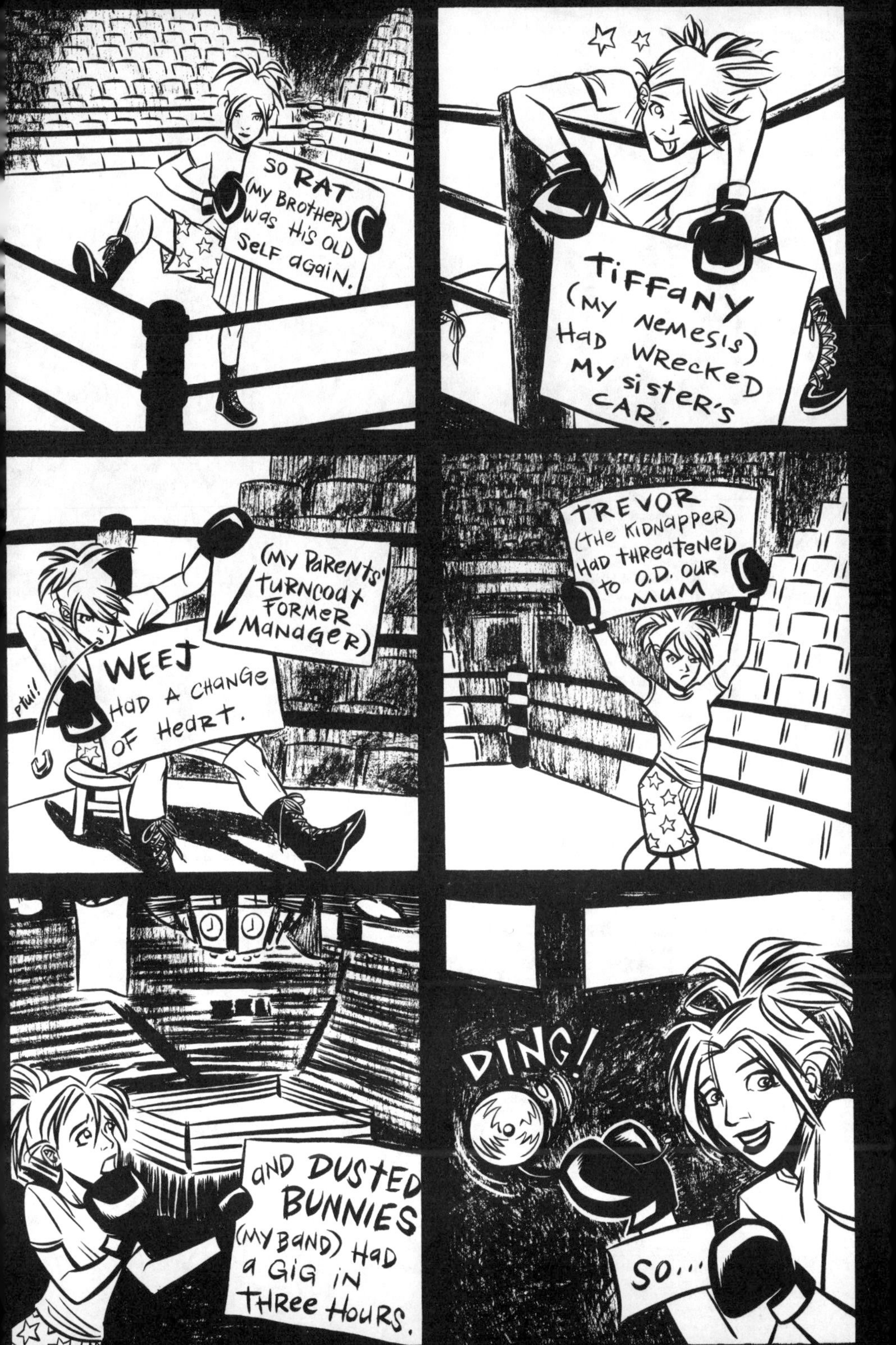
SO RAT (MY BROTHER) WAS HIS OLD SELF AGAIN.
TIFFANY (MY NEMESIS) HAD WRECKED MY SISTER'S CAR.
(MY PARENTS' TURNCOAT FORMER MANAGER)
WEEJ HAD A CHANGE OF HEART.
PTUI!
TREVOR (THE KIDNAPPER) HAD THREATENED TO O.D. OUR MUM
AND DUSTED BUNNIES (MY BAND) HAD A GIG IN THREE HOURS.
DING!
SO...

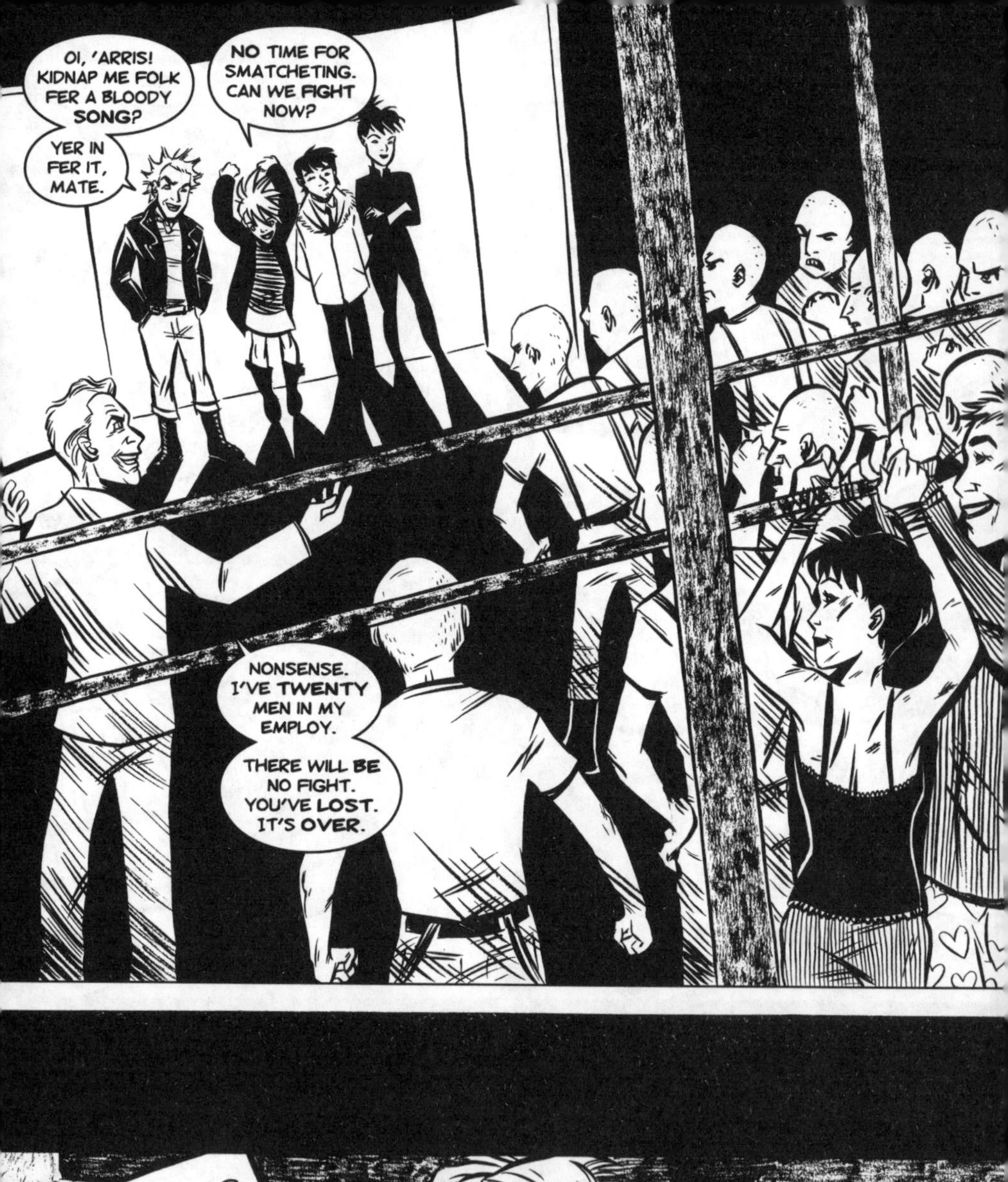
OI, 'ARRIS! KIDNAP ME FOLK FER A BLOODY SONG?
YER IN FER IT, MATE.
NO TIME FOR SMATCHETING. CAN WE FIGHT NOW?
NONSENSE. I'VE TWENTY MEN IN MY EMPLOY.
THERE WILL BE NO FIGHT. YOU'VE LOST. IT'S OVER.

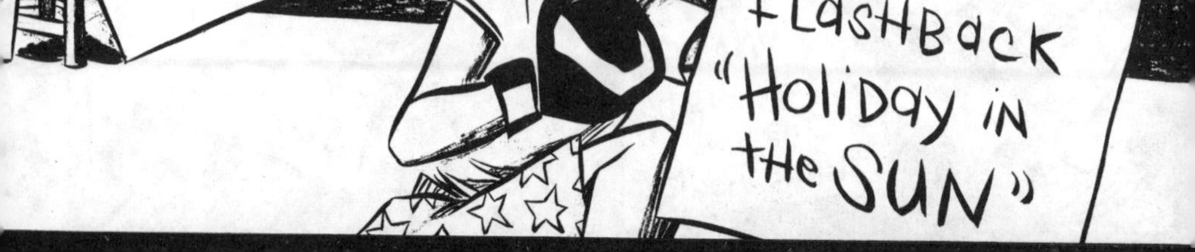
He's JOKING, RIGHT?
FLASHBack "Holiday in the SUN"

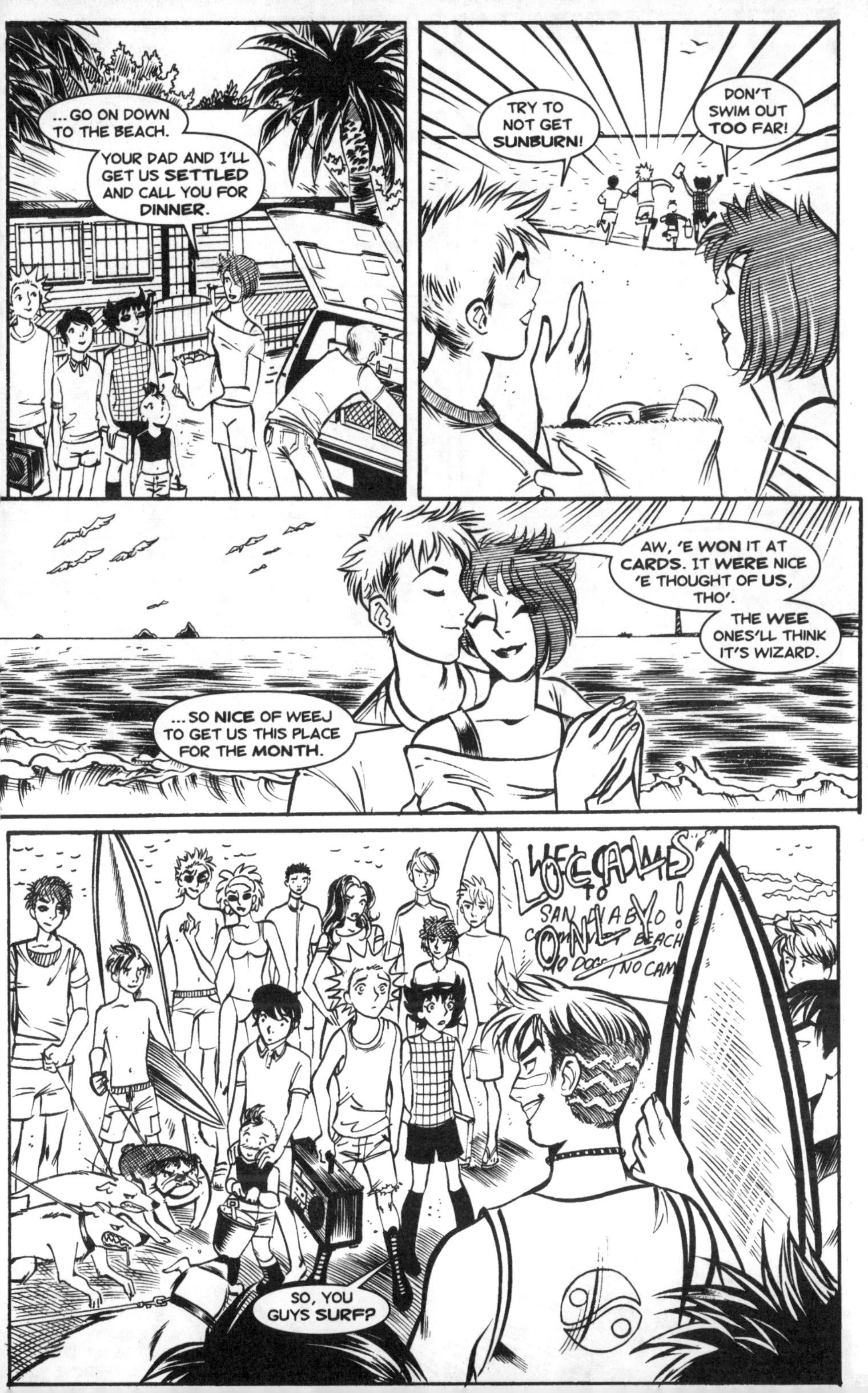

...GO ON DOWN TO THE BEACH.
YOUR DAD AND I'LL GET US SETTLED AND CALL YOU FOR DINNER.
TRY TO NOT GET SUNBURN!
DON'T SWIM OUT TOO FAR!
...SO NICE OF WEEJ TO GET US THIS PLACE FOR THE MONTH.
AW, 'E WON IT AT CARDS. IT WERE NICE 'E THOUGHT OF US, THO'.
THE WEE ONES'LL THINK IT'S WIZARD.
LOCALS ONLY!
SO, YOU GUYS SURF?

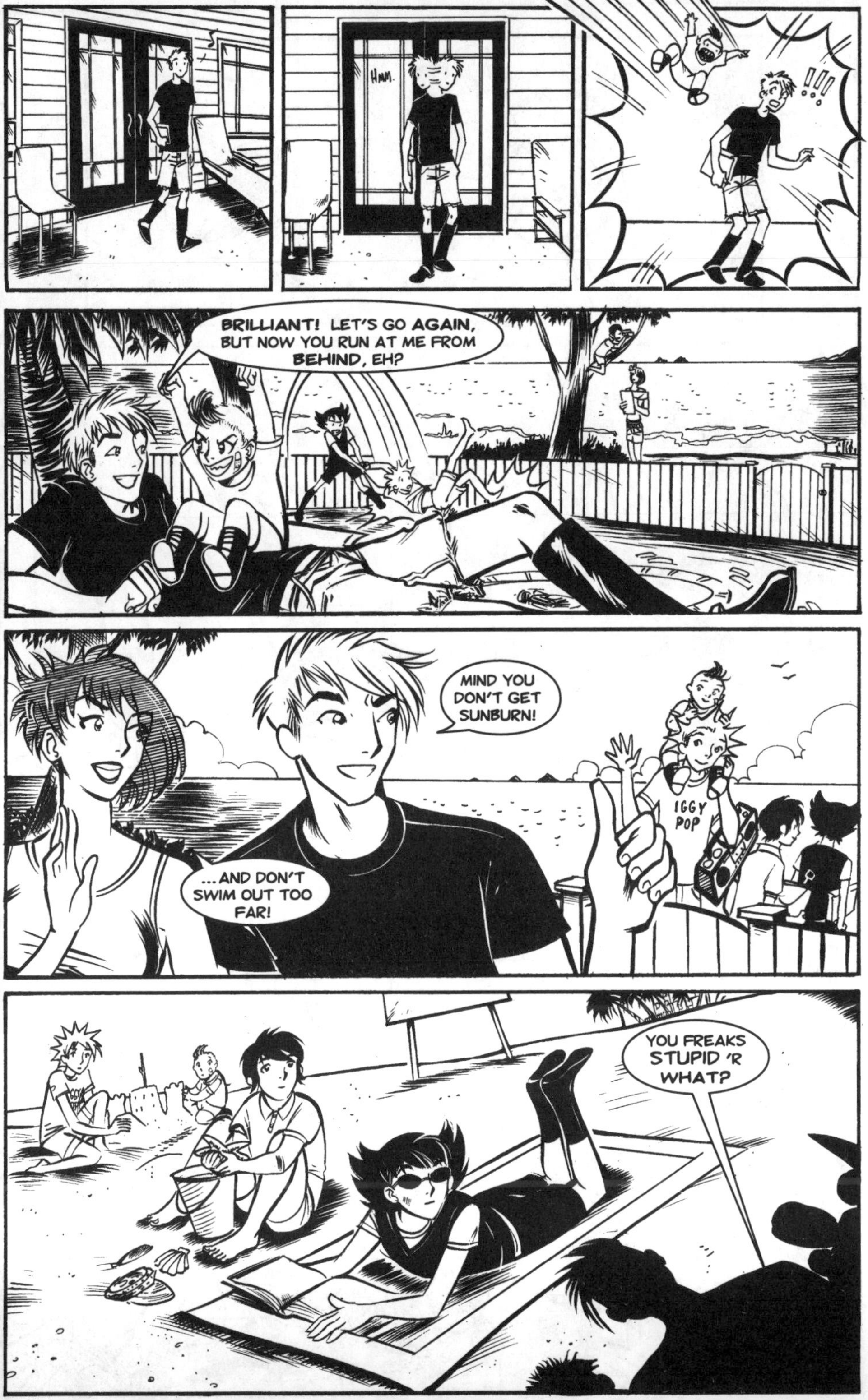
HMM.
!!!
BRILLIANT! LET'S GO AGAIN, BUT NOW YOU RUN AT ME FROM BEHIND, EH?
MIND YOU DON'T GET SUNBURN!
...AND DON'T SWIM OUT TOO FAR!
IGGY POP
YOU FREAKS STUPID 'R WHAT?

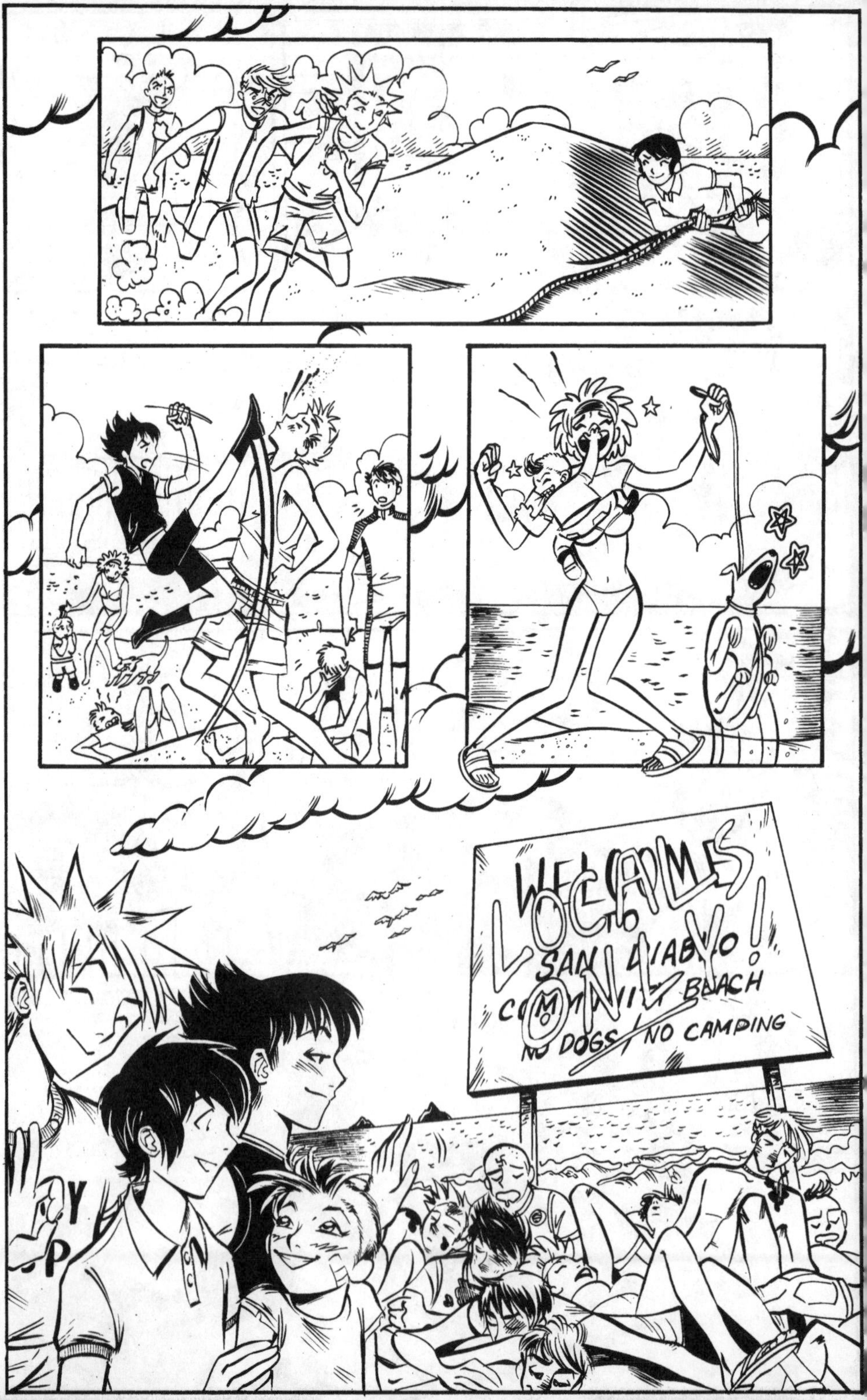
LOCALS ONLY!
NO DOGS / NO CAMPING

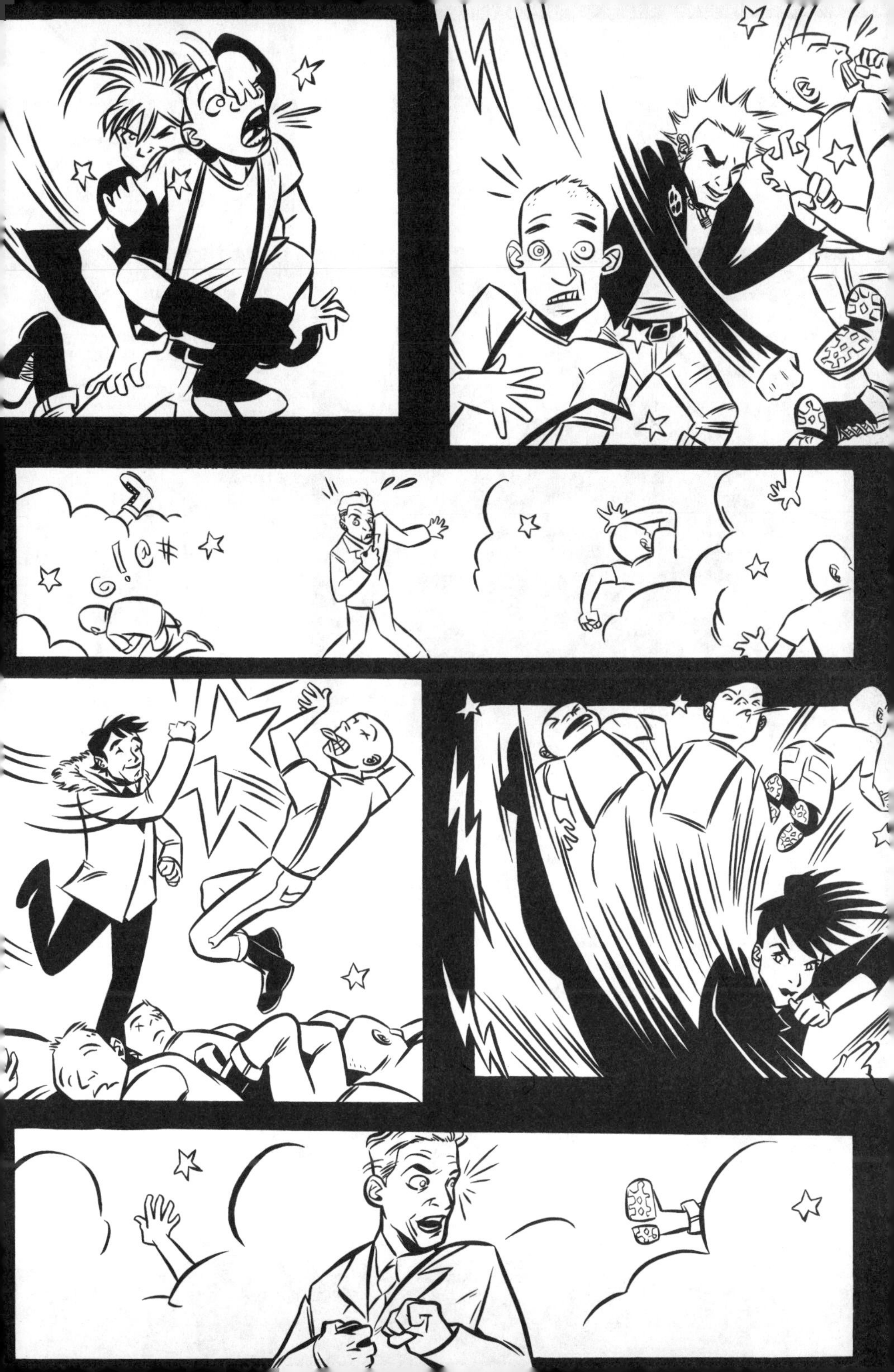
!@#

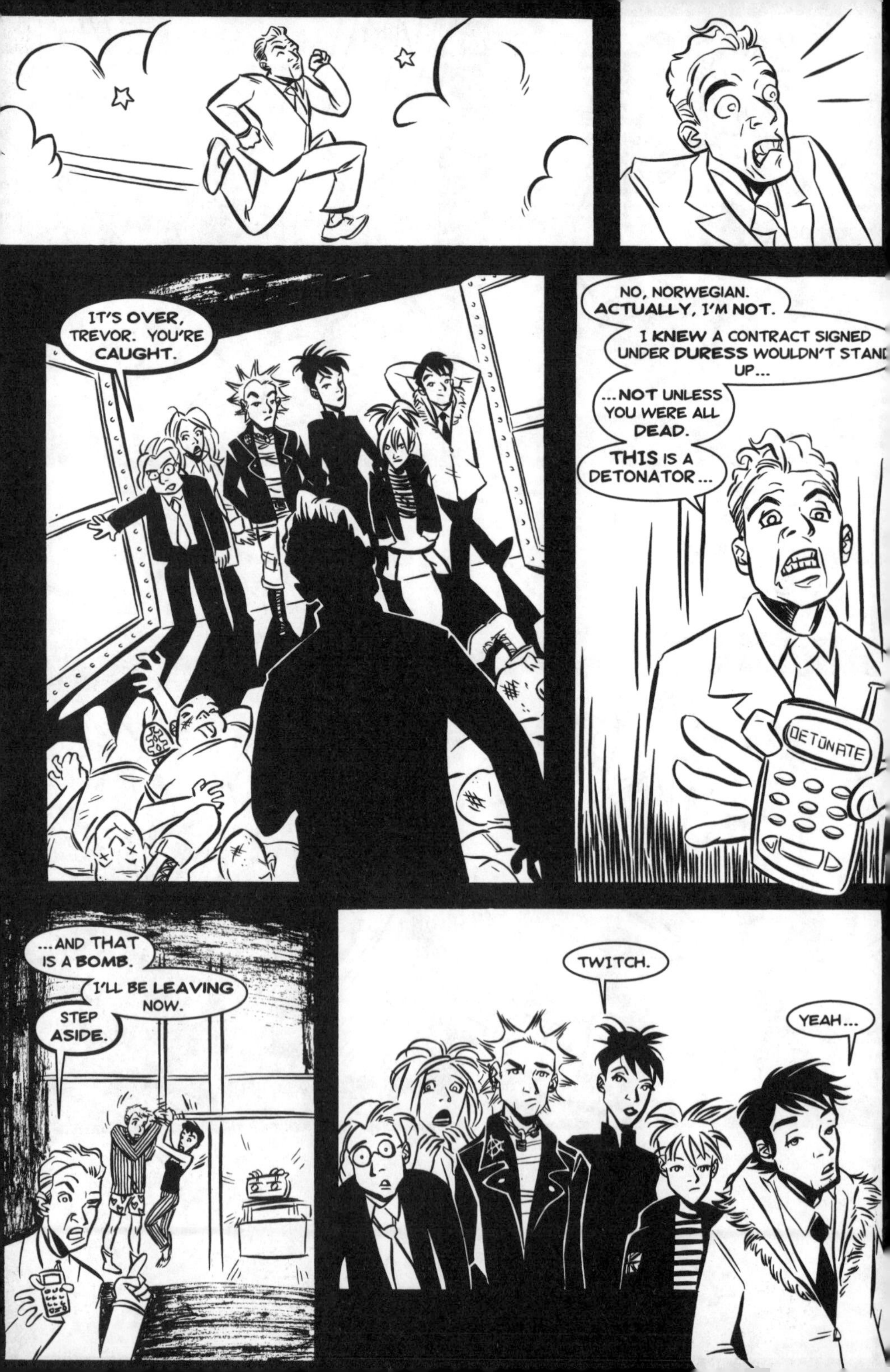
IT'S OVER, TREVOR. YOU'RE CAUGHT.
NO, NORWEGIAN. ACTUALLY, I'M NOT.
I KNEW A CONTRACT SIGNED UNDER DURESS WOULDN'T STAND UP...
...NOT UNLESS YOU WERE ALL DEAD.
THIS IS A DETONATOR...
DETONATE
...AND THAT IS A BOMB.
I'LL BE LEAVING NOW.
STEP ASIDE.
TWITCH.
YEAH...

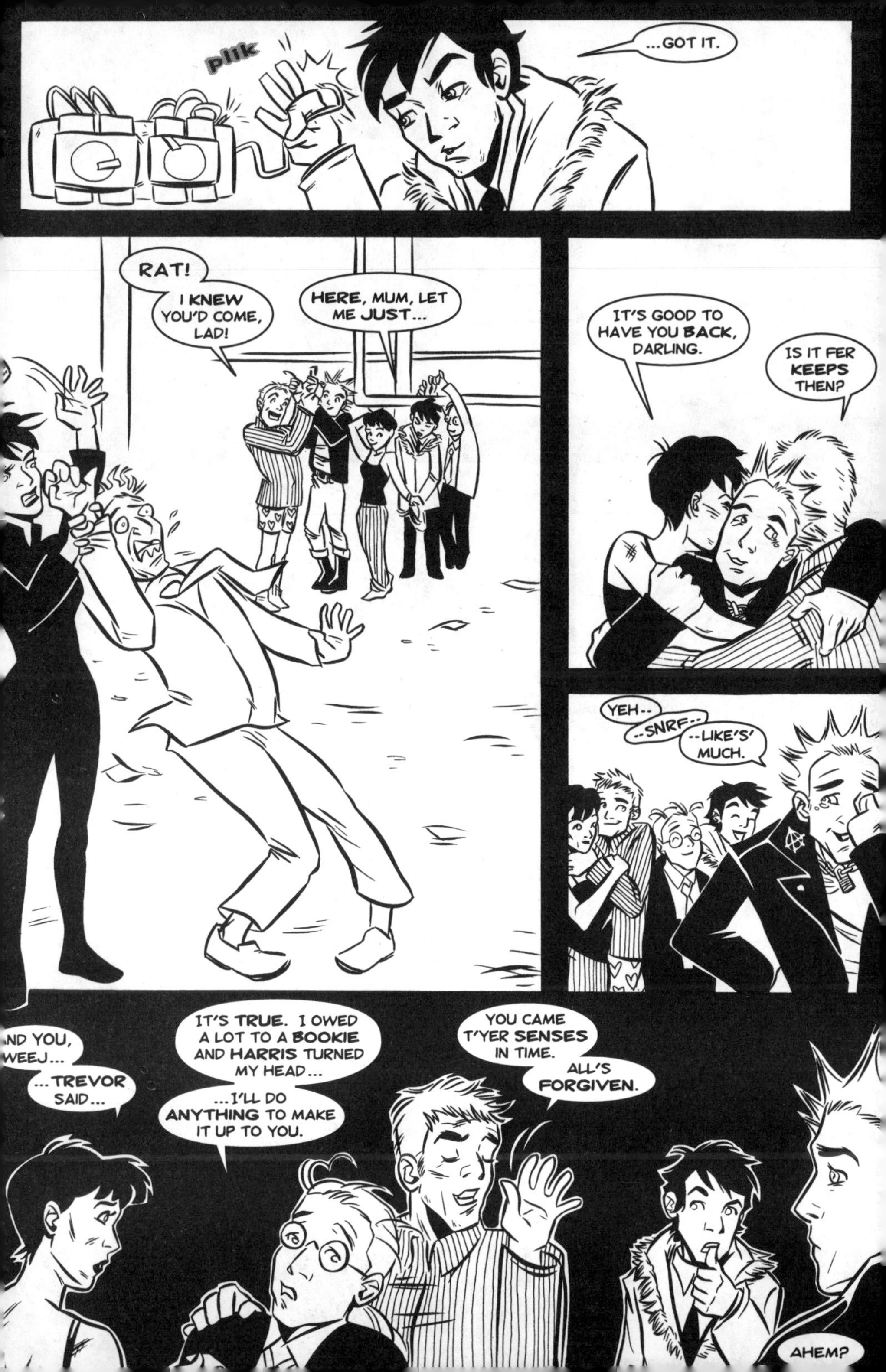
plik
...GOT IT.
RAT!
I KNEW YOU'D COME, LAD!
HERE, MUM, LET ME JUST...
IT'S GOOD TO HAVE YOU BACK, DARLING.
IS IT FER KEEPS THEN?
YEH--
--SNRF--
--LIKE'S' MUCH.
ND YOU, WEEJ...
...TREVOR SAID...
IT'S TRUE. I OWED A LOT TO A BOOKIE AND HARRIS TURNED MY HEAD...
...I'LL DO ANYTHING TO MAKE IT UP TO YOU.
YOU CAME T'YER SENSES IN TIME.
ALL'S FORGIVEN.
AHEM?

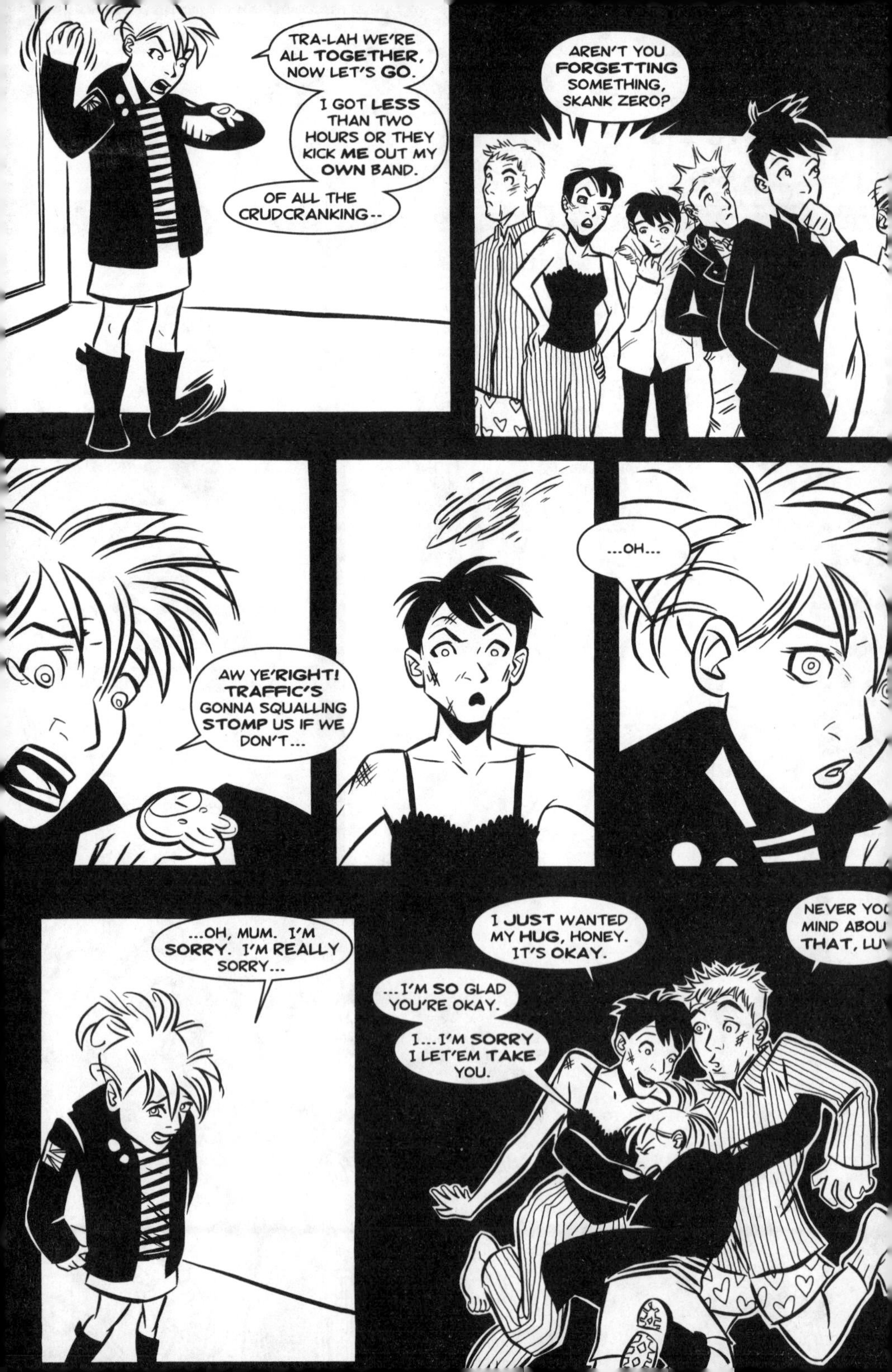
TRA-LAH WE'RE ALL TOGETHER, NOW LET'S GO.
I GOT LESS THAN TWO HOURS OR THEY KICK ME OUT MY OWN BAND.
OF ALL THE CRUDCRANKING--
AREN'T YOU FORGETTING SOMETHING, SKANK ZERO?
AW YE'RIGHT! TRAFFIC'S GONNA SQUALLING STOMP US IF WE DON'T...
...OH...
...OH, MUM. I'M SORRY. I'M REALLY SORRY...
I JUST WANTED MY HUG, HONEY. IT'S OKAY.
...I'M SO GLAD YOU'RE OKAY.
I...I'M SORRY I LET'EM TAKE YOU.

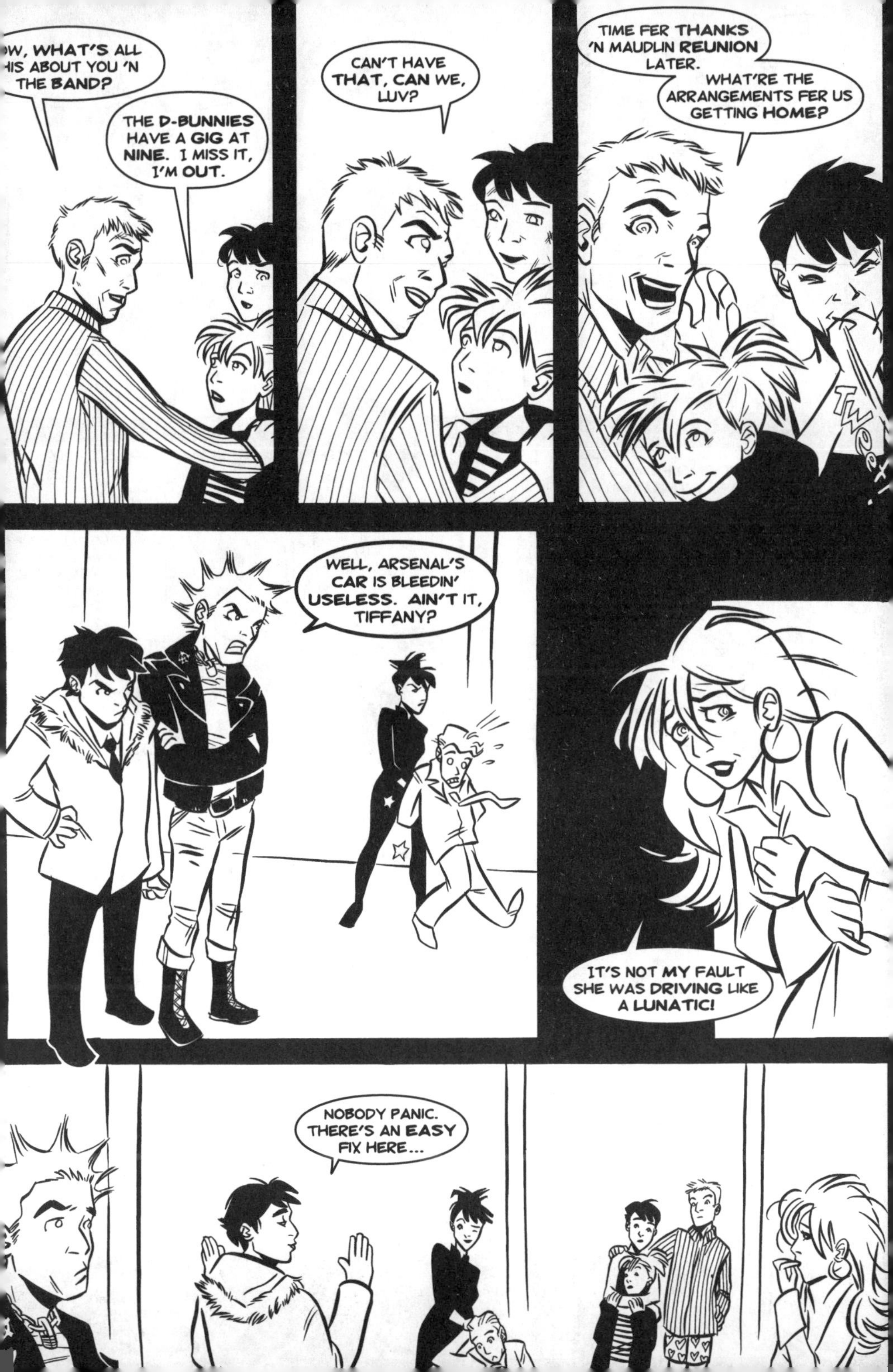

OW, WHAT'S ALL THIS ABOUT YOU 'N THE BAND?
THE D-BUNNIES HAVE A GIG AT NINE. I MISS IT, I'M OUT.
CAN'T HAVE THAT, CAN WE, LUV?
TIME FER THANKS 'N MAUDLIN REUNION LATER.
WHAT'RE THE ARRANGEMENTS FER US GETTING HOME?
TWEET!
WELL, ARSENAL'S CAR IS BLEEDIN' USELESS. AIN'T IT, TIFFANY?
IT'S NOT MY FAULT SHE WAS DRIVING LIKE A LUNATIC!
NOBODY PANIC. THERE'S AN EASY FIX HERE...

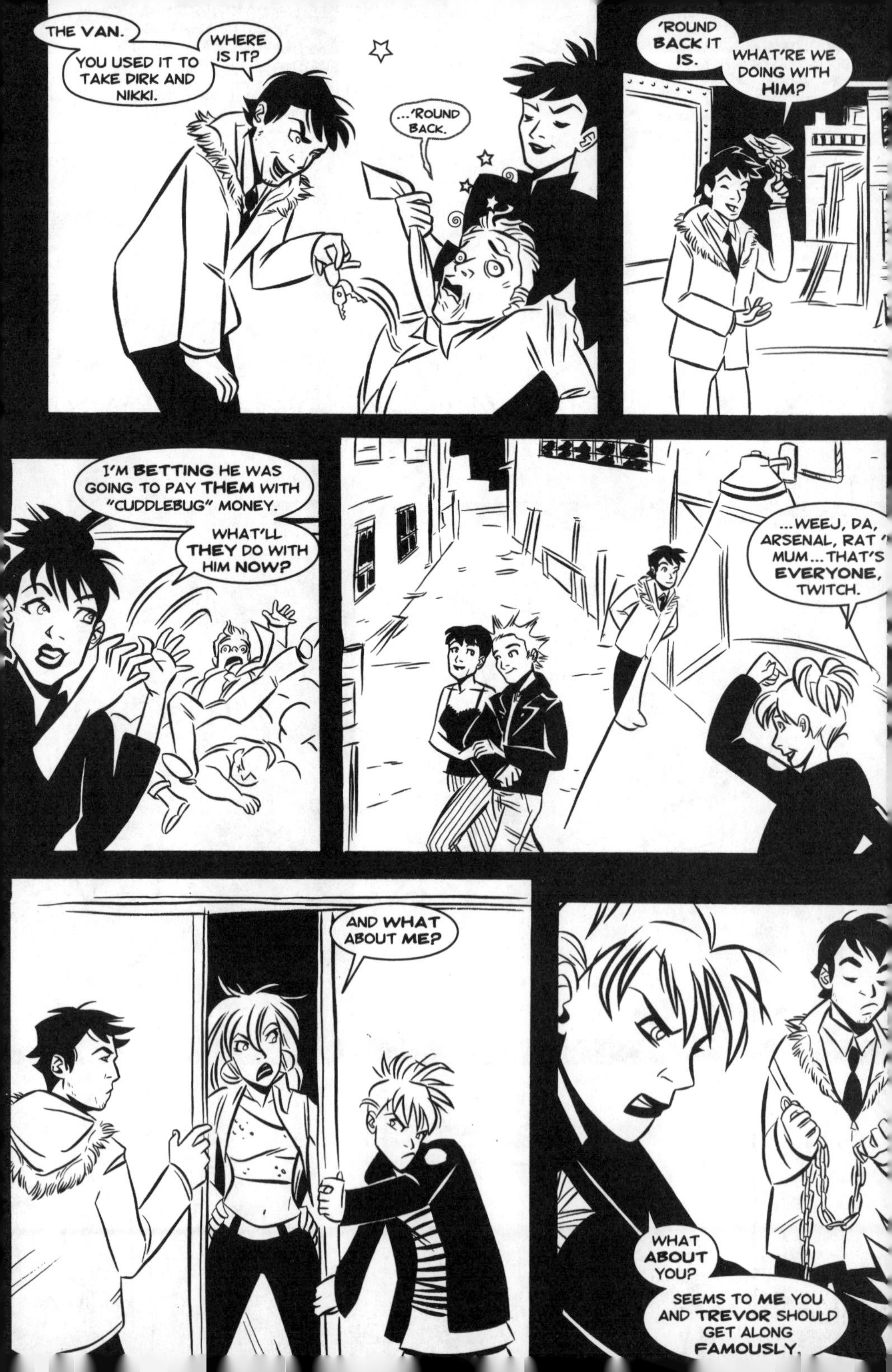
THE VAN.
YOU USED IT TO TAKE DIRK AND NIKKI.
WHERE IS IT?
...'ROUND BACK.
'ROUND BACK IT IS.
WHAT'RE WE DOING WITH HIM?
I'M BETTING HE WAS GOING TO PAY THEM WITH "CUDDLEBUG" MONEY.
WHAT'LL THEY DO WITH HIM NOW?
...WEEJ, DA, ARSENAL, RAT 'N MUM... THAT'S EVERYONE, TWITCH.
AND WHAT ABOUT ME?
WHAT ABOUT YOU?
SEEMS TO ME YOU AND TREVOR SHOULD GET ALONG FAMOUSLY.

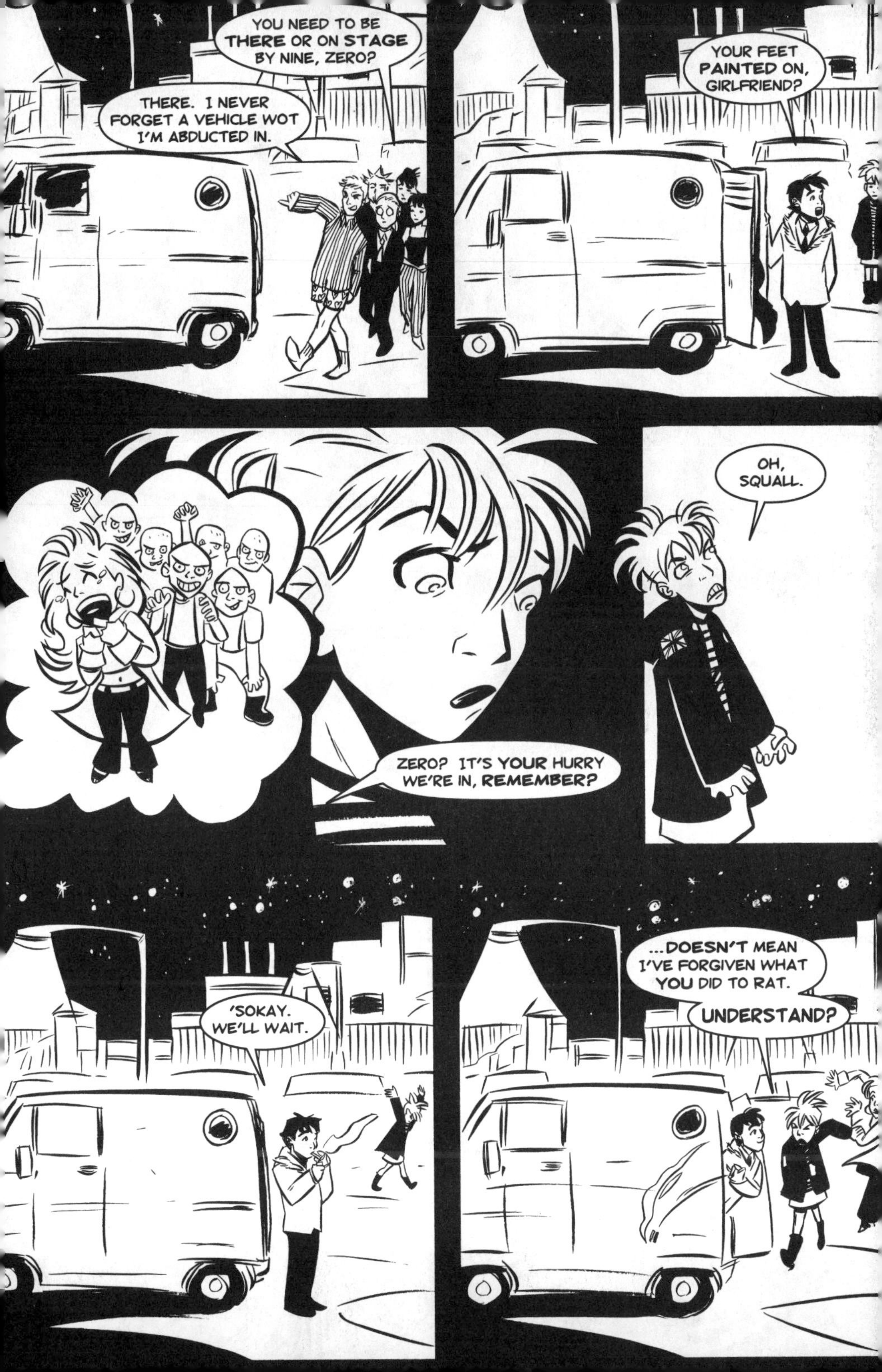
YOU NEED TO BE THERE OR ON STAGE BY NINE, ZERO?
THERE. I NEVER FORGET A VEHICLE WOT I'M ABDUCTED IN.
YOUR FEET PAINTED ON, GIRLFRIEND?
OH, SQUALL.
ZERO? IT'S YOUR HURRY WE'RE IN, REMEMBER?
'SOKAY. WE'LL WAIT.
...DOESN'T MEAN I'VE FORGIVEN WHAT YOU DID TO RAT.
UNDERSTAND?

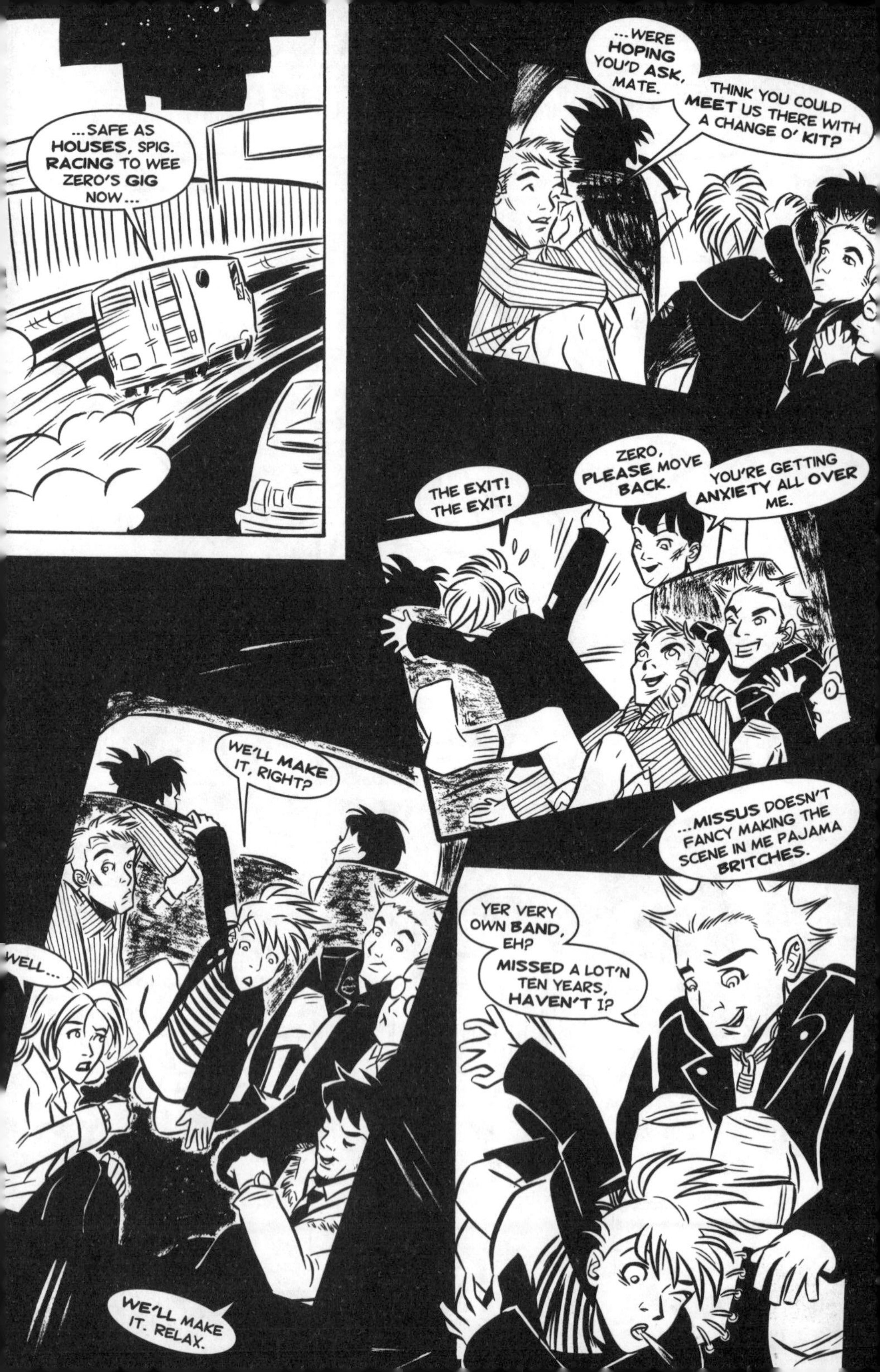
...SAFE AS HOUSES, SPIG. RACING TO WEE ZERO'S GIG NOW...
...WERE HOPING YOU'D ASK, MATE.
THINK YOU COULD MEET US THERE WITH A CHANGE O' KIT?
THE EXIT! THE EXIT!
ZERO, PLEASE MOVE BACK.
YOU'RE GETTING ANXIETY ALL OVER ME.
...MISSUS DOESN'T FANCY MAKING THE SCENE IN ME PAJAMA BRITCHES.
WE'LL MAKE IT, RIGHT?
WELL...
WE'LL MAKE IT. RELAX.
YER VERY OWN BAND, EH?
MISSED A LOT'N TEN YEARS, HAVEN'T I?

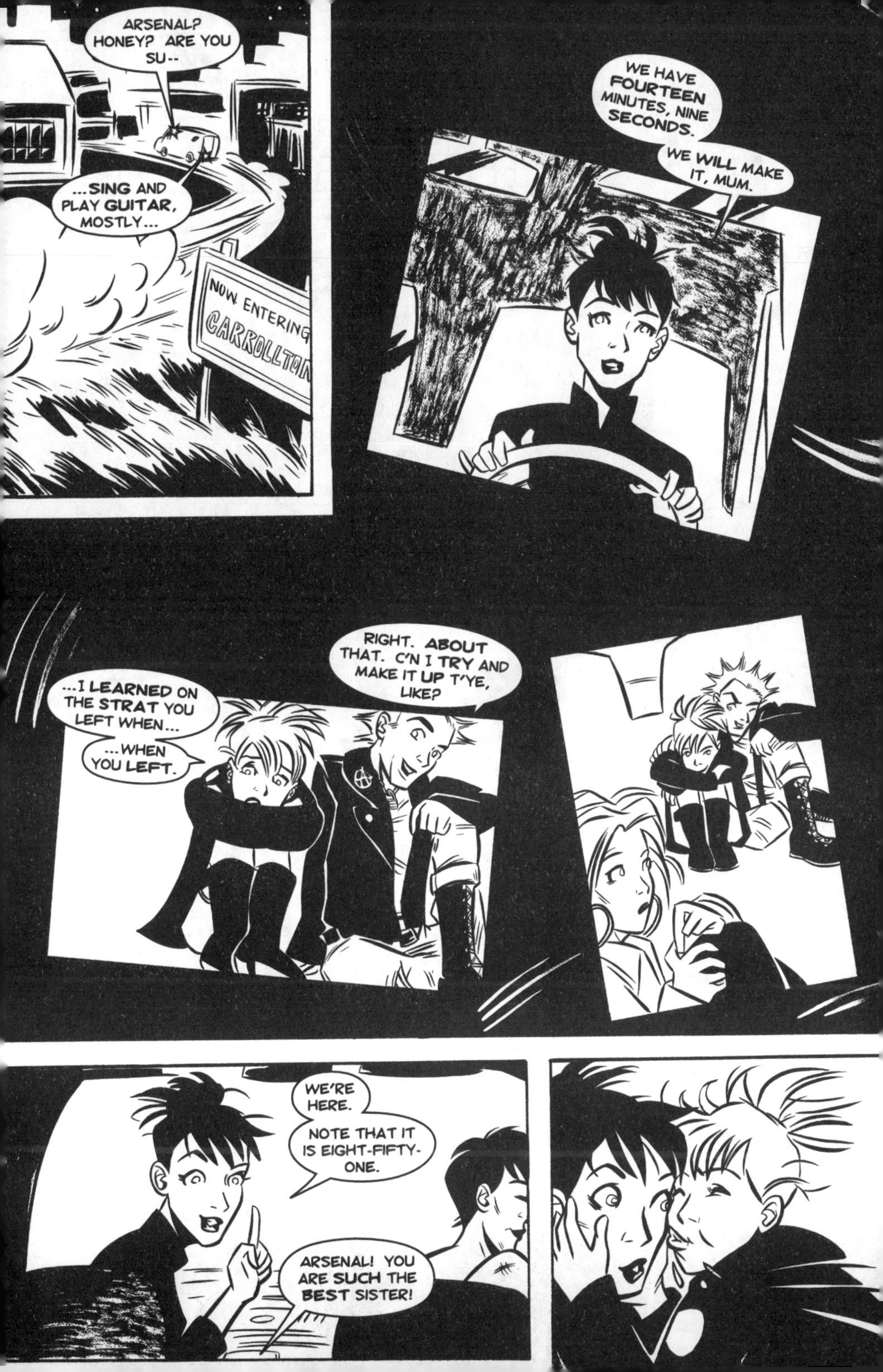
ARSENAL? HONEY? ARE YOU SU--
...SING AND PLAY GUITAR, MOSTLY...
NOW ENTERING CARROLLTON
WE HAVE FOURTEEN MINUTES, NINE SECONDS.
WE WILL MAKE IT, MUM.
...I LEARNED ON THE STRAT YOU LEFT WHEN...
...WHEN YOU LEFT.
RIGHT. ABOUT THAT. C'N I TRY AND MAKE IT UP T'YE, LIKE?
WE'RE HERE.
NOTE THAT IT IS EIGHT-FIFTY-ONE.
ARSENAL! YOU ARE SUCH THE BEST SISTER!

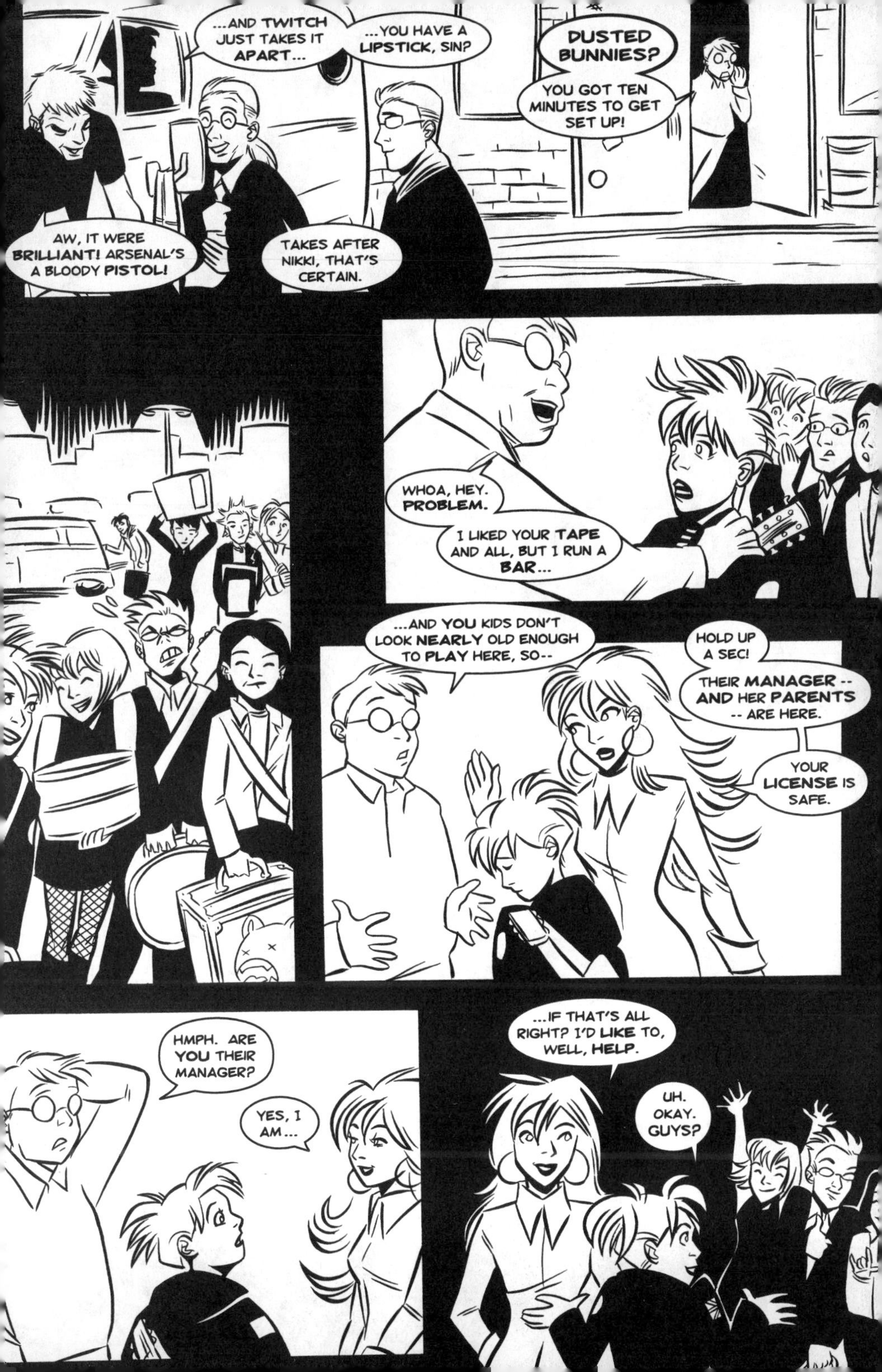
...AND TWITCH JUST TAKES IT APART...
AW, IT WERE BRILLIANT! ARSENAL'S A BLOODY PISTOL!
...YOU HAVE A LIPSTICK, SIN?
TAKES AFTER NIKKI, THAT'S CERTAIN.
DUSTED BUNNIES?
YOU GOT TEN MINUTES TO GET SET UP!
WHOA, HEY. PROBLEM.
I LIKED YOUR TAPE AND ALL, BUT I RUN A BAR...
...AND YOU KIDS DON'T LOOK NEARLY OLD ENOUGH TO PLAY HERE, SO--
HOLD UP A SEC!
THEIR MANAGER -- AND HER PARENTS -- ARE HERE.
YOUR LICENSE IS SAFE.
HMPH. ARE YOU THEIR MANAGER?
YES, I AM...
...IF THAT'S ALL RIGHT? I'D LIKE TO, WELL, HELP.
UH. OKAY. GUYS?

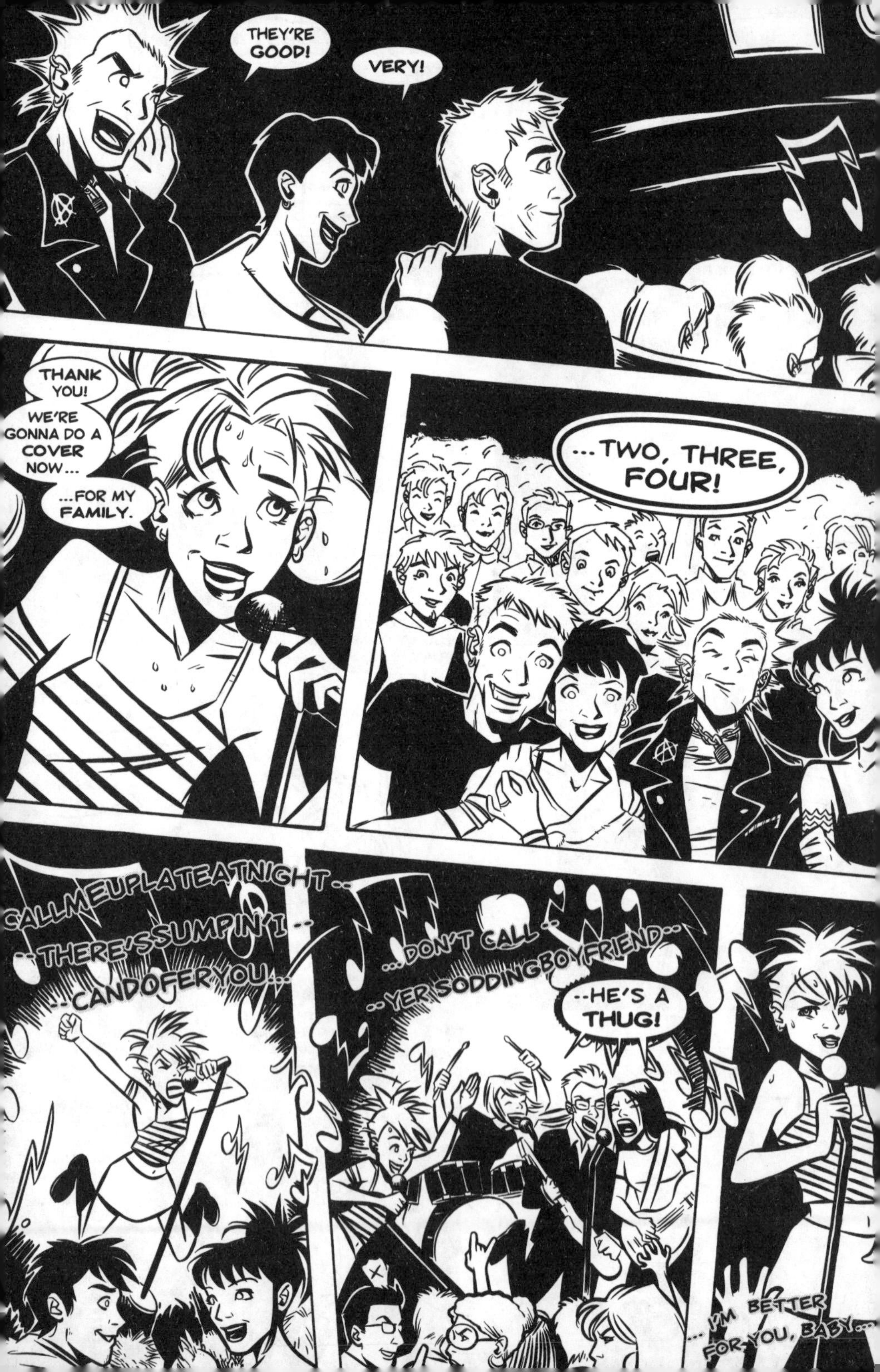
THEY'RE GOOD!
VERY!
THANK YOU!
WE'RE GONNA DO A COVER NOW...
...FOR MY FAMILY.
...TWO, THREE, FOUR!
CALLMEUPLATEATNIGHT--
--THERE'SSUMPIN'I--
--CANDOFERYOU...
...DON'T CALL--
--YER SODDINGBOYFRIEND--
--HE'S A THUG!
...I'M BETTER FOR YOU, BABY...

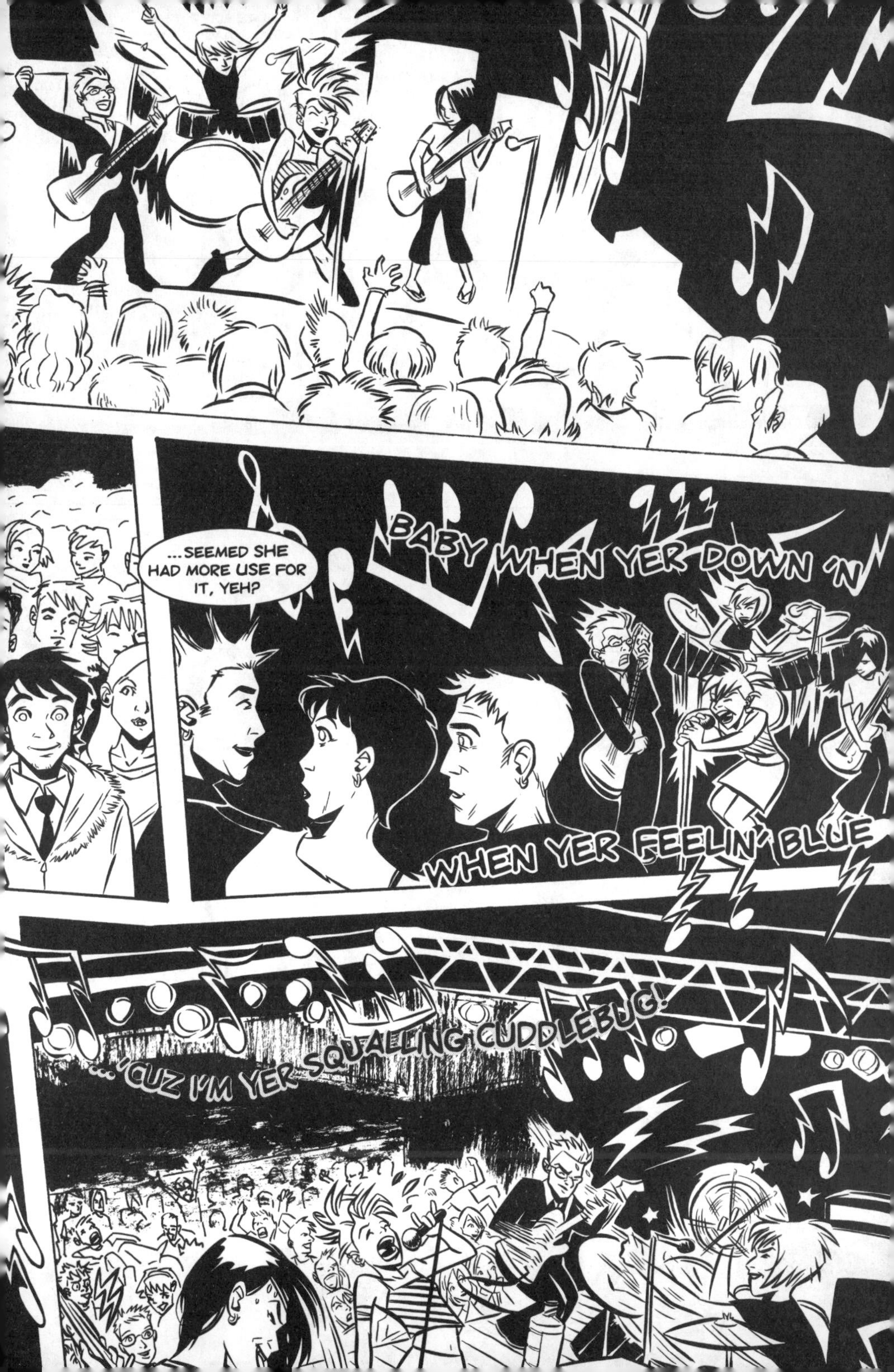
...SEEMED SHE HAD MORE USE FOR IT, YEH?
BABY WHEN YER DOWN 'N
WHEN YER FEELIN' BLUE
...'CUZ I'M YER SQUALLING CUDDLEBUG!

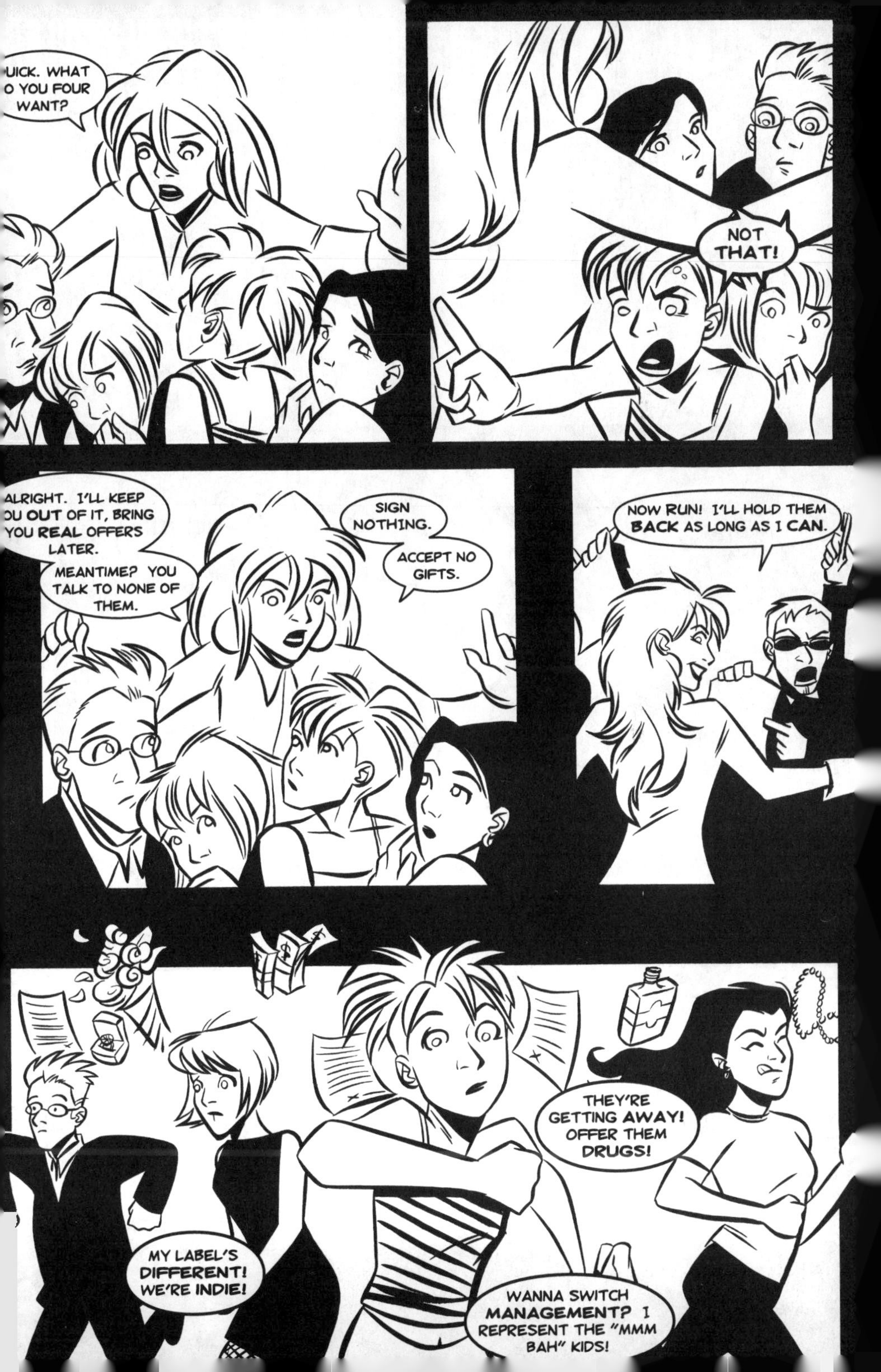

UICK. WHAT
O YOU FOUR
WANT?
NOT
THAT!
ALRIGHT. I'LL KEEP
OU OUT OF IT, BRING
YOU REAL OFFERS
LATER.
MEANTIME? YOU
TALK TO NONE OF
THEM.
SIGN
NOTHING.
ACCEPT NO
GIFTS.
NOW RUN! I'LL HOLD THEM
BACK AS LONG AS I CAN.
THEY'RE
GETTING AWAY!
OFFER THEM
DRUGS!
MY LABEL'S
DIFFERENT!
WE'RE INDIE!
WANNA SWITCH
MANAGEMENT? I
REPRESENT THE "MMM
BAH" KIDS!

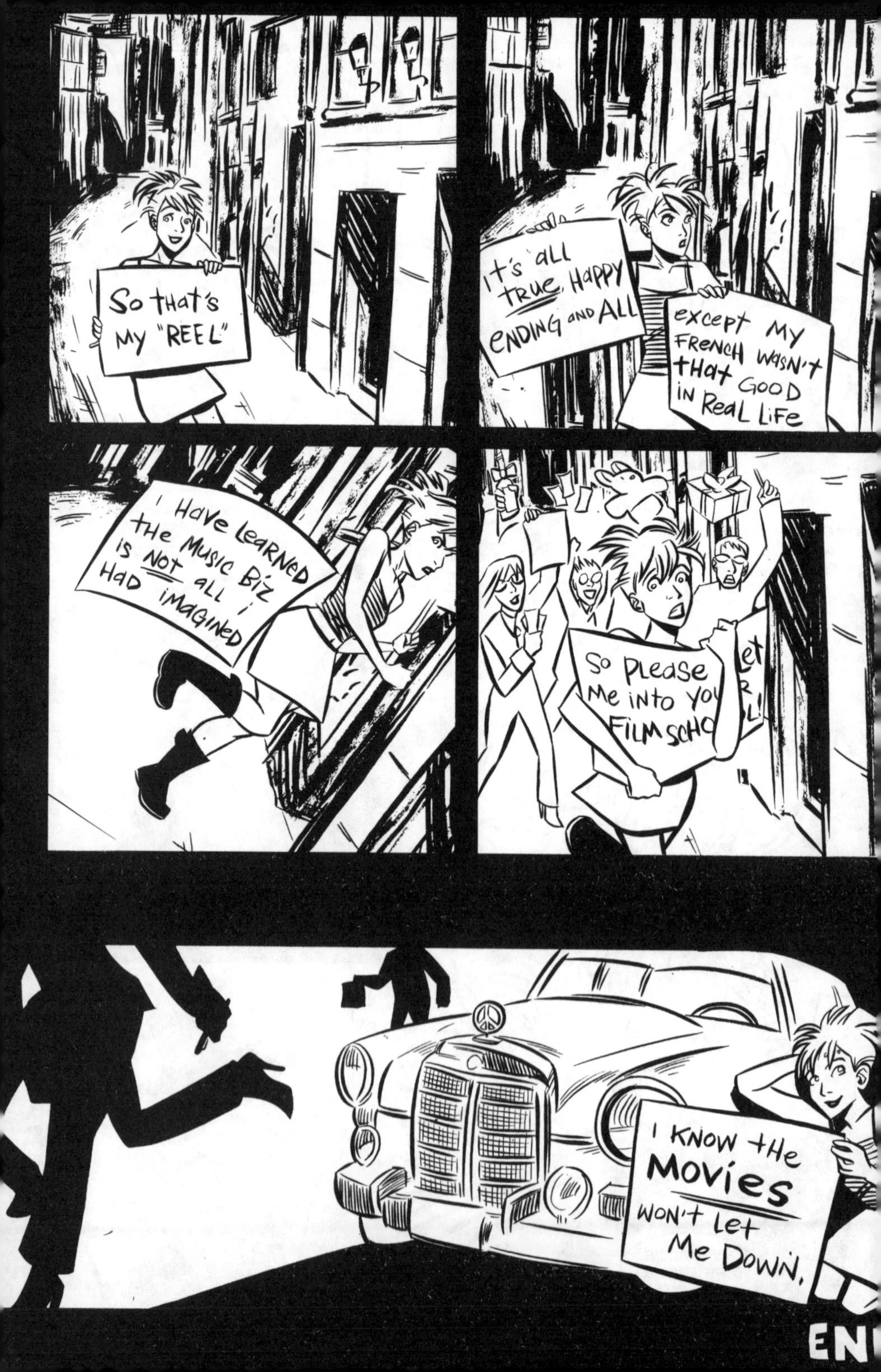
So that's my "REEL"
It's all TRUE, Happy ending and all
except my French wasn't that good in Real life
I have learned the Music Biz is NOT all I had imagined
So please let me into your film school!
I know the Movies won't let me down.
END

GALLERY

The following pages contain Christine Norrie's developmental sketches done in preparation for the series. Many of these were also used as design elements throughout this collection.

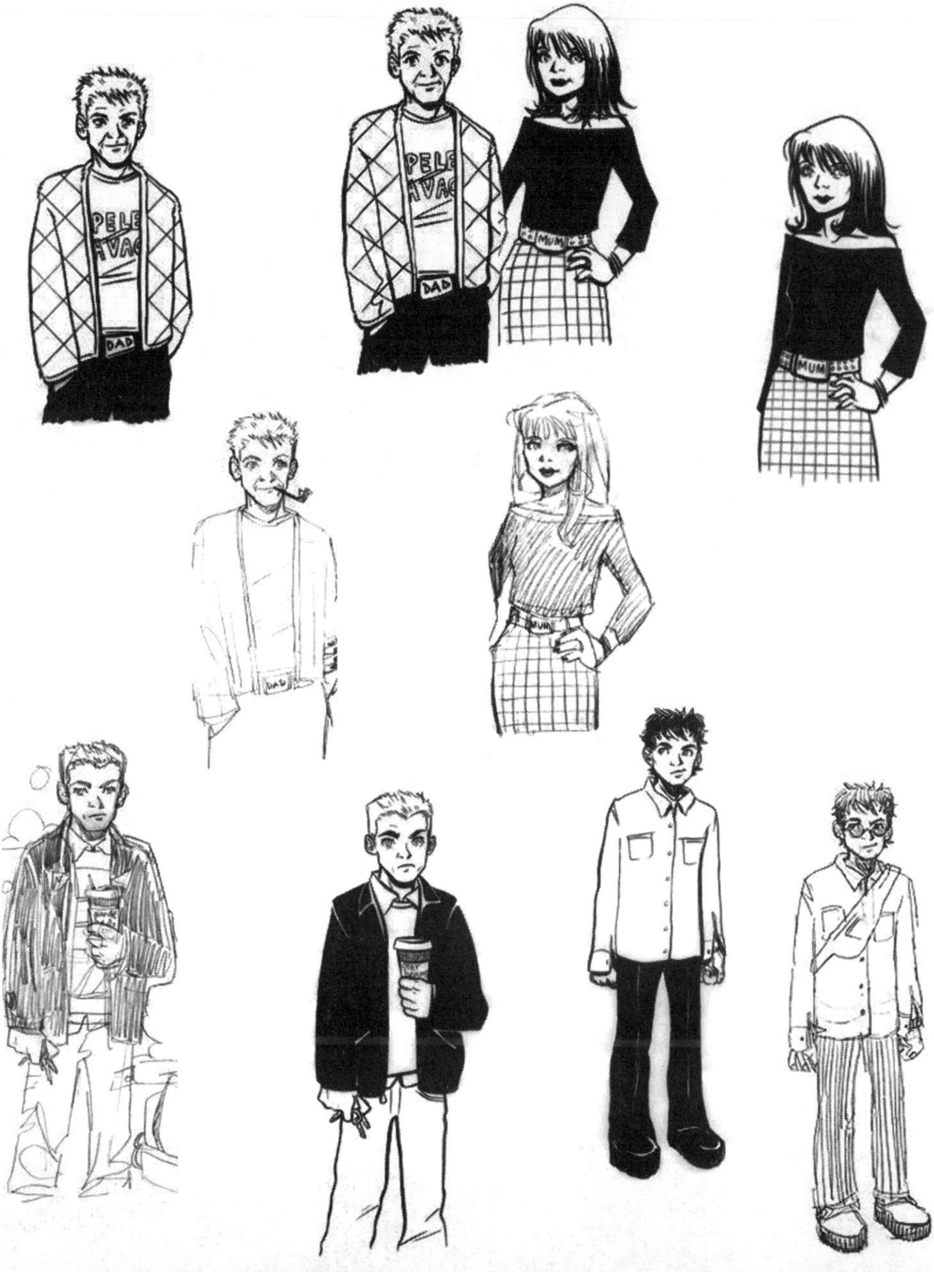
DAD
MUM

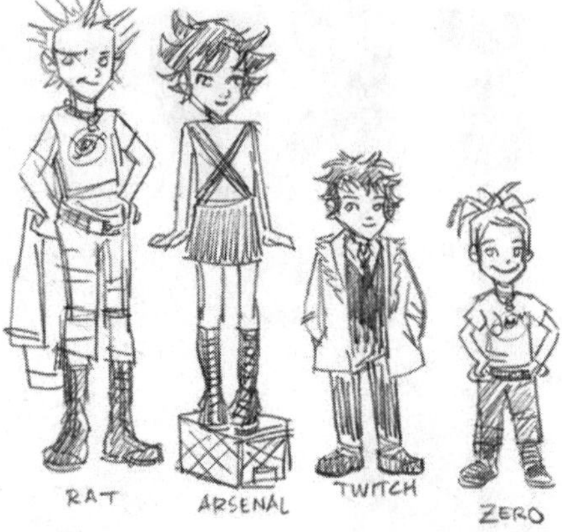
RAT
ARSENAL
TWITCH
ZERO

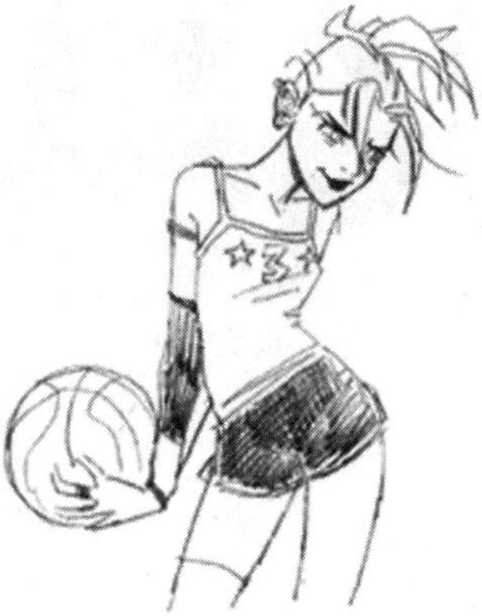

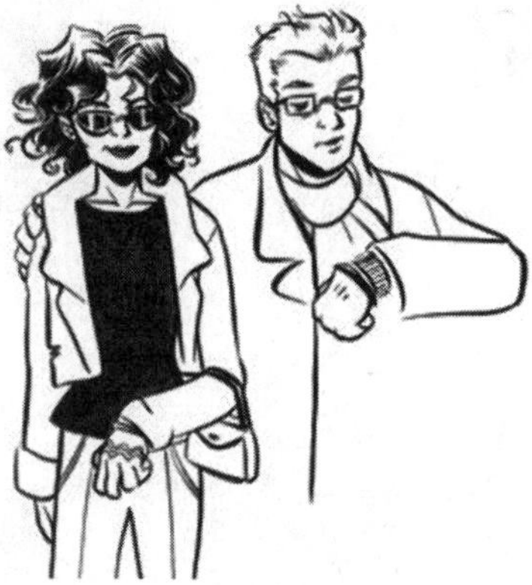

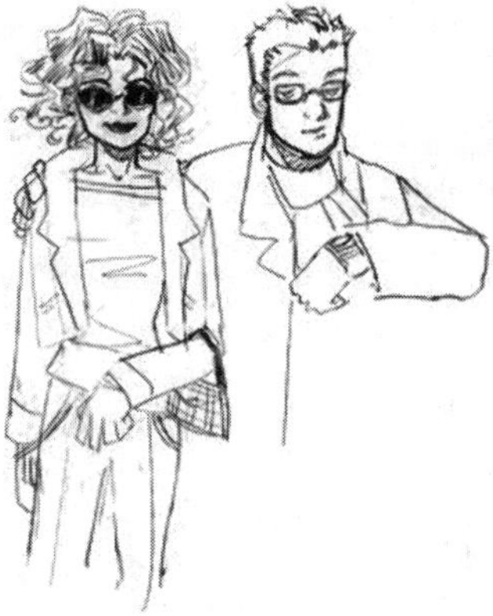

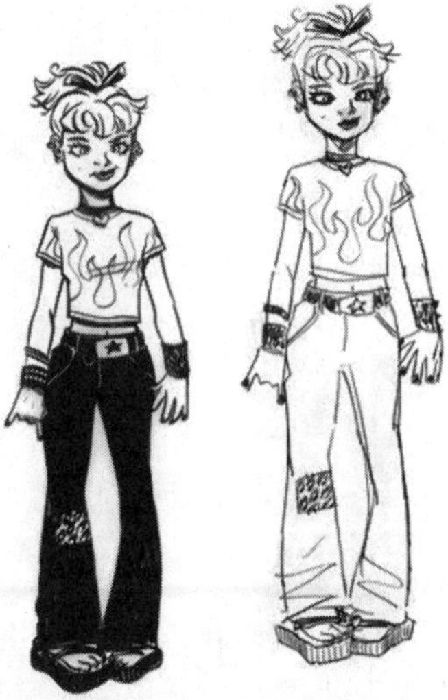

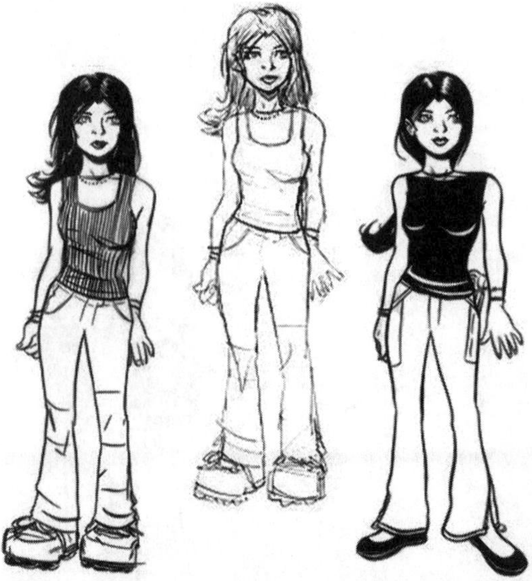

Thumbnail layouts by Clugston-Major and Norrie.

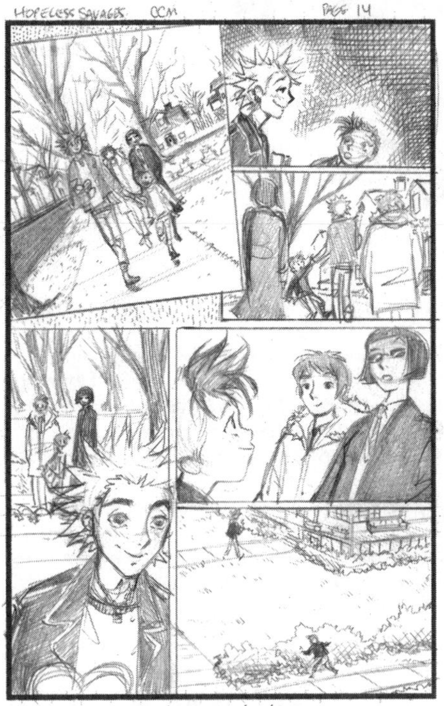
HOPELESS SAVAGES
CCM
PAGE 14

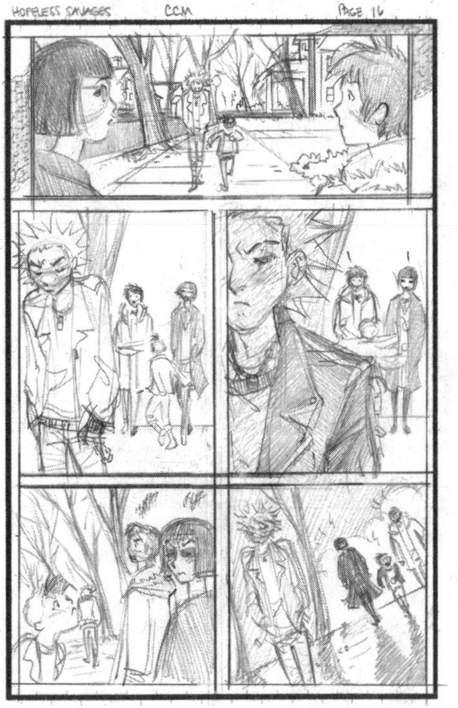
HOPELESS SAVAGES
CCM
PAGE 16

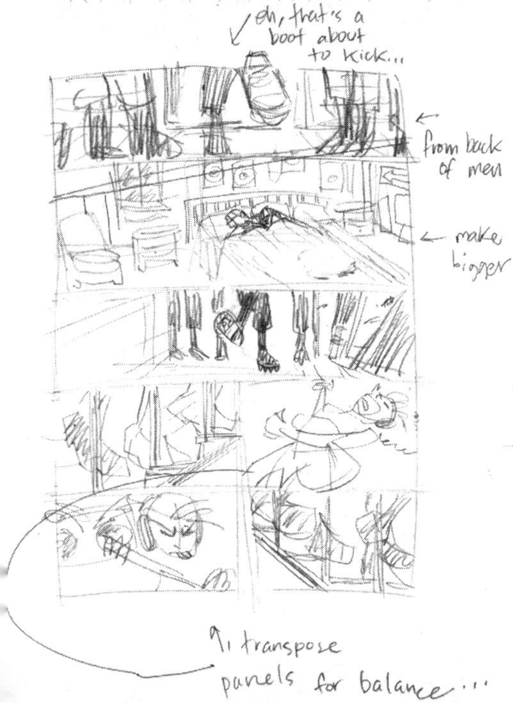
oh, that's a boot about to kick...
from back of men
make bigger
↑ transpose panels for balance...
(hope that's ok)

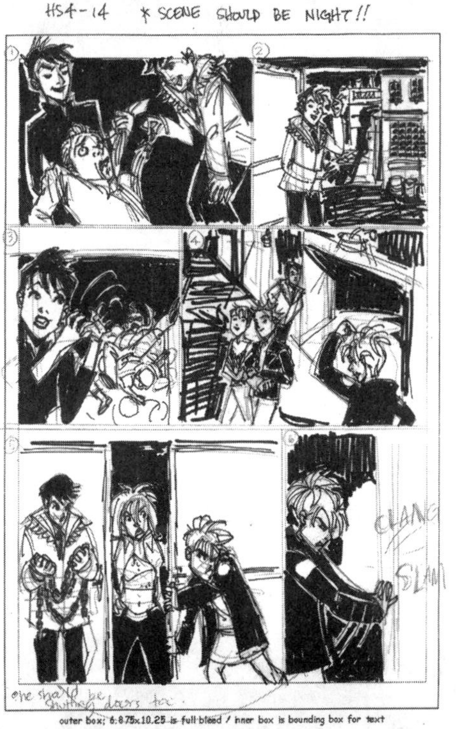
HS4-14
* SCENE SHOULD BE NIGHT!!
CLANG
SLAM
she should be shutting doors too
outer box; 6.875x10.25 is full bleed / inner box is bounding box for text

ACKNOWLEDGEMENTS

Jen thanks:

Daria Penta and David and Jasper Laur, Jennifer Mosier and Roger Billery-Mosier, Nunzio DeFilippis & Christina Weir, Jamie S. Rich, Joe Nozemack, James Lucas Jones, Andi Watson, Chynna Clugston-Major and Christine Norrie. Also, and always, thanks to my family for their love, support and inspiration.

This book is for Greg and Elliot, with my love.

Christine thanks:

Catherine Norrie, my sister, for our childhood of drawing in front of the TV; my supercool family; Anchovy, Crease, Luby, Tim and Jeremy for those teenage late nights sketching; Evan & Sarah and Jimmy Mahfood for getting me started; Nick, Ivan, Scott and the DC Kids; Little Mikey; Joyce, Bob and the crew; Ned, Sarah and Agnes; my neighborhood and the Dogs of St. George; the kitties; Orwell the Hound, for getting me through every day.

...and Andy who bribed me with the dog to pursue my true passion in comics.

Jen, for being so fun and amazing to work with; Andi and Chynna, whom I'm honored to stand beside; and Oni Press for making all my hopes and dreams possible.

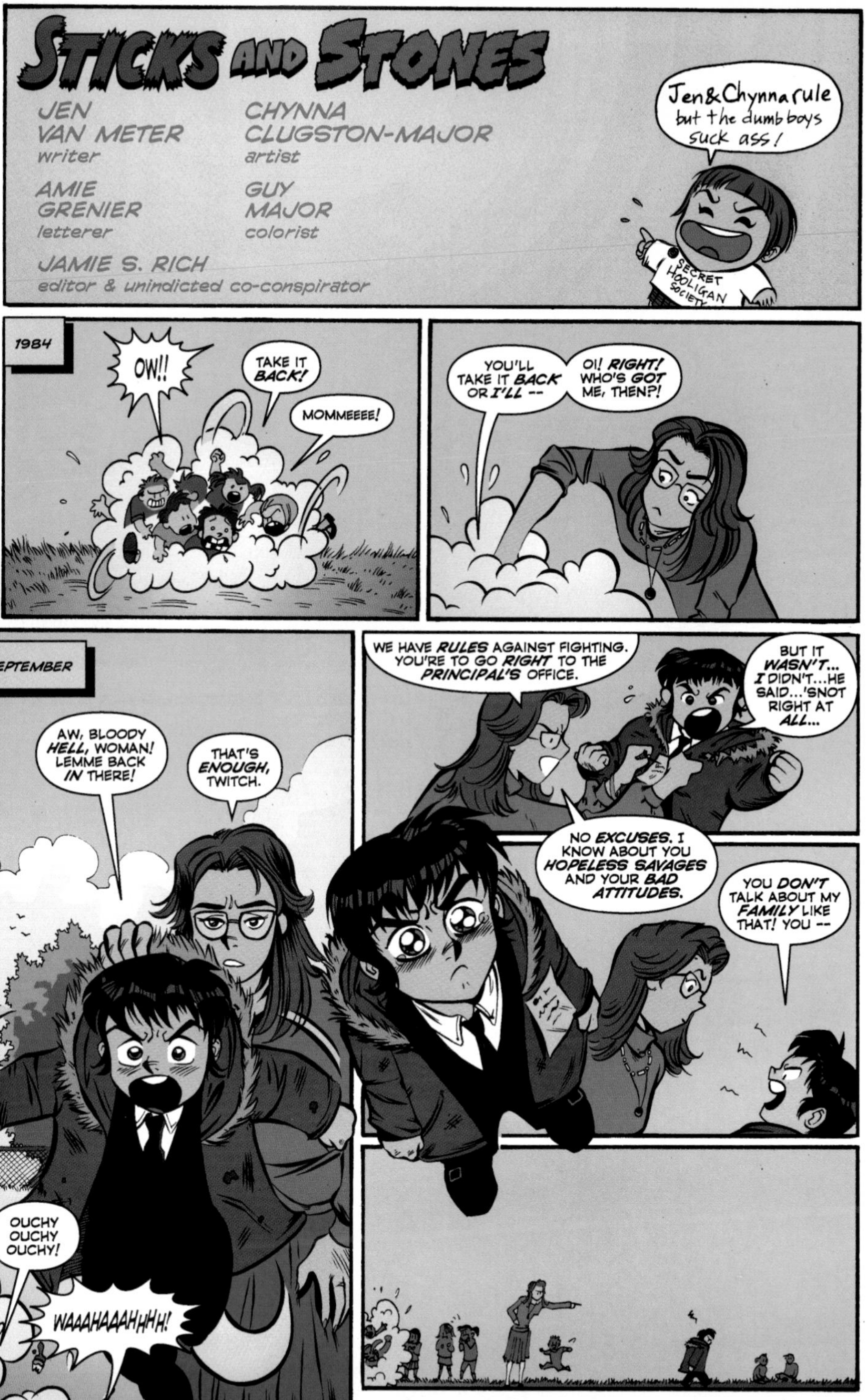

STICKS AND STONES
JEN VAN METER
writer
CHYNNA CLUGSTON-MAJOR
artist
AMIE GRENIER
letterer
GUY MAJOR
colorist
JAMIE S. RICH
editor & unindicted co-conspirator
Jen&Chynna rule but the dumb boys suck ass!
SECRET HOOLIGAN SOCIETY
1984
OW!!
TAKE IT BACK!
MOMMEEEE!
YOU'LL TAKE IT BACK OR I'LL --
OI! RIGHT! WHO'S GOT ME, THEN?!
SEPTEMBER
AW, BLOODY HELL, WOMAN! LEMME BACK IN THERE!
THAT'S ENOUGH, TWITCH.
OUCHY OUCHY OUCHY!
WAAAHAAAHHHH!
WE HAVE RULES AGAINST FIGHTING. YOU'RE TO GO RIGHT TO THE PRINCIPAL'S OFFICE.
BUT IT WASN'T... I DIDN'T...HE SAID...'SNOT RIGHT AT ALL...
NO EXCUSES. I KNOW ABOUT YOU HOPELESS SAVAGES AND YOUR BAD ATTITUDES.
YOU DON'T TALK ABOUT MY FAMILY LIKE THAT! YOU --

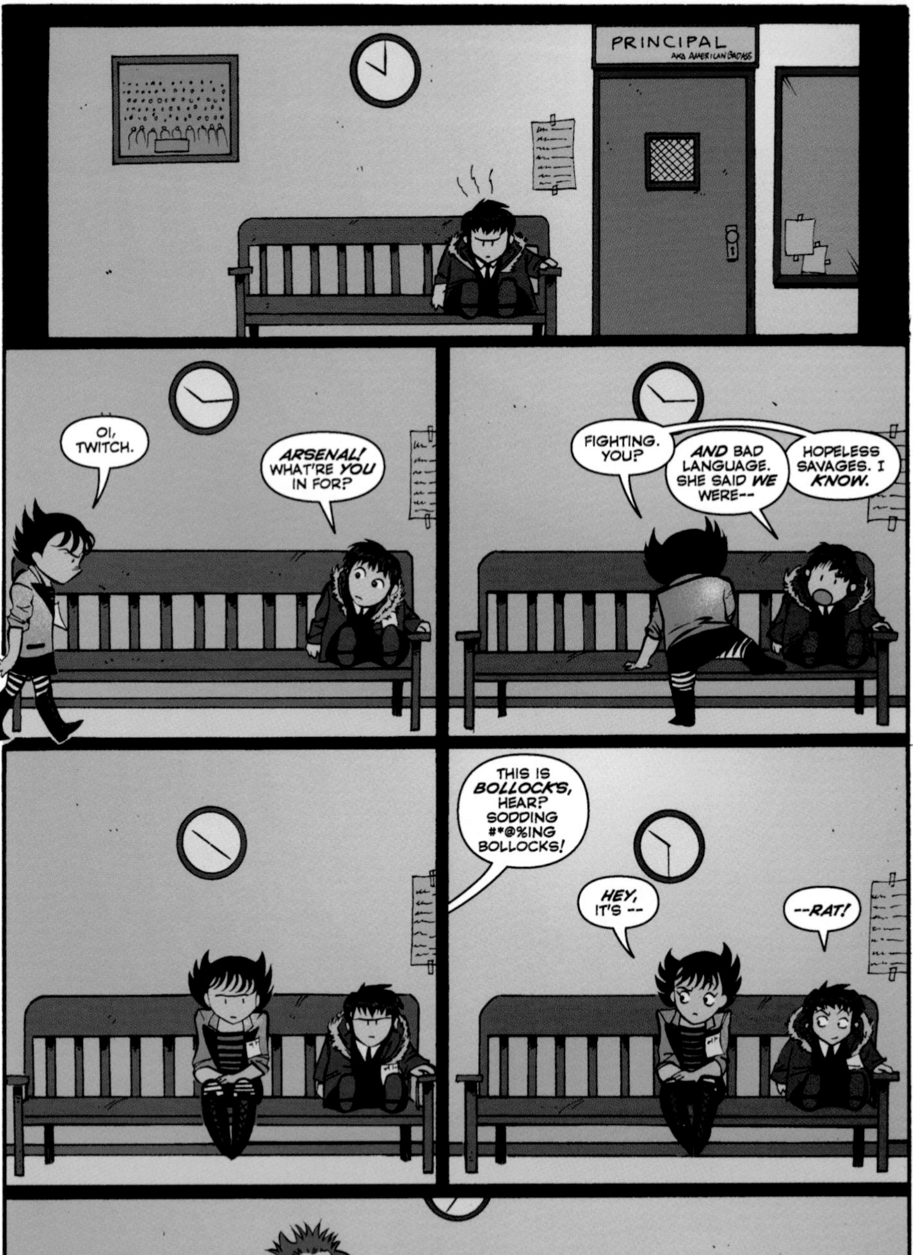
PRINCIPAL
AKA AMERICAN BADASS
OI, TWITCH.
ARSENAL! WHAT'RE YOU IN FOR?
FIGHTING. YOU?
AND BAD LANGUAGE. SHE SAID WE WERE--
HOPELESS SAVAGES. I KNOW.
THIS IS BOLLOCKS, HEAR? SODDING #*@%ING BOLLOCKS!
HEY, IT'S --
--RAT!

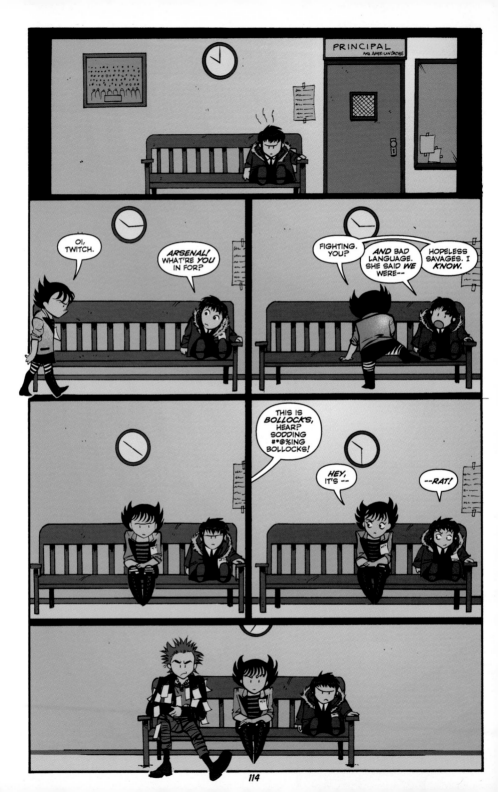

115

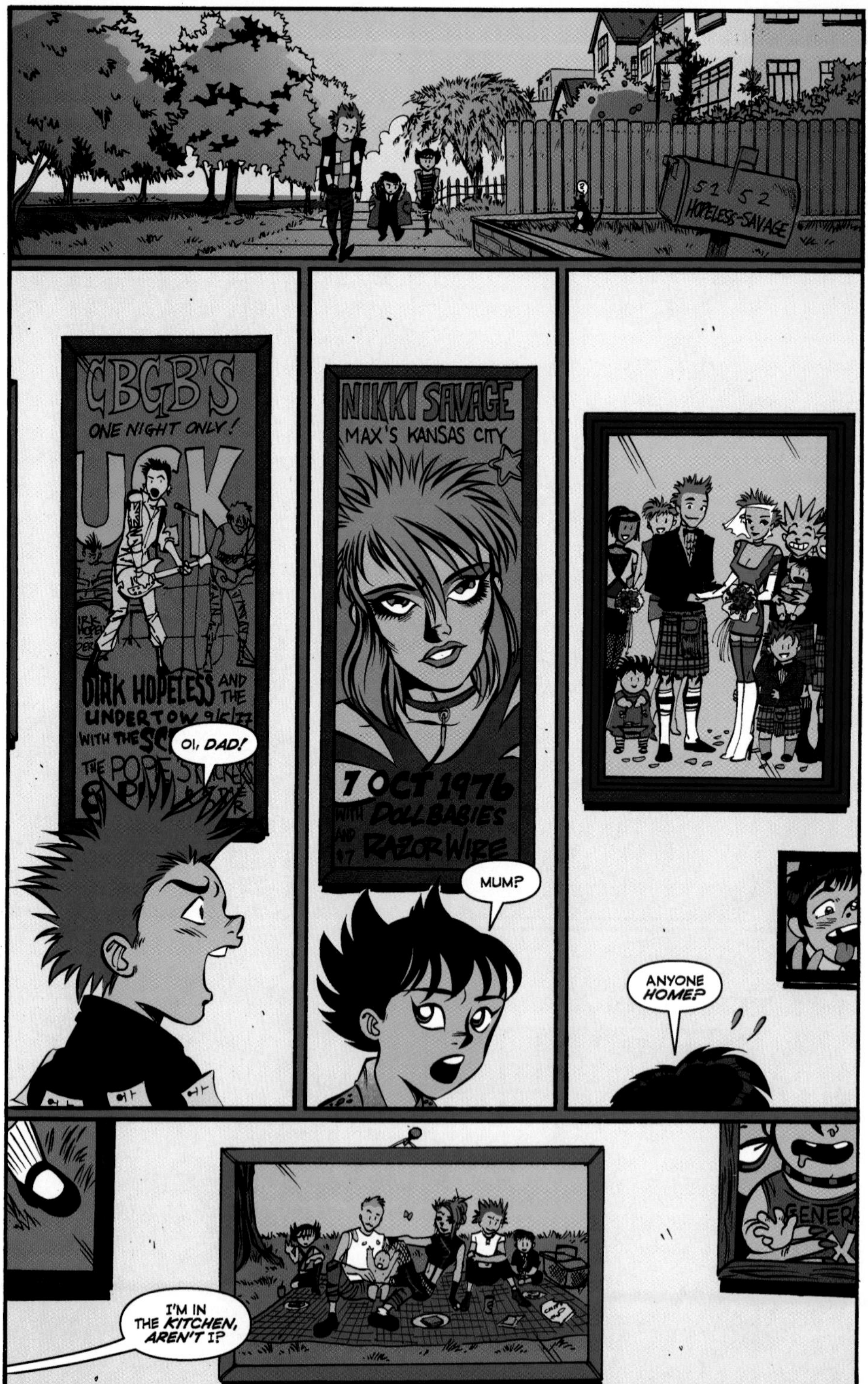

51 52
HOPELESS-SAVAGE
CBGB'S
ONE NIGHT ONLY!
DIRK HOPELESS AND THE UNDERTOW 9/5/77
NIKKI SAVAGE
MAX'S KANSAS CITY
7 OCT 1976
DOLL BABIES
RAZOR WIRE
OI, DAD!
MUM?
ANYONE HOME?
I'M IN THE KITCHEN, AREN'T I?

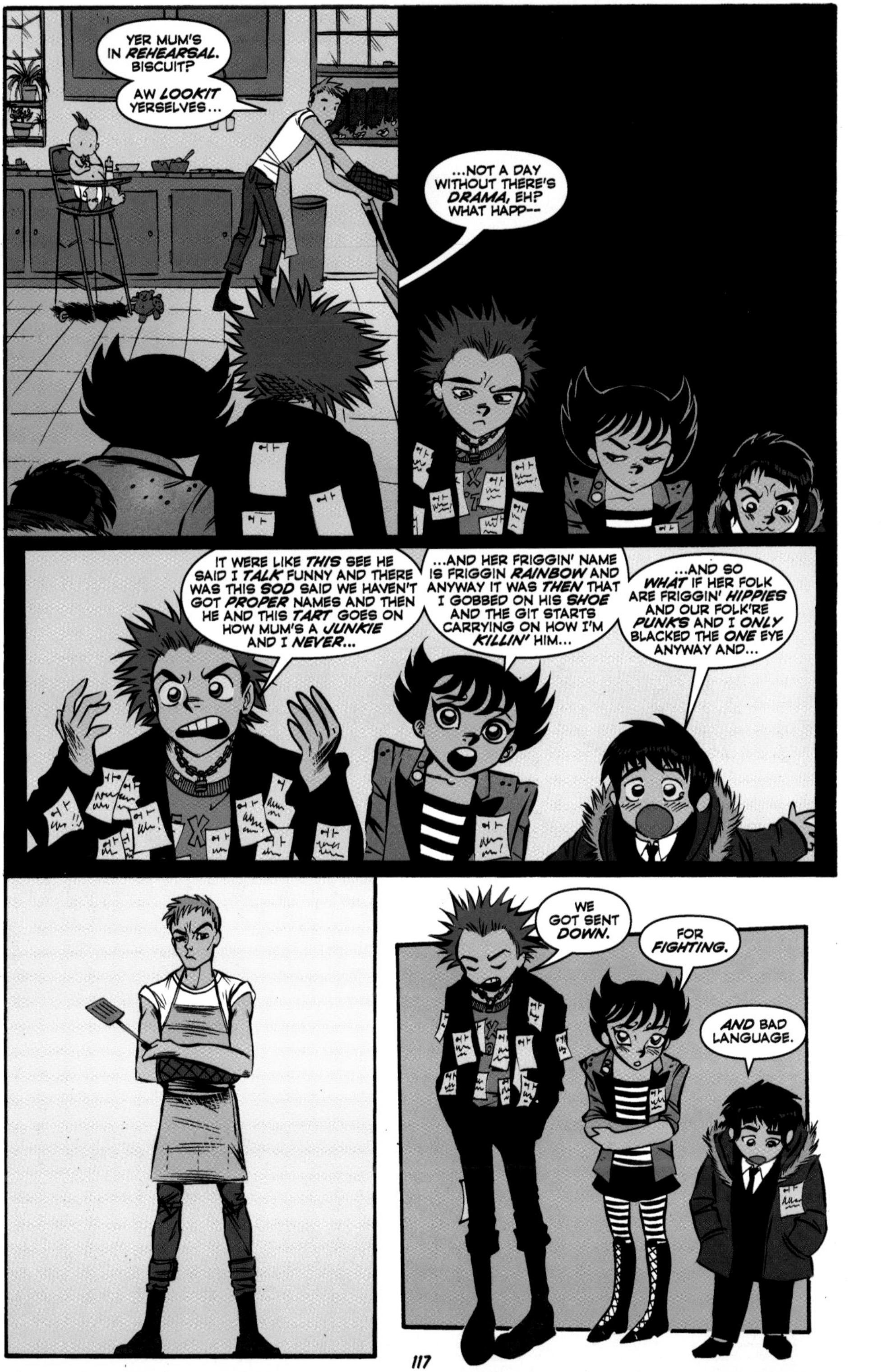
YER MUM'S IN REHEARSAL. BISCUIT?
AW LOOKIT YERSELVES...
...NOT A DAY WITHOUT THERE'S DRAMA, EH? WHAT HAPP--
IT WERE LIKE THIS SEE HE SAID I TALK FUNNY AND THERE WAS THIS SOD SAID WE HAVEN'T GOT PROPER NAMES AND THEN HE AND THIS TART GOES ON HOW MUM'S A JUNKIE AND I NEVER...
...AND HER FRIGGIN' NAME IS FRIGGIN RAINBOW AND ANYWAY IT WAS THEN THAT I GOBBED ON HIS SHOE AND THE GIT STARTS CARRYING ON HOW I'M KILLIN' HIM...
...AND SO WHAT IF HER FOLK ARE FRIGGIN' HIPPIES AND OUR FOLK'RE PUNKS AND I ONLY BLACKED THE ONE EYE ANYWAY AND...
WE GOT SENT DOWN.
FOR FIGHTING.
AND BAD LANGUAGE.

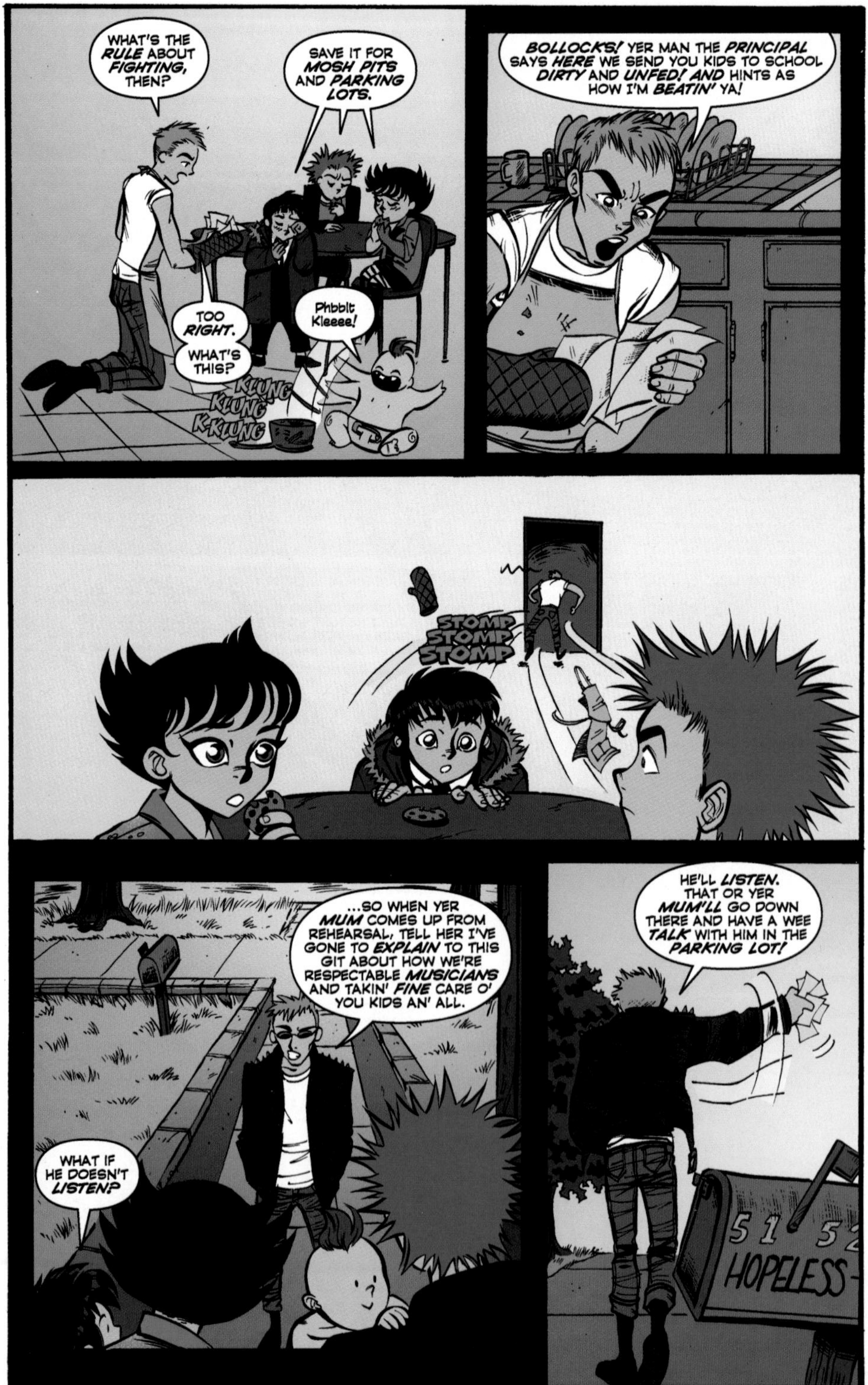
WHAT'S THE RULE ABOUT FIGHTING, THEN?
SAVE IT FOR MOSH PITS AND PARKING LOTS.
TOO RIGHT.
WHAT'S THIS?
Phbblt Kleeee!
KLUNG KLUNG K-KLUNG
BOLLOCKS! YER MAN THE PRINCIPAL SAYS HERE WE SEND YOU KIDS TO SCHOOL DIRTY AND UNFED! AND HINTS AS HOW I'M BEATIN' YA!
STOMP STOMP STOMP
...SO WHEN YER MUM COMES UP FROM REHEARSAL, TELL HER I'VE GONE TO EXPLAIN TO THIS GIT ABOUT HOW WE'RE RESPECTABLE MUSICIANS AND TAKIN' FINE CARE O' YOU KIDS AN' ALL.
WHAT IF HE DOESN'T LISTEN?
HE'LL LISTEN. THAT OR YER MUM'LL GO DOWN THERE AND HAVE A WEE TALK WITH HIM IN THE PARKING LOT!
51 52
HOPELESS

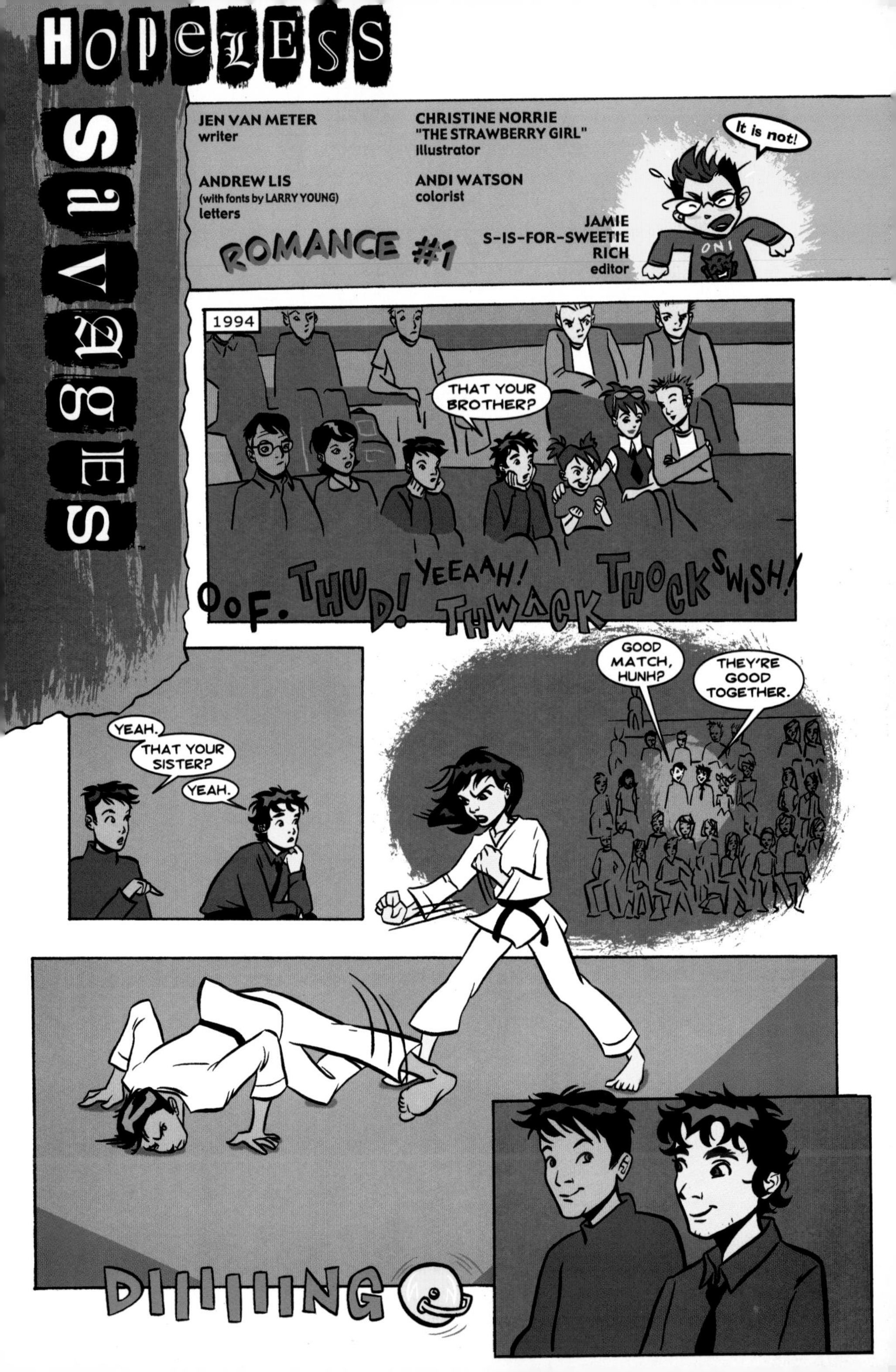
HOPELESS SAVAGES
JEN VAN METER
writer
CHRISTINE NORRIE
"THE STRAWBERRY GIRL"
illustrator
ANDREW LIS
(with fonts by LARRY YOUNG)
letters
ANDI WATSON
colorist
JAMIE
S-IS-FOR-SWEETIE
RICH
editor
It is not!
ROMANCE #1
1994
THAT YOUR BROTHER?
OOF. THUD! YEEAAH! THWACK THOCK SWISH!
YEAH.
THAT YOUR SISTER?
YEAH.
GOOD MATCH, HUNH?
THEY'RE GOOD TOGETHER.
DIIIIIING

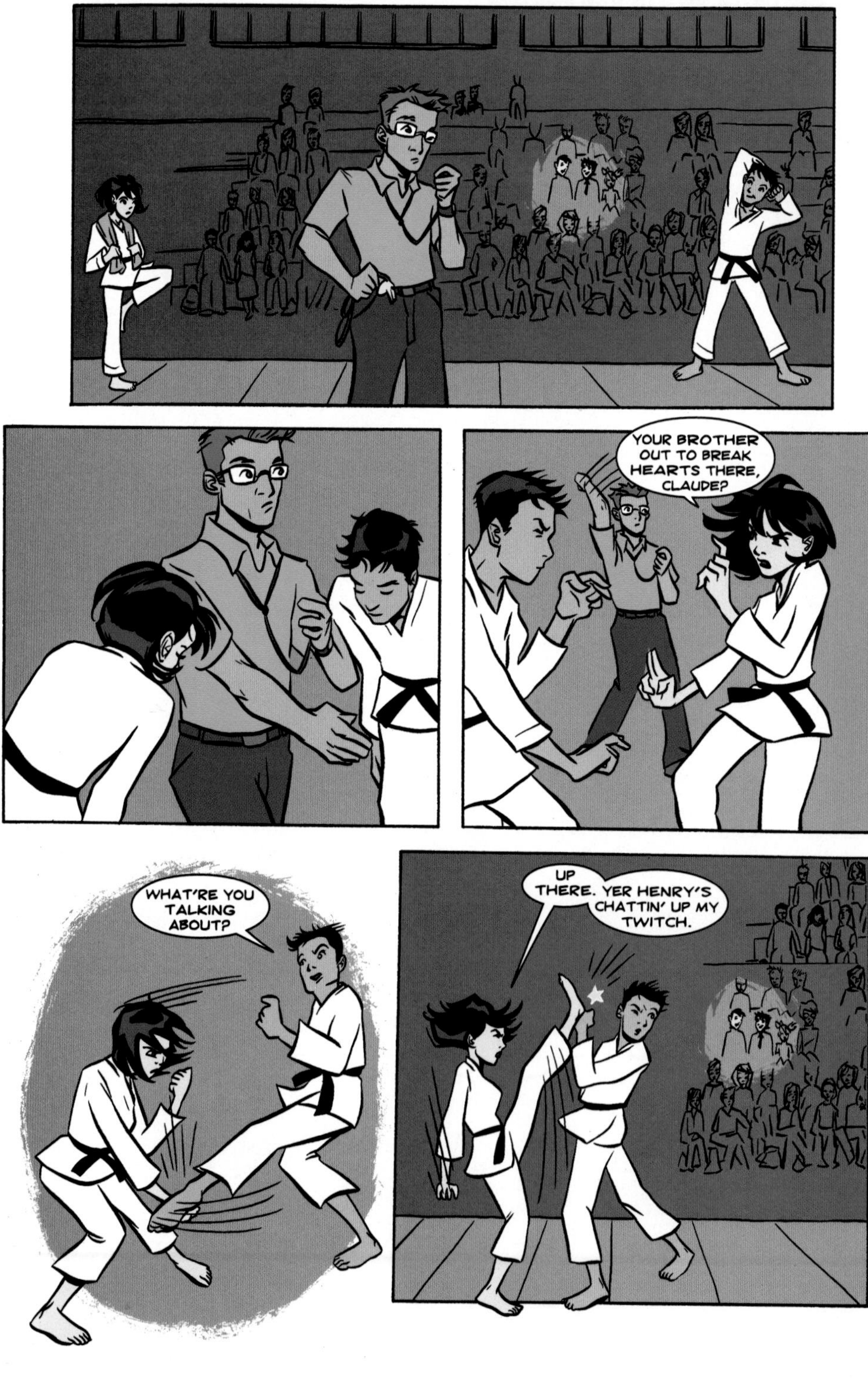
YOUR BROTHER OUT TO BREAK HEARTS THERE, CLAUDE?
WHAT'RE YOU TALKING ABOUT?
UP THERE.
YER HENRY'S CHATTIN' UP MY TWITCH.

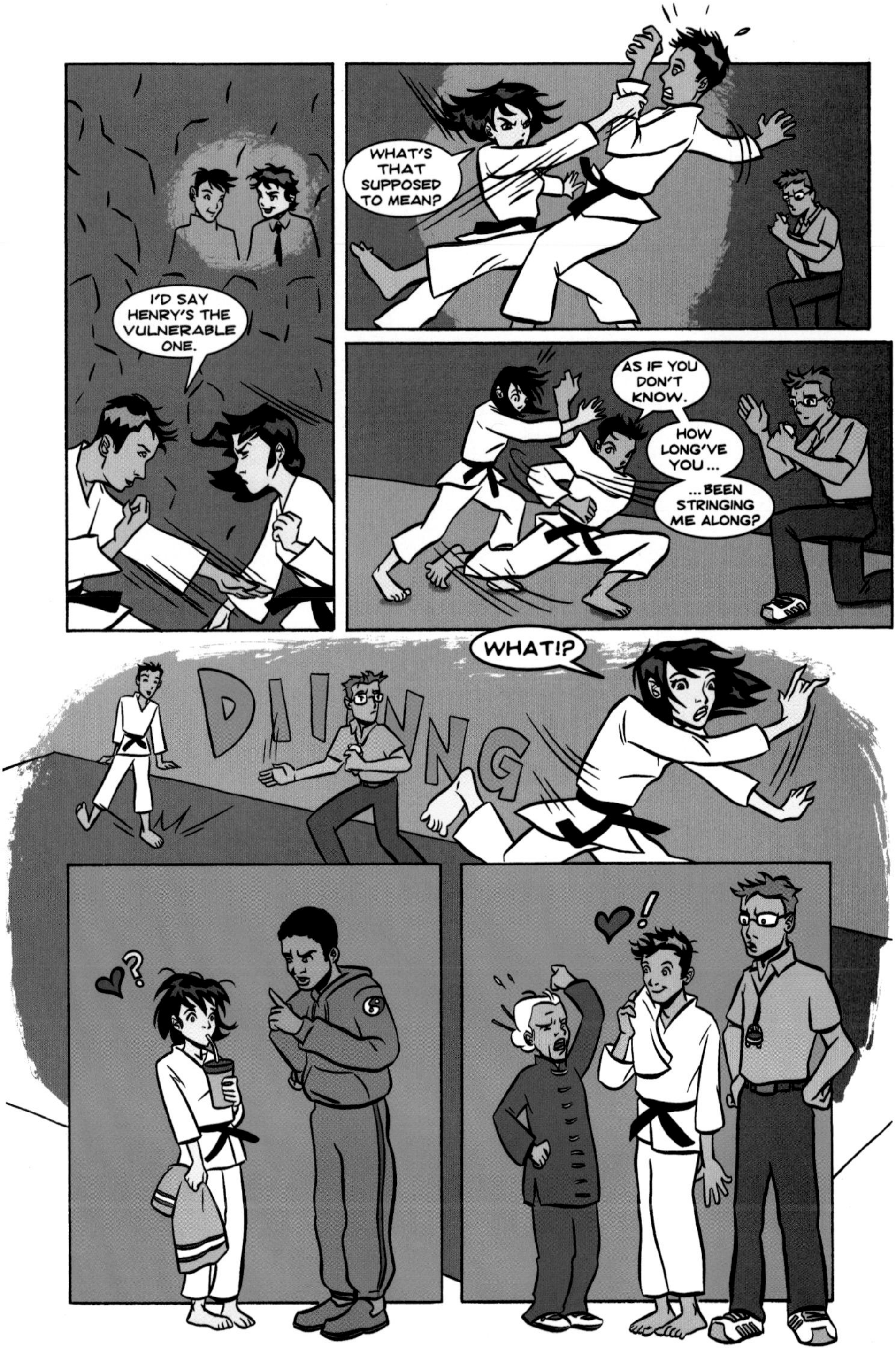
I'D SAY HENRY'S THE VULNERABLE ONE.
WHAT'S THAT SUPPOSED TO MEAN?
AS IF YOU DON'T KNOW.
HOW LONG'VE YOU...
...BEEN STRINGING ME ALONG?
WHAT!?
DIINNG

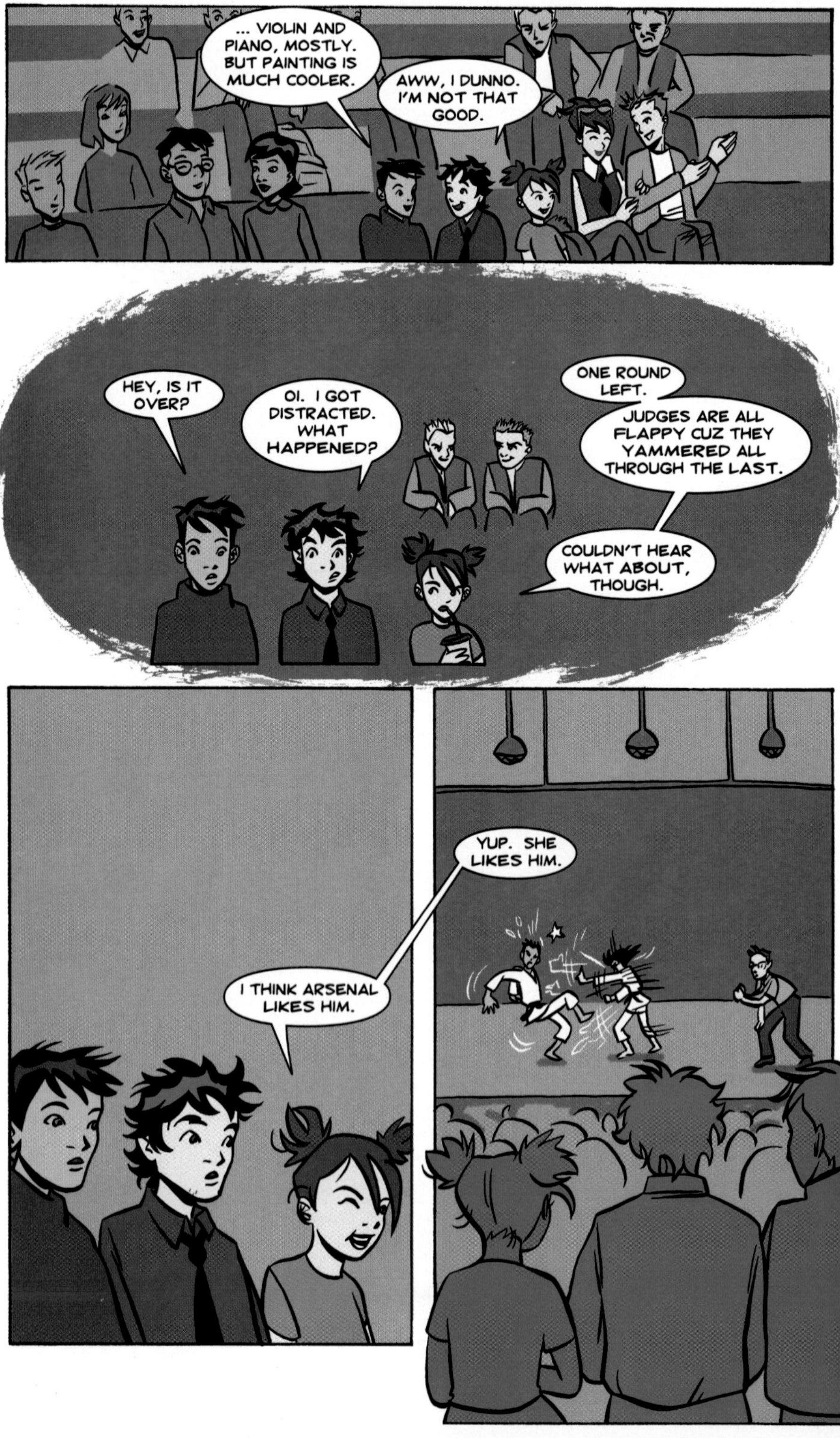
... VIOLIN AND PIANO, MOSTLY. BUT PAINTING IS MUCH COOLER.
AWW, I DUNNO. I'M NOT THAT GOOD.
HEY, IS IT OVER?
OI. I GOT DISTRACTED. WHAT HAPPENED?
ONE ROUND LEFT.
JUDGES ARE ALL FLAPPY CUZ THEY YAMMERED ALL THROUGH THE LAST.
COULDN'T HEAR WHAT ABOUT, THOUGH.
I THINK ARSENAL LIKES HIM.
YUP. SHE LIKES HIM.

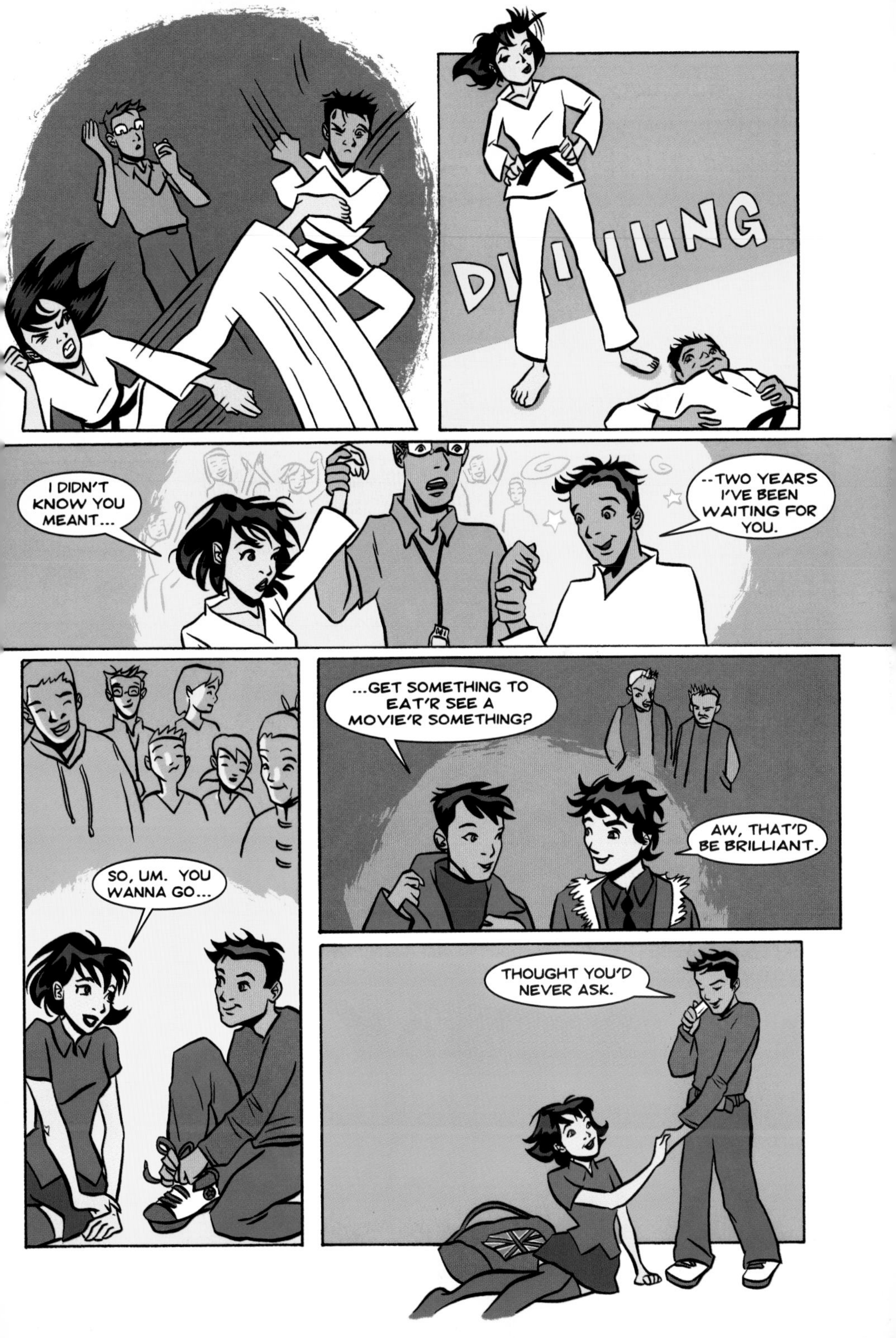
DIIIIIING
I DIDN'T KNOW YOU MEANT...
--TWO YEARS I'VE BEEN WAITING FOR YOU.
SO, UM. YOU WANNA GO...
...GET SOMETHING TO EAT'R SEE A MOVIE'R SOMETHING?
AW, THAT'D BE BRILLIANT.
THOUGHT YOU'D NEVER ASK.

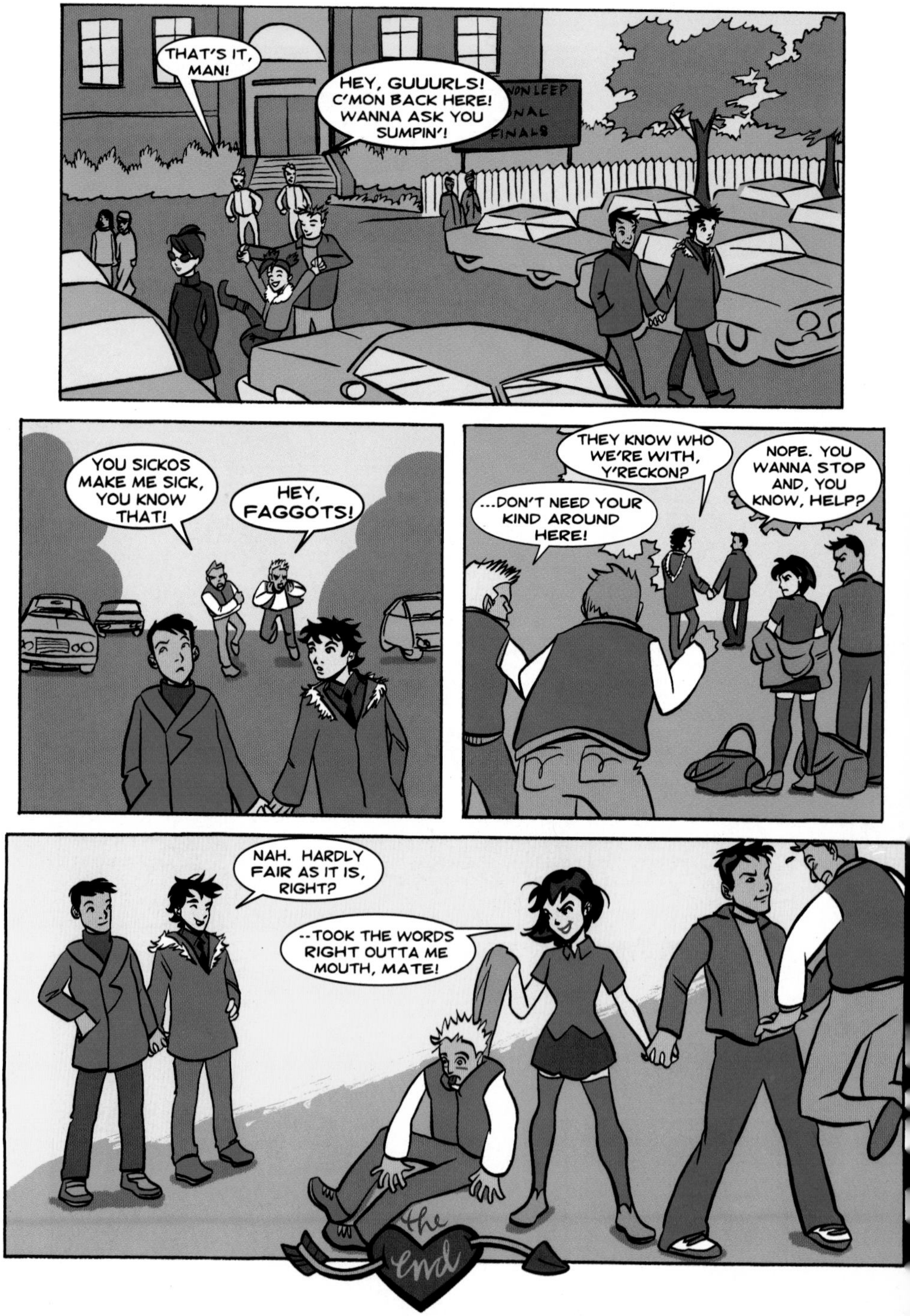
THAT'S IT, MAN!
HEY, GUUURLS! C'MON BACK HERE! WANNA ASK YOU SUMPIN'!
YOU SICKOS MAKE ME SICK, YOU KNOW THAT!
HEY, FAGGOTS!
...DON'T NEED YOUR KIND AROUND HERE!
THEY KNOW WHO WE'RE WITH, Y'RECKON?
NOPE. YOU WANNA STOP AND, YOU KNOW, HELP?
NAH. HARDLY FAIR AS IT IS, RIGHT?
--TOOK THE WORDS RIGHT OUTTA ME MOUTH, MATE!
the end

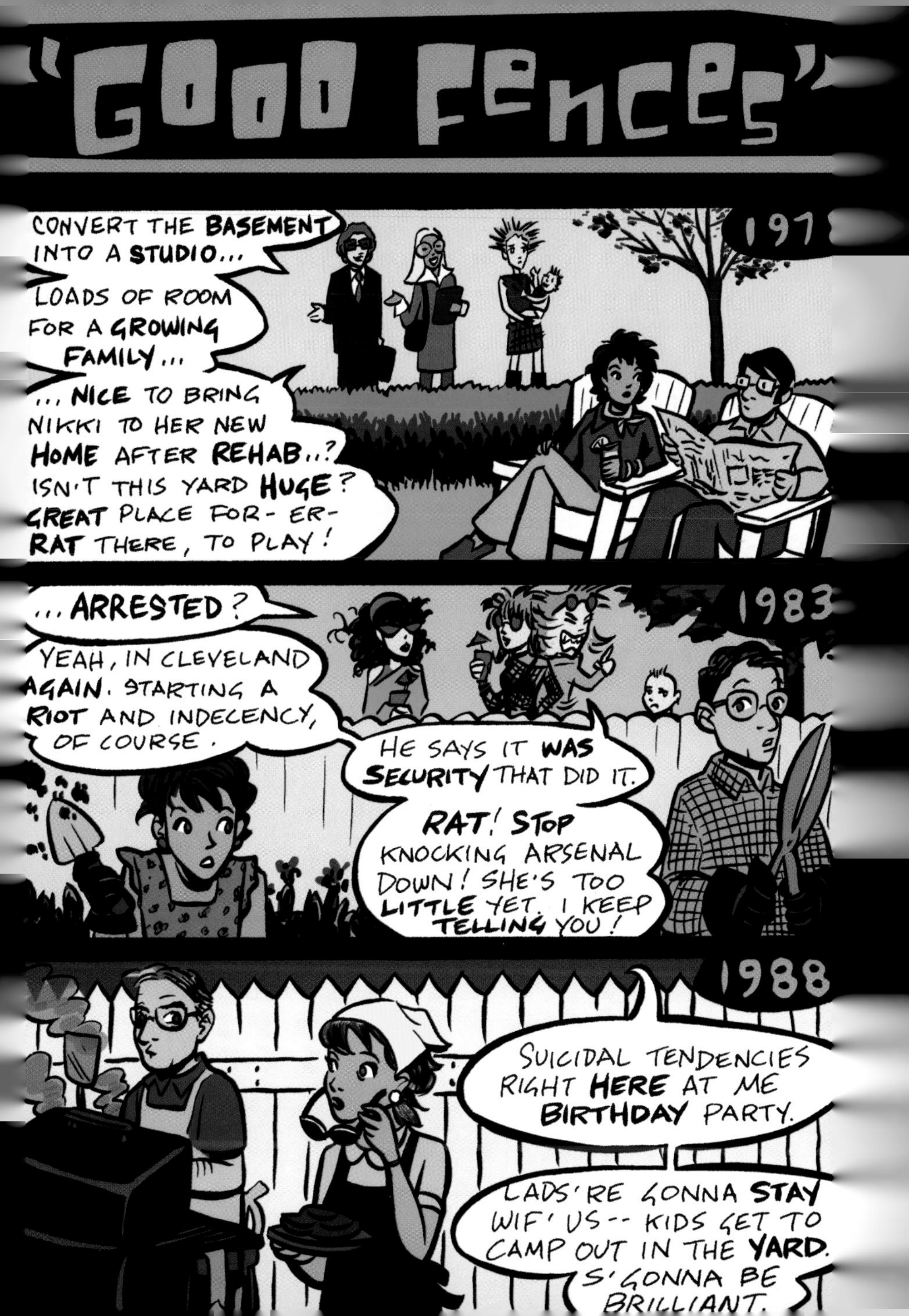

"GOOD FENCES"
1978
CONVERT THE BASEMENT INTO A STUDIO...
LOADS OF ROOM FOR A GROWING FAMILY...
...NICE TO BRING NIKKI TO HER NEW HOME AFTER REHAB..? ISN'T THIS YARD HUGE? GREAT PLACE FOR- ER- RAT THERE, TO PLAY!
1983
...ARRESTED?
YEAH, IN CLEVELAND AGAIN. STARTING A RIOT AND INDECENCY, OF COURSE.
HE SAYS IT WAS SECURITY THAT DID IT.
RAT! STOP KNOCKING ARSENAL DOWN! SHE'S TOO LITTLE YET. I KEEP TELLING YOU!
1988
SUICIDAL TENDENCIES RIGHT HERE AT ME BIRTHDAY PARTY.
LADS'RE GONNA STAY WIF' US-- KIDS GET TO CAMP OUT IN THE YARD. S'GONNA BE BRILLIANT.

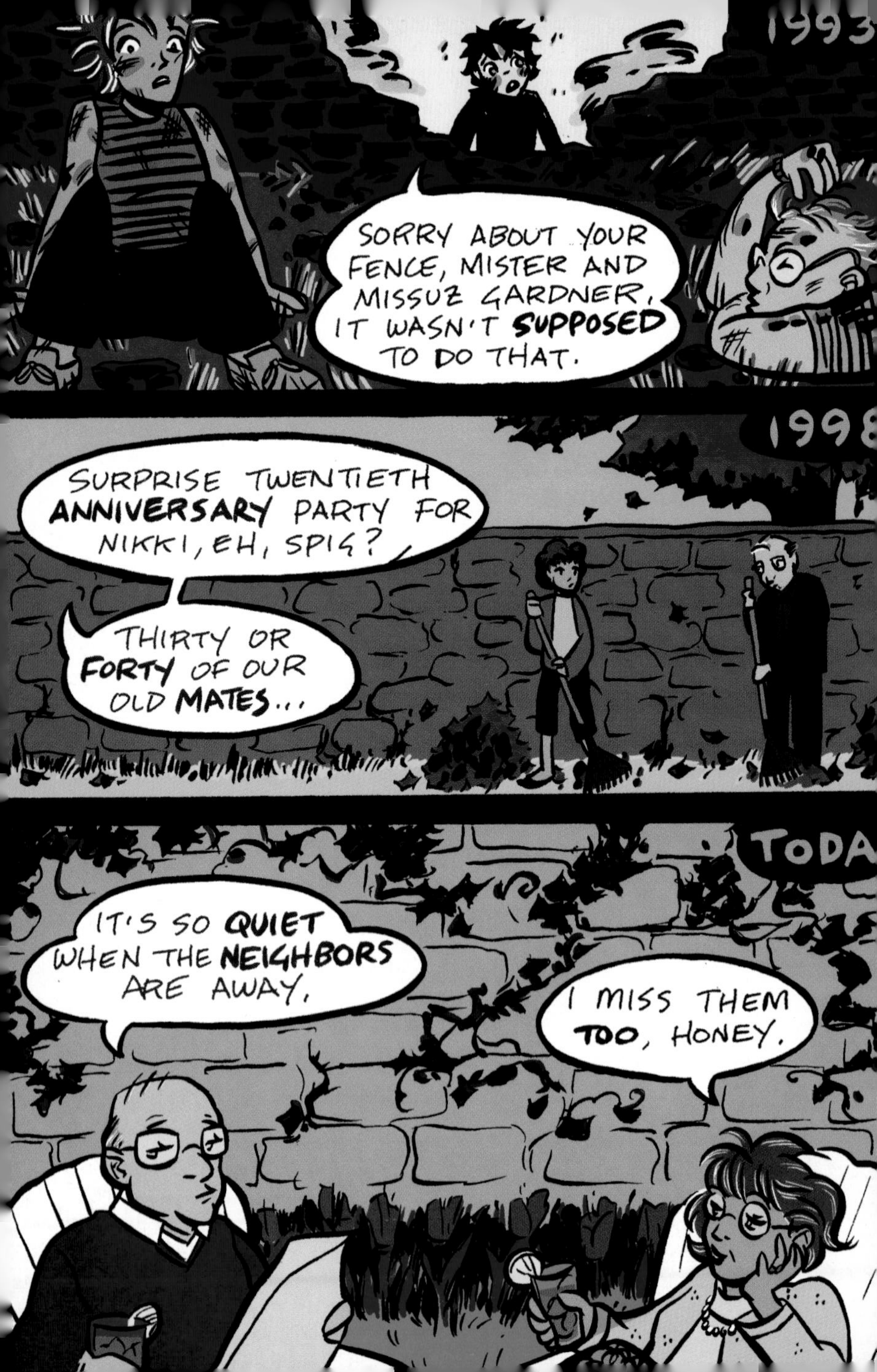
1993
SORRY ABOUT YOUR FENCE, MISTER AND MISSUZ GARDNER, IT WASN'T SUPPOSED TO DO THAT.
1998
SURPRISE TWENTIETH ANNIVERSARY PARTY FOR NIKKI, EH, SPIG?
THIRTY OR FORTY OF OUR OLD MATES...
TODA
IT'S SO QUIET WHEN THE NEIGHBORS ARE AWAY.
I MISS THEM TOO, HONEY.